The Illusion of Ignorance

Constructing the American Encounter with Mexico, 1877–1920

Janice Lee Jayes

UNIVERSITY PRESS OF AMERICA,® INC.
Lanham • Boulder • New York • Toronto • Plymouth, UK

Library of Congress Control Number: 2010939551
ISBN: 978-0-7618-5354-1 (paperback : alk. paper)
eISBN: 978-0-7618-5355-8

Cover image: President Grant on a Banana Plantation in Mexico.
Source: William E. Curtis, *Capitals of Spanish America*,
(NY: Harper, 1888): 15. (Courtesy of Slippery Rock University)

Contents

**PART III   "MEXICO, THE WONDERLAND OF
              THE SOUTH!"**

Preface and Acknowledgments

Like many projects, this book grew in response to personal experiences. As a university student I was fortunate to spend a year in Mexico City immersed in the study of historic and contemporary Mexico. Coming back to the U.S., I was sad that so few U.S. Americans seemed to have more than rudimentary knowledge of the Mexico I had begun to know. I chalked up the discrepancy to poor communication and limited contact between the nations and blithely assumed that time and increased contact would improve relations.

In the years that followed I returned to Mexico, but also had opportunities to live and work in other countries and on other continents and I began to think about the puzzle at the heart of this book. How is it, I repeatedly found myself asking, that U.S. citizens have such an intense level of involvement with the world through business, migration and foreign relations, and yet preserve an almost perverse form of cultural isolationism? The mental map that most Americans maintain of the world, with its vast stretches of blank space in which little but earthquakes catch national attention, bears little relationship to the U.S.'s engagement with the world. Gradually my focus shifted from questioning why Americans remain mired in this irrational and uneven ignorance, to trying to understand what purpose this ignorance serves in American culture and how Americans unconsciously conspire to preserve it.

I chose to explore this question by returning to the study of U.S.-Mexican relations both because it is such a powerful example of the American cultural disconnect with the reality of its foreign relations, and because I think that it was in Porfirian Mexico that Americans first learned the art of maintaining the illusion of ignorance. Both the U.S. and Mexico sought to reinvent relations in the 1870s and 1880s, both had goals for exploiting the potential of the changing international arena, and yet very concrete Mexican public relations campaigns were ineffective in reaching the American audience. For Americans were not merely learning how to relate politically and economically to the world, they were learning how to understand those relations in ways that were consistent with the American national identity they had chosen to nurture. Only the illusion of ignorance protected that vision of America at home and abroad from the inconvenient realities of the world.

Exploring this cultural puzzle through the lens of Mexican-American relations during the Porfiriato has both advantages and disadvantages, as does the research framework I chose. To begin with I chose to examine a wide variety of cultural interactions (diplomatic, commercial, touristic, and journalistic) rather than explore the question through a single frame of contact. It would have been possible to shape this investigation around any one of those fields of interaction, and indeed there are some masterful monographs on U.S.-Mexican relations that do just that, but I think that laying out the parallel problems in cultural relations across of a wide array of contacts offers different insights into the puzzle of American ignorance.

In addition, these forms of contact did take place simultaneously, and juxtaposing them helps readers envision the larger context of changing relations in the Porfirian era. The new world accessible through travel and trade was not experienced through discrete interactions, but through a messy barrage of political, cultural and business notices. Finally, I have tried to make this a book that would be accessible to students of U.S. history as well as to students of U.S.-Mexican relations by immersing the reader in the logistics of the nineteenth century world. It is certainly entertaining to read about the trials of business travel in 1880, but I think it also helps us imagine the human dilemma of trying to incorporate new sights and experiences into familiar narratives of personal and national life.

While I enjoyed writing the descriptive passages on American encounters with Mexico, I recognize that in some ways I have committed the same ethnocentric errors as my subjects. I have written a book not about Mexico, but about Americans thinking about Mexico. There is enough from the Mexican side to show that the Díaz administration had clear objectives for shaping cultural relations as part of their larger foreign policy goals, but this is primarily a book about American interpretations of Mexico, which is not at all the same thing as a book about Mexico. A parallel book centered on how the Mexicans responded to and interpreted their changing relations with the outside world would be welcome.

There is no adequate way to thank the many people who helped make this book possible, but I will try to do for others what they did for me. Some of those tasks will be easier than others, such as buying students coffee or lunch and listening to their thoughts. I do not think I will ever find a way to help the librarians I have bothered, all the way from the Library of Congress to the local library in Madison, South Dakota. I cannot tell some of my favorite professors, like Charlie McLaughlin or James Mooney how much their teaching awoke my curiosity because they have passed away, but I think of them whenever I begin a new semester. I couldn't even number the many Mexicans who helped me learn Spanish and cooked for me, but I hope I have repaid them by working with those learning English here at home. Ruby and Alfonso, Lupita and Ania, and Terry and Francisco deserve especially tender thanks. Some of the chapters here emerged from my dissertation, and I am sure that my readers Michael Kazin, Eileen Findlay, Barbara Tenenbaum and my advisor Peter Kuznick, appreciate not having to have read the final version of this text until it was beyond comment!

Finally I have to thank my family and friends. My dear friends Hyde and Elizabeth, and the thirty-six people that make up my siblings and in-laws and nieces and nephews have cleverly known when to ask about the book, and when not to ask. My husband's parents, Dr. Theodore Walwik and Barbara Walwik, and my parents, Robert and Dorothy Jayes, have been kind and generous with affection and more practical things. My children, Kirby, Martin and Madeleine are anxious for this to be finished so I can write a truly meaningful book (perhaps about poodles, pirates or dragons) and my husband, Joseph Walwik, is still kind, and smart, and makes me laugh.

Timeline of Key Events in U.S. Mexican Relations, 1821–1920

1810–1821 Mexican War for independence from Spain.

1827–29 U.S. Minister to Mexico Joel Poinsett offers to purchase Texas, Mexico refuses. Poinsett expelled after interfering in Mexican politics.

1835–36 American and Mexican residents of Texas declare independence from Mexico. The Lone Star Republic established following a war with Mexico.

1845 Texas annexed to the U.S., Mexico breaks off relations with the U.S.

1846 President James Polk sends envoy to Mexico to buy California and New Mexico, Mexico refuses. The U.S. declares war on Mexico after border skirmishes.

1847 U.S. troops occupy Mexico City.

1848 The Treaty of Guadalupe Hidalgo ends the war and confirms Mexican cession of territory that will become California, New Mexico, Arizona, and part of Utah, Colorado, Texas and Wyoming.

1853 In the Gadsden Purchase the U.S. gains territory that will become southern New Mexico and Arizona for 10 million dollars. The treaty is bitterly condemned by the Mexican people.

1857 A Mexican Liberal Constitution passes, but civil war follows (1858-1861). Liberals triumph over Conservatives and Benito Juarez elected President.

1861–1865 U.S. Civil War, some Confederates seek exile in Mexico.

1862–67 Great Britain, Spain and France take advantage of the Mexican and American civil strife to invade Mexico in support of the Conservatives. French troops are defeated by the Liberals in Puebla, 5 May 1862, but one year later occupy Mexico City, allowing Archduke Maximilian of Austria to arrive and rule as emperor in Mexico City.

1867 The Conservative-French alliance defeated, Maximilian executed, and Juárez restored to the presidency.

1872 Juarez dies in office, Supreme Court Chief Sebastián Lerdo de Tejada succeeds Juárez, but his claim to the presidency disputed by General Porfirio Diaz.

1873 Minister John W. Foster arrives in Mexico City to represent the U.S.

1876 Porfirio Díaz leads a revolt against President Lerdo's attempt to claim a second term. Díaz takes power November 1876, but the U.S. denies recognition to his government.

1877 Porfirio Diaz elected to the Presidency, but U.S. still denies recognition. Border troops of both nations placed on alert. Manuel Zamacona, Díaz's commercial agent in the U.S., coordinates public relations campaign for Mexico in the U.S.

1878 In February the U.S. recognizes the Diaz government after intense public pressure.

1878 Public insult of U.S. Minister John Foster in Mexico City, September 15.

1879 The American Industrial Deputation visits Mexico in January.

1880 Former president Ulysses S. Grant visits Mexico in January, Minister Foster transferred to Moscow; Díaz leaves the Presidency at the end of his term.

1884 Completion of first rail lines from Mexico City to the U.S.

1884–1911 Porfirio Diaz re-elected to the Presidency, remains in office.

1885 Mexico participates in the New Orleans Cotton Centennial Exposition.

1895 U.S. involvement in the Venezuela boundary dispute leads Díaz to become more wary of growing U.S. power in the region.

1898 The Spanish American War leads to U.S. occupation of Cuba and Puerto Rico. Mexico counters growing U.S. influence with overtures to Europe, Central America.

1910 Mexico celebrates its centenary. The Revolution begins as Francisco Madero spearheads political opposition to Diaz.

1911 Diaz leaves for European exile. Madero elected President, but faces growing armed opposition across the political spectrum.

1912–13 American reporters gather along the northern border to watch the Revolution unfold. American expatriates and Mexican refugees flee north.

1913 Violent political struggles disrupt Mexico City in February. Madero appoints General Victoriano Huerta to restore order; Huerta betrays and murders Madero. Defenders of the republican constitution (*Constitucionalistas*) rise up to lead revolts against Huerta and his Federal troops (the *Federales*). In the north, Francisco (Pancho) Villa, Alvaro Obregon and Venustiano Carranza lead Constitutionalist armies, while Emiliano Zapata leads the revolt against Huerta in the south. Incoming U.S. President Woodrow Wilson follows policy of "Watchful Waiting."

1913 Journalist Ambrose Bierce vanishes in Mexico. Journalist John Reed slips across the border to follow Constitutionalist troops for 5 months, interviewing Pancho Villa and Venustiano Carranza.

1914 In April American troops occupy Veracruz and encounter fierce resistance. In July Huerta resigns and flees the capital. War breaks out in Europe in August and U.S. troops are withdrawn from Veracruz by November.

1915 Struggles between former allies Villa, Carranza, and Zapata continue. In October US recognition of Venustiano Carranza's government is followed by aid; Villa outraged.

1916 Pancho Villa leads raid on Columbus, New Mexico in March. U.S. General John J. Pershing leads 10,000 American troops into northern Mexico in the Punitive Expedition; withdrawn after eighteen months without apprehending Villa.

1917 Constitution establishes new revolutionary government for Mexico.

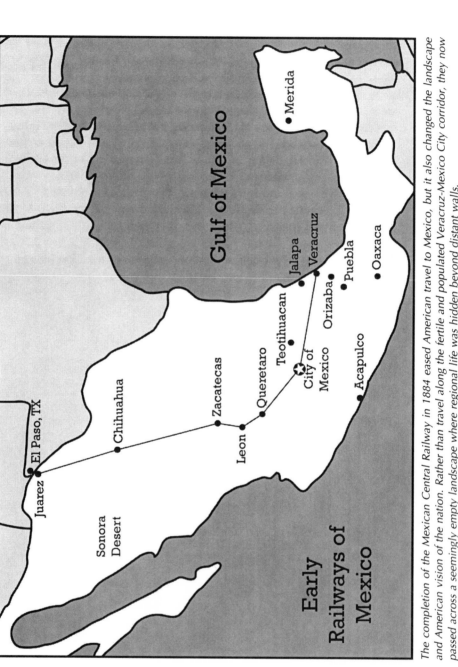

The completion of the Mexican Central Railway in 1884 eased American travel to Mexico, but it also changed the landscape and American vision of the nation. Rather than travel along the fertile and populated Veracruz-Mexico City corridor, they now passed across a seemingly empty landscape where regional life was hidden beyond distant walls.

Introduction:
Donkeys and Diplomats

THE ILLUSION OF IGNORANCE: CONSTRUCTING THE AMERICAN ENCOUNTER WITH MEXICO, 1877–1920[1]

In 1877 an American resident in Mexico complained to a visiting U.S. journalist that "Americans know as little about the interior of Mexico as the interior of Africa."[2] The journalist, John Finerty, agreed that American knowledge of Mexico was atrocious, but he, like other Americans and Mexicans of the era, was confident that the growth of commerce would create new patterns of contact and promote a new age of understanding. The following decades did bring an explosion of contact as American investors, tourists and diplomats flooded into Mexico, and Mexican exhibits, people and products flowed north across the border, but the change in relations had little effect on American understanding of Mexico. More than a century after Finerty's journey the U.S.-Mexican Bilateral Commission still identified 'pervasive cultural misunderstandings' as a continuing impediment to better relations.[3] The persistent cultural gulf only underscores the continuing tragedy of U.S.-Mexican relations; while the two nations are drawn ever closer through trade, migration, tourism, and other issues, the Mexican people still appear as strangers—indistinct, misunderstood and mysterious figures on the fringes of the American imagination.

In the 1870s it might have been reasonable to attribute U.S. citizens' overwhelming disregard for Mexican history, culture, and politics to a lack of contact, but it is hardly an acceptable excuse in today's world. Economically, the U.S. and Mexico have maintained a formidable relationship for more than a century. Mexico is consistently one of the top trade partners of the U.S. and a leading international tourist destination for Americans. The two countries share one of the longest and most interactive borders in the world, and have mutual interests in a variety of resulting concerns, including migration, transnational crime and the environment. There is frequent contact at every level of the relationship, from high-level political consultations to package tours. Americans dance to Mexican music, eat Mexican food and celebrate Mexico's "Cinco de Mayo" holiday at their local bars, yet the Mexico Americans think they know bears little resemblance to the nation the Mexicans know as home.

This book argues that most Americans know little of Mexico beyond her food and beaches not because they have had no opportunity or cause to learn more, but because they have chosen not to do so. Instead, they have chosen to cling to a comforting but stereotyped pattern of interaction whose origins lie in the era of the Porfiriato, named for Mexican President Porfirio Díaz, who dominated Mexican politics from 1876–1910. The Porfiriato witnessed a sea change in relations between the two nations, when the two moved from a relationship dominated by periodic military confrontations over disputed territory into a relationship of political and economic cooperation. The older cultural framework of hostility and suspicion was hardly adequate for the needs of a new age of commerce, and both nations struggled to reinvent their visions of their neighbor. Ultimately, contact with late nineteenth century Mexico challenged Americans to elaborate new visions both of their relationship with Mexico and of their nation's place in the world. The pattern of interpretation established in response to this challenge not only remains with Americans today, but offers clues to understanding the United States' continuing pattern of intense international interaction combined with cultural isolation that persists today, not only in U.S. relations with Mexico, but in U.S. cultural relations with the world in general.

The unhappy history between the United States and Mexico made the task of reinventing relations especially complicated. Both before and after Mexican independence from Spain in 1821 Americans and Mexicans struggled for control of the continent. Florida slipped from the control of Mexico City to Washington D.C. in the course of the Mexican struggle for independence, leading Mexico City to redouble its efforts to retain control over the northern province of Texas. But in the mid 1830s Mexican and American residents of Texas joined in a revolt and proclaimed their independence. During the next decade the growing presence of U.S. traders and settlers began to threaten Mexican authority over the lands of California and New Mexico, and in 1846 U.S. President James Polk seized upon a minor border clash in disputed territory as a pretext for a declaration of war against Mexico. Many Porfirian era officials, including Porfirio Díaz himself, were old enough to recall the U.S. invasion of Mexico in 1846 and the humiliating occupation of Mexico City in 1847. The war not only resulted in the U.S. annexation of Mexico's northern states, but plunged Mexico into a bitter cycle of civil war and European intervention that only concluded in the 1870s. As the Porfirian era opened the Mexicans had ample reason to remain resentful of their neighbors to the north.

The Americans remembered the past century in a different manner. Americans had justified their expansion into Florida, Texas and the Southwest as the natural course of civilization, or the "manifest destiny" of the nation in the vocabulary of the era. Proponents of expansion argued that U.S. control of the continent was inevitable and depicted Mexicans as being incapable of bringing order or industry to the land. These accusations conveniently disqualified Mexican claims to the territory in American eyes. In the years after the American Civil War, however, Americans were less enamored with the prospect of territorial expansion. Disputes over the legal and social place of freed African Americans and European immigrants in U.S. society absorbed American discussion, while persistent conflict with Native American tribes on the western plains lessened the enthusiasm for military campaigns. The U.S., wary of annexing additional territory with culturally alien and potentially hostile populations, began to rethink its assumption that commercial expansion required territorial annexation. As the Porfirato opened Americans were shifting rapidly to visions of commercial, as opposed to political expansion, but the legacy of racist depictions of Mexican character made it difficult for Americans to engage with Mexican diplomats and traders as equals in the new bi-national arena.

The following chapters explore the way in which both Mexicans and Americans struggled with the need to reinvent cultural relations during this time of profound change. Porfirian-era Mexicans were well aware of the dangers of international disregard for their nation. They had only to open the newspapers of the day to read accounts of European nations dividing up the continent of Africa or of Americans resettling tribes on the western frontier to be reminded that failure to win nation-state recognition on Western terms could carry fatal consequences. In response, the Mexican state structured a defensive cultural diplomacy aimed at replacing American ignorance and disdain with respect for the rich history and culture of Mexico. On the American side the process was less organized. Americans were entering a new phase of international activism that changed both the terms of and the participants in international contact. American diplomats, investors, missionaries, and tourists served as the pioneers of the new era, both in exploring the newly available opportunities abroad and in guiding American understanding of the new internationalism in the context of American culture. The American vanguard in Mexico invented a manner of relating not merely to Mexico, but to the unsettling world beyond U.S. borders.

This book examines three areas of interaction central to the birth of the modern era in U.S.-Mexican relations. Part I, "Diplomatic Fictions," explores cultural competition in the diplomatic sphere by reexamining the myth and reality of U.S. Minister to Mexico John W. Foster's confrontation with Mexican president Porfirio Díaz. Foster's status as America's "first professional diplomat" rests in large part on the reputation he cultivated for having recruited Mexico into a trade partnership with the U.S. during his diplomatic appointment in the 1870s. The reality was somewhat different; Minister Foster was consistently outmaneuvered by the Díaz administration in the late 1870s and ended his mission to Mexico in 1880 in disgrace. Foster's experience in Mexico illustrates how diplomats competed to influence cultural relations as part of their foreign policy strategy, but it also highlights the inaccuracies of American national memory. The gap between Foster's disheartening experience and his iconic place in American popular culture allowed Americans to create a fictitious narrative of U.S. foreign policy mastery over the international realm.

Part II, "A War of Words: Rewriting the Vocabulary of U.S.-Mexican Relations," examines the Díaz administration's efforts to reshape American images of Mexican economic and political life. The Mexican preparations for the American trade mission of 1879 and the visit of former American President Ulysses S. Grant to Mexico in 1880 clearly revealed the nationalist agenda of the Mexican state, but the American response was disappointing. While the Díaz administration sought to highlight Mexican credentials as a progressive and republican partner and win both increased investment and new international respect for Mexican sovereignty, the Americans consistently interpreted Mexico as a disciple, not a colleague in the march toward progress. The tragic consequence of this condescension, which echoed and reinforced the simultaneous rise of new forms of racial stratification within the U.S. itself, appeared in American support for the increasingly brutal style of the Díaz regime.

Part III, "Mexico: The Wonderland of the South," focuses on the leisure realms of the tourist, the fairgoer and the writer. Despite Porfirian attempts to shape itineraries and narratives in these fields and present Mexico as a modernizing nation with a complex culture and history, tourists and fairgoers patronized experiences that relegated the Mexican nation to the role of a timeless paradise. This revealed another failure of Porfirian objectives, but also the institutionalization of an alternative theme in American interaction with the world. Mexico, and later other non-European nations, provided Americans with a locus for their ambivalence toward American-style progress. However, American fascination with a primitive Mexican wonderland never encouraged serious consideration of an alternative development path, instead, it promoted a generic image of a static, non-western world doomed only to stagnation or Americanization.

This vision even survived the watershed of the Mexican Revolution of 1910. The revolution challenged every assumption of Western culture in its explicit rejection of American and European cultural models, its flirtation with socialism, and perhaps most importantly, its violent challenge to American visions of progress, but the U.S. model for relating to Mexico survived virtually unscathed. The Revolution was converted in the American mind into one more exotic but unviable relic of the primitive. Americans indulged in the energy of the Revolution, but they brought home only souvenirs and stories, not ideology.

This study has been able to draw upon a rich array of earlier scholarship on U.S.-Mexican relations, to which it contributes both by extending cultural inquiry into new realms of contact and juxtaposing different categories of interaction.[4] Comparing the activities of diplomats, travel writers, tourists, and merchants illustrates the multiple points of contact that shaped the new U.S. relationship with Mexico and highlights the ubiquity of cultural competition across this spectrum. Battles over interpretation of national character, whether encountered in diplomatic notes or tourist guidebooks, expose the struggles of individuals and nations to both shape and come to terms with the changing international horizons of the era. In juxtaposing these different forms of interaction this book aims to create not so much a history of U.S.-Mexican relations, as a case study of the American encounter with the world in this time of dramatic change.

Juxtaposing these different channels of contact also allows this study to explore more fully the links between debates on domestic and international issues in late-nineteenth century America. Certainly the explosion of contact with the outside world, experienced firsthand by missionaries, diplomats, investors and tourists, and secondhand by those who read their accounts, followed their negotiations and bought their products, challenged Americans' comfortable illusion of physical and cultural quarantine from the world and provided Americans with opportunities to discuss not only international but domestic issues such as race, governance, class, or immigration as well.[5] Studying the American encounter with Mexico provides insights into American domestic cultural debates just as it does into American foreign relations.

While this study focuses on the U.S. experience, this is also a study of an important moment in Mexican history. The U.S. may in part recall its history as one of expansion into a static and submissive world, but the following chapters emphasize the dynamism of an era of rapidly changing commercial and political possibilities for Mexico as well. Even before Díaz took power in 1876, Mexican leaders had begun debating the best means of protecting the nation's future and had chosen strategic engagement with the U.S. as a defensive measure. By pursuing U.S. trade and investment the early Porfirian leaders hoped to reduce Mexico's dangerous dependence on European credit and markets and spur the desperately needed domestic modernization that would protect Mexico from future invasions. To ignore this vision and portray Mexico as a passive victim of American expansionism would merely create an updated version of 19th century stereotypes of indolent, un-enterprising Mexicans pushed aside by the energy of American manifest destiny.

Ironically, despite the greater attention given by American scholars to the expansion of U.S. cultural hegemony during the era, the Mexican leadership had a far more coherent and proactive vision of the cultural politics of the encounter than did the Americans, as can be seen in the following chapters. For Porfirian Mexico cultural diplomacy was no luxury, but central to winning recognition as a valid nation-state entity. Mexico, having been repeatedly subject to invasion and annexation, enjoyed no illusions of isolation, and for the Díaz administration establishing the unquestionable legitimacy of Mexico City as both national capital and international actor was not merely a matter of national pride, but of national survival.

Unfortunately, recalling the intense nationalism that drove the campaigns of the early Porfiriato only makes Mexico's later failure to strengthen national sovereignty through trade and modernization more poignant. This study does not discount the immense human tragedies wreaked through the excesses of this era, or the distortions provoked by the growing U.S. orientation of the Mexican economy, but it does argue for a more complicated vision of the U.S. and Mexican roles in the encounter. Ignoring the nationalistic motives of the early Porfirian state leaves Americans with a simplistic and self serving memory of the era that implicitly blames Mexico for the sad outcome of the Porfirian partnership with the U.S. Reexamining the 1870s and 1880s from the Porfirian perspective reminds us that there was no realistic option for Mexico to cloister herself away from the new forms of international contact; the challenge was to find the most advantageous strategy for Mexico within the changing world system. Mexican leaders were neither fools nor traitors; their plans for strengthening the nation through foreign linkages were ultimately defeated by the uneven distribution of political and economic influence in the emerging system. The way in which the Mexican side of the story vanished from U.S. national memory is but another casualty of that inequitable relationship.

The Illusion of Ignorance is an inquiry not only into the roots of contemporary U.S.-Mexican cultural relations, but into the continuing dynamics of the American vision of the U.S. role in the world, a pattern that first emerged in this era of cultural adjustment and competition. In order to achieve the commerce both desired, Mexico and the U.S. conspired to reinvent cultural relations and replace the hostile framework of the past with a new model of alliance. Beneath the cooperative veneer, however, fundamental differences remained. While Mexicans sought to strengthen national sovereignty and increase respect for the Mexican nation-state before the world, the Americans always assumed the underlying goal was "Americanization" and the subsequent establishment of an American-centered international system. In constructing their encounter with Mexico, and their memory of that encounter, Americans created a reassuring, and still appealing, fiction of their controlling role in the world around them. Mexico, reflected journalist John Kenneth Turner at the close of the Porfiriato, was a country "divided from ours only by a shallow river and an imaginary geographical line," but during this era of international reinvention it provided Americans with the stuff dreams are made of.[6]

NOTES

1. Although the term "Americans" applies to all residents of the Western Hemisphere, in common usage in the U.S. and Mexico it often refers to the people of the United States of America, and for the sake of brevity will be employed as such in this work.

2. John F. Finerty, *John F. Finerty Reports from Porfirian Mexico*, edited by Wilbert Timmons (El Paso: Western Press, 1974), 41.

3. The Bilateral Commission on the Future of United States-Mexican Relations, "Education for New Understanding," chapter in *The Challenge of Interdependence: Mexico and the United States* (New York: University Press of America, 1989), 173–205.

4. There are many excellent studies of U.S.-Mexican/Latin cultural relations, personal favorites include Helen Delpar, *The Enormous Vogue of Things Mexican: Cultural Relations between the U.S. and Mexico, 1920–1935* (Tuscaloosa: University of Alabama, 1992); Robert Johannsen, *To the Halls of the Montezumas: The Mexican War in the American Imagination* (New York: Oxford, 1985); Benjamin Keen, *The Aztec Image in Western Thought* (New Brunswick: Rutgers, 1971); Carlos Monsivais, "Los Viajeros y la Invención de México" *Aztlán* 15 (Fall 1985): 201–30; Frederick B. Pike, *The U.S. and Latin America: Myths and Stereotypes of Civilization and Nature* (Austin: University of Texas, 1992); and David J. Weber, *Myth and the History of the Hispanic Southwest* (Albuquerque: University of New Mexico, 1988).

5. See Amy Kaplan, *The Anarchy of Empire in the Making of U.S. Culture*, (Cambridge: Harvard, 2002); and Matthew Frye Jacobson, *Barbarian Virtues: The United States Encounters Foreign Peoples at Home and Abroad, 1876–1917*, (NY: Hill and Wang, 2000).

6. John Kenneth Turner, *Barbarous Mexico*, (Chicago: C.H. Kern, 1911), 135.

Part I

DIPLOMATIC FICTIONS: JOHN W. FOSTER'S MISSION TO MEXICO, 1873–1880

Introduction: Of Missions and Memoirs

September 15, 1878 was an emotional evening in Mexico City. On this date the residents of Mexico City planned to commemorate the anniversary of Mexico's defiant rejection of Spanish colonial rule in 1810, but the preparations for celebration were tinged with anxiety. Many worried that Mexican independence would soon be endangered by yet another disastrous war with Mexico's northern neighbor, the United States. Throughout that long summer the frontier armies of both the U.S. and Mexico had remained on alert, drilling within sight and hearing of one another along the international boundary. Accounts of military movements along the border circulated in Mexico City while mysterious foreigners roamed the capital streets whispering rumors of Washington's plan to annex the northern Mexican states. The newspapers of both nations contributed to the atmosphere of impending crisis by printing denunciations of one another's motives and drawing parallels between the contemporary situation and the eve of the U.S. Mexican War of 1846–1848.[1]

The U.S. Minister to Mexico, John Watson Foster, was well aware of the intense sentiments of the moment, but he, along with other members of the diplomatic community, had been invited to attend an evening of patriotic poetry and song and resolutely committed himself to attend. Foster knew that the theatre would be filled with the prominent citizens and administration officials he had dealt with every day during the past five years since his appointment as Minister in 1873 and he hoped that his attendance would be accepted as a sign of his respect for the Republic of Mexico, if not for the administration of the current Mexican President, Porfirio Díaz. It was well known in Mexico City that Foster had little love for Díaz, whom Foster regarded as a revolutionary militant who had illegitimately ousted the elected government in 1876.

Disregarding the international tension and his personal history of confrontation with the Mexican president, Foster entered the theatre with his wife and children on the evening of the 15th. Unfortunately, the audience did not see his attendance as a sign of solidarity with the Mexican people, as Foster had hoped, but as a provocation. The U.S. Minister was subjected to a lengthy and insulting poem detailing American treachery, followed by a thundering chorus of voices shouting, "Death to the Yankees!" from the surrounding galleries. Stone-faced and stoic, Foster awaited the resumption of the program, then withdrew quietly with his family.[2]

During the days that followed Mexican newspapers debated the significance of the incident and the meaning of Foster's withdrawal from the theatre. While the *Trait d'Union* insisted that Foster's limited knowledge of the Spanish language had insulated him from the offense and that only the "excessive heat of the theatre" had prompted his departure, the *Voz de México* and the *Diario Oficial* asserted that the hostile outburst was an unmistakable insult to the American minister. Accounts of the event raced through Mexican society and encouraged wild speculation on the consequences, even prompting rumors that Foster had demanded the return of his passport from the Foreign Ministry prior to his departure and certain American retaliation.

In reality Foster and the Foreign Ministry cooperated quickly to minimize the impact of the incident. Foster informed Mexican Foreign Minister Eleuterio Avila that he in no way considered the crowd's outburst an official act of the government, but merely one of those "unpremeditated demonstrations that are likely to occur in times of popular excitement in any country." Minister Avila returned the courtesy, noting that President Díaz was "well acquainted" with Foster's high intelligence and never for a moment believed that Foster would grant importance to the unfortunate display. The exchange of notes was published in the principal newspapers of the city and gradually the incident was forgotten.

Although the incident did not incite a new stage of conflict between the two nations, in retrospect it clearly signaled the final chapter of Foster's mission to Mexico. As the crowd in the theatre revealed, Foster had become an unwelcome symbol of American treachery, an image the Díaz administration encouraged as it turned to implementing a new foreign relations strategy that circumvented the representative from Washington while simultaneously saddling him with the blame for poor relations between the two nations. Although Foster remained one more year as Minister in the Mexican capital, it was an increasingly uncomfortable tenure. He enjoyed little esteem within either Mexico City or Washington circles and seemed increasingly alienated from the negotiating tables. His diplomatic posting to Mexico ended in 1880 under humiliating circumstances and Foster left the State Department soon afterwards. Foster's diplomatic career appeared to be at an end.

Yet Foster did not disappear, instead he finished life as an honored elder statesman of American foreign relations. He rehabilitated his career through private legal work and later returned to the diplomatic service, even serving briefly as Secretary of State. More surprisingly, Foster also repaired his relationship with Mexico and his former adversary, Porfirio Díaz, and became Mexico's most important legal counselor and public affairs agent in the U.S. By the end of his career Foster was lauded as the paragon of the diplomatic representative.

Ironically, Foster's enduring reputation as America's "first professional diplomat" rested in large part upon his supposed role in fashioning the U.S.-Mexican alliance of the late nineteenth century, an interpretation Foster institutionalized in his memoirs.[3] In *Diplomatic Memoirs*, first published in 1909, Foster portrayed himself as the calm and fatherly professional, guiding the former enemies into a glorious new alliance. Foster returned even to the scene of his public humiliation and converted the events of September 15, 1878 into a testimony to his forbearance during a time of international tension. In Foster's account the spotlight is on the Minister's self control, not the stage; the anger of the Mexican crowd merely sets off Foster's self portrait of the skilled diplomat in control of a tricky situation. The *Memoirs* reinterpreted Foster's mission to Mexico as an unalloyed success and provided the capstone to Foster's professional rejuvenation.

Foster is hardly the first autobiographer guilty of rewriting the past, but his symbolic place in his nation's memory of American international expansion and U.S.-Mexican relations lends more than personal significance to his story. In the *Memoirs*, Foster created a version of events that was flattering not only to himself, but to his nation. The American public conspired with Foster and forgot that the Díaz administration had consistently bested both Foster and the U.S. in the diplomatic contests of 1876–1880. The reinterpretation required little effort, for by 1909, when the *Memoirs* were published, the early nationalist successes of the Porfirian administration had been long forgotten, overshadowed by the distortions of the late Porfirian state and post Spanish-American War U.S. interventions in the Caribbean. It was easy for Americans to accept Foster's historical portrait of the earlier era, epitomized by the image of the composed American statesman before the volatile crowds of Mexico, calmly erecting a new framework of world affairs. Americans found in Foster a hero for the new age, but only by fabricating inaccurate memories of a distraught and malleable Mexico awaiting American guidance. Unfortunately, that fantasy did little to prepare Americans for the violent backlash of revolution in 1910.

Foster's place in American memory has wider significance than just the history of U.S.-Mexican relations for it exposes the fragile underpinnings of one of America's favorite creation narratives. Americans prefer to remember their history and their relationship with the world as a series of challenges met and mastered (for better or worse) through formal U.S. initiatives. This narrative, boxed in by the debates between those who celebrate and those who decry the history of American expansionism, perpetuates itself through myopic fixation on official American actors abroad. Other actors and other nations occupy the shadowy margins of these morality plays. Like the nationalists of early Porfirian Mexico, the role of informal and non-U.S. forces in shaping the modern international system has been forgotten, replaced by a myth of masterful U.S. unilateralism. In the case of Foster in Mexico, the state-centered conventions of diplomatic history and the cultural preferences of Americans combined to create an illusion of American government control that simply does not match the experiences of "America's First Professional Diplomat" in Mexico.

Foster's curious career provides the perfect starting point for an inquiry into the matrix of diplomatic, economic and cultural relations between America and the world in this era. While Foster's professional role in U.S.-Mexican affairs has been documented by biographers and diplomatic historians, the cultural implications of his humiliation and rehabilitation remain unexamined. Contrasting the contentious reality of Foster's confrontation with the early Díaz administration with the later ascendance of Foster as icon of triumphant American diplomacy highlights the illusions underpinning the American vision of world order during this key moment in the expansion of American empire. Foster, representing the U.S., lost the political and diplomatic battles of the late 1870s to Diaz, but ultimately, as his legend showed, Foster and the U.S. won the cultural war to shape American visions of world order.

Foster's experience exemplifies the illusions of U.S. memory. The interpretation of the era that Foster offered and Americans preferred did leave them with a culturally coherent vision of their own purposeful action in a pliant world, but it was a dangerous and misleading vision that only obscured the messy reality of the international arena. Foster's early confrontation with Porfirian policy, his later accommodations, and the triumphant reclamation of his reputation tell the story of one man's professional collision with the uncooperative reality of Mexico, but it also suggests a way of understanding the broader American encounter with Mexico and the world beyond. Foster's story offers evidence not merely of what Americans experienced in Mexico, but, more importantly, of what they fashioned from that experience.

NOTES

1. Newspaper coverage of the crisis is reproduced in Clementina Díaz y de Ovando, *Crónica de una Quimera: Una Invasión Norteamericana en México, 1879* (México: Coordinación de Humanidades, Universidad Nacional Autónoma de México, 1989), 10, 31–49.

2. John Watson Foster, *Diplomatic Memoirs*, vol. 1 (New York: Houghton Mifflin, 1909), 101–2; John W. Foster to William Evarts, 21 September 1878, *Diplomatic Dispatches from Mexico* (DDM), RG 59, National Archives, Washington, D.C. Mexican newspaper coverage reviewed in "El Señor Foster," *Diario Oficial,* 19 September, 1878; *Two Republics*, 20 September 1878. The American press did not report on the event until December, when it classified the outburst as characteristic of Mexico's "mixed race, who have always shown themselves incapable of self government, of common sense or common justice." *New York Times*, 15 December 1878.

3. See J. Fred Rippy, *The U.S. and Mexico* (New York: Crofts, 1926); James Morton Callahan, *American Foreign Policy in Mexican Relations* (New York: MacMillan, 1926); William Gibbs, "Spadework Diplomacy: United States-Mexican Relations during the Hayes Administration, 1877–1881" (Ph.D. diss., Kent State University, 1973); as well as the contemporary reviews of *Diplomatic Memoirs* in *Dial*, 16 May 1910, *Nation,* 20 January 1910; and *North American Review*, May 1910, 655.

Chapter One

"The Most Difficult Mission on the Western Hemisphere"

John Watson Foster arrived in Mexico in June 1873 to assume the post of Envoy Extraordinary and Minister Plenipotentiary from the United States to the Republic of Mexico. The formal title contrasted ironically with the haphazard history of American diplomatic missions to Mexico. In the five decades since Mexico had won independence from Spain in 1821, U.S. representation in the southern republic had been characterized by inconsistent and uninformed policies, typically voiced by unskilled envoys. In contrast, Foster's seven year tenure as chief of the U.S. Mission to Mexico was marked by a steady increase in the professional conduct of diplomacy. In part the shift reflected the orderly character of Foster himself, who approached his work in a consistently conscientious manner, but it also reflected the growing importance attached to foreign relations by each nation. During this era both the U.S. and Mexico began to recognize the linkages between external and domestic policy goals, while changes in communication and transportation made it increasingly possible for national capitals to follow and implement foreign actions. Foster's seven year posting to Mexico bridged the transition from the virtual absence of peaceful contact between the two nations to the birth of an important political and economic alliance between the U.S. and Mexico.[1]

Foster's preparation for a diplomatic career was typical of his era. The Minister unashamedly admitted that at the time of his appointment he had little knowledge of international affairs. The thirty seven year old had practiced law, edited a newspaper, and served as an officer in the Union Army, but, most importantly for his new career path, he had been an ardent supporter of the Republican Party in his home state of Indiana. In 1872 Foster travelled to Washington and called upon his Senator, Oliver Morton, and former army colleagues William Tecumseh Sherman, now General-In Chief of the Army, and Ulysses S. Grant, the newly elected President, to request an appointment in the U.S. civil service. Foster hinted to his patrons that a stay in Europe might be "pleasant and useful," but European posts were not available and, after rejecting Japan as "too remote," Foster settled upon the American Mission in Mexico as his next residence.

While many ambassadorships continue to be filled by political appointees even today, there now exists an institutionalized support staff of career foreign service professionals that can guide an Ambassador's encounter with the host nation. Foster, like other minister's of his age, had no such luck. He would have had to depend on his own knowledge supplemented, if he were lucky, by a trusted secretary/translator and perhaps a local consul, to handle his orientation to the ongoing issues and political networks of the new post. There would be little guidance from distant Washington; communication was sporadic and, even if a telegraph network were in place, the reservoir of knowledge on foreign relations and practices was meager even within the Department of State. For a careless appointee the situation could be disastrous.

For Foster, the isolated post was not intimidating, but invigorating. As even the title, 'diplomatic' memoirs, suggested, Foster dated his professional life from his ministerial debut in Mexico. His earlier career was reduced to mere prologue and preparation for his true vocation as diplomat. Even Foster's brief and nostalgic account of his family's pioneer background served merely to cast a glow of inevitability over Foster's new endeavors. The description of his father traversing the nation from New York to the wilds of Indiana, contained within the chapter, "How I Entered the Diplomatic Service," echoed in the succeeding description of Foster setting out from New Orleans to the land of Montezuma with his own family. Mexico was clearly the new frontier for Foster.

In 1873, however, success was in no ways assured. Despite Foster's assertion that the Mexican post was considered the "most difficult mission on the Western Hemisphere" and thus far superior to his previously contemplated European choices, few in 1873 would have envied Foster his new position. Just a few years before Foster's arrival, the incoming U.S. Minister had travelled only as far as the port city of Veracruz before rethinking his appointment and retreating to New Orleans.[2] American fears of tropical disease certainly contributed to Mexico's 'difficult' reputation, but Foster's comment suggested more along the lines of sensitive negotiations and secret communiqués. In reality, apart from the nagging negotiation of claim suits remaining from the U.S.-Mexican War and the perennial headaches of border security, Washington showed little interest in Mexican affairs in 1873. U.S. ministers and consuls in Mexico before Foster's era appeared immersed in the same rote work as other U.S. missions: bailing out indigent Americans and burying the dead, presenting and pursuing damage claims, and, all too frequently, following up on their own business interests in the host country. Mexico was hardly seen as a critical arena for U.S. policy in 1873 and certainly not as a promising steppingstone for an ambitious professional like Foster. Foster, however, would prove to be a man with a mission in more than one sense and within a few years of his arrival Mexican questions had moved to the front line of American foreign policy.

Foster's first challenge as Minister was in transporting himself and his family to Mexico. Despite Mexico's contiguity with the U.S., Mexico City was harder to reach than most European capitals. Overland travel between the U.S. border and Mexico City could take weeks over rough and dangerous roads, and, if one chose to travel by sea, there was not a single direct steamship line between the two nations. Most commonly travelers bound from the U.S. for Mexico departed from New York aboard a British steamer and made interim stops in a variety of Caribbean ports before finally docking in Veracruz. Foster had no desire to prolong his stay in a region of yellow fever and hurricanes and was thankful when a U.S. naval vessel was appointed to convey him, his wife Mary Parke, and his two daughters directly to the new post. It was fitting (not to mention more convenient), noted Foster, that the new Minister arrive upon a vessel flying the flag of his own nation.

Arriving in Veracruz Foster must have been relieved to find that the new rail line, completed only months before, spirited travelers up over the mountains to the central plateau of the capital within twelve hours, eliminating several days of bone wrenching travel by mule or stage.[3] Yet even seated in the plush comfort of the new train coaches gazing out at the novel scenery, Foster must have felt discouraged by the enormity of the challenges facing the Mexican republic and his own appointment. The countryside still suffered visible scars from the power struggles that had engulfed Mexico since independence in 1821. The train passed through territory that had hosted battles between Mexican, British, Spanish, American, and French troops during the past half century. Most poignant for Foster may have been the scenes of the U.S. invasion route from the war of 1846–48. While Americans had largely erased the memory of the Mexican war from their thoughts, Mexico lived still with the legacy of the humiliating occupation and annexation of Mexican territory. The aftermath of the war produced both the proudest moments in Mexican history (the Liberal Reform led by Benito Juarez) and the most shameful (the conservative alliance with the invading forces of the French Empire). Although liberal republicanism eventually triumphed with Juarez's victory over Emperor Maximilian, his French troops, and the Mexican monarchists in 1867, the decade of conflict had militarized Mexican politics and discontent and uncertainty simmered throughout the system and political stability remained elusive. In 1873 President Sebastián Lerdo de Tejada remained under the close scrutiny of critics, including another Liberal hero of the war against the French, General Porfirio Díaz. And even if Lerdo de Tejada had enjoyed the support of political bosses like Díaz, it would have been hard for him to claim that he ruled the whole of the Mexican nation. The vastly different cultures, languages and economics of Mexico's many regions challenged Lerdo's visions of the nation and called into question Mexico City's ability to claim authority over and demand allegiance from distant populations. Minister Foster arrived in 1873 to find that he was accredited to an administration with only nominal control over the varied territory and peoples of Mexico.

The preceding decades of war also left devastating legacies in the field of foreign relations. Upon arrival Foster noted that Mexico was both financially and diplomatically isolated from the outside world. Juarez's repudiation of loans contracted by the monarchist supporters of the French intervention had led to a European embargo on credit and stunted the ability of the Mexican government to repair war damage or initiate new public works. Diplomatic relations broken during the wars had not all been reestablished and Foster found that he was responsible not only for representing American concerns, but for providing diplomatic services for citizens of Great Britain, France, Austria, Belgium, Switzerland, and Russia as well.

Foster's tasks were complicated by the fact that Mexicans remained angry with and suspicious of the U.S. Although Americans may have thought of Mexico as a distant nation, the Mexican people had no similar impression. Mexicans were bitterly conscious of the long history of U.S. political interference in Mexico, including the machinations of a former U.S. Minister to Mexico, Joel Poinsett, in the 1820s, the treasonous revolt of American immigrants to the Mexican province of Texas in the 1830s, and the aggressive American expansion that culminated in the U.S.-Mexican War of 1846. Relations were not improved when a later U.S. Minister to Mexico, James Gadsden, conspired to buy a tract of land the size of the state of Pennsylvania from President Antonio López de Santa Anna in 1852. The Mexicans found it easy to unseat Santa Anna in protest, but impossible to reverse the land transfer. A few years later Foreign Minister Sebastián Lerdo de Tejada (President of Mexico at the time of Foster's arrival) resisted heavy pressure from Washington to grant the U.S. "transit rights" across the southern Isthmus of Tehuantepec. Finally, many Mexicans remained bitter in the conviction that the U.S. had offered neither material nor moral support to the Republic during her struggle against the French empire of Napoleon III, and his proxy, Maximilian, during the 1860s.[4]

In dealing with this complex history Foster could expect little guidance from Washington, in fact he could expect little news from Washington at all. The near total "absence of facilities of communication with the outer world"

was a considerable surprise to the new minister, who found no reliable telegraph or mail service to the United States. The monthly steamer from Europe
brought the only regular news of the outside world to the capital city. Communication within Mexico was almost as uneven and infrequent. Yet in John
Foster's later recollection of the era, the isolation, disorder and overwhelming
caseload of his new position posed only challenges, not obstacles, and the
Memoirs records only enthusiasm for the tasks ahead.

After presenting his credentials to President Lerdo on June 16, Foster
delved immediately into rehabilitating the representation of the U.S. in Mexico. Foster's recent experiences as political party organizer and his childhood
memories of life in newly established frontier towns certainly influenced his
approach and Foster quickly embarked upon a campaign to rouse the few
resident Americans from their lethargy and create an American community
out of the disparate exiles. Foster arrived in Mexico City in mid-June and
committed himself to hosting a Fourth of July dinner, at which he was "pleasantly surprised" to find fifty of his compatriots gathered about the tables. The
occupations of the guests reflected the narrow range of American interest in
Mexico in 1873. The few merchants, teachers and railroad mechanics were
joined by the Reverend William Butler and the publisher George W. Clarke.
Butler, who offered the blessing over the meal, had established a Methodist
church in Mexico only a few months before. Although Protestant churches
had been invited into Mexico during the presidency of Juarez in 1857, they
had made little headway and Butler's small congregation consisted primarily
of fellow Americans. George Clarke, another community leader, owned and
edited the *Two Republics*, an English-language daily in Mexico City. Clarke
was an ex-confederate officer and one of the many American Southerners
who had fled to Mexico following the Civil War in the hopes of recreating
a plantation society under the empire of Maximilian. When the Confederate
colonies failed most of the Americans returned north but a few, like Clarke,
remained.[5]

The new U.S. Minister greeted Clarke, Butler and the other guests warmly
and urged them to join with him in raising the American profile in Mexico.
Foster used the meeting to present himself and his services to the community
and expressed his hope that "we might become better acquainted with each
other, promote social intercourse and in some manner elevate the standard
of American citizenship in the place of our present residence." The Minister
admonished his guests gently, having "regretted to learn" that there had been
no general observance of the U.S. national anniversary for several years. The
appearance of the American cemetery had been sadly neglected as well, Foster pointed out, insulting the memory of those American soldiers for whom
it had originally been established. Finally, Foster proposed the formation of

an American Benevolence Society to assist needy Americans residing in or traveling through Mexico. It was shameful, felt Foster, for those confronted with misfortune to have to appeal for charity to the Mexican government when their own compatriots were available to assist them.[6]

After the speeches the banquet descended into a flurry of toasts as Americans offered cups to "The President of the U.S.," "The President of Mexico," "The Memory of Washington," "The Honor of Country," and "The Enterprise of America," As the banquet continued they cheerily progressed through "hips," for Mrs. Foster, the ladies of America, the ladies of Mexico, the American ladies in Mexico, Mexican ladies in the U.S., and, not surprisingly, ladies in general. The following day Editor Clarke published an effusive thanks to the Minister for reviving the fraternal spirit of the American community in Mexico and ushering in a splendid new era in its history.

Foster's approach certainly reflected his experience in political party organizing back home, but it also reflected common American assumptions about morality and national identity. In Foster's opinion, the local American community was not only disorganized, but dissolute, given its members' adaptation to local customs. Throughout his years in Mexico, Foster invariably judged Americans he met by their ability to preserve American religious and social customs despite their immersion in the Mexican environment. As chaperone of the American community it was both politically expedient and morally fitting that Foster struggle to "elevate the standard of American civilization" in the Mexican capital and recall American residents in Mexico to their national identity. The organizations Foster founded and promoted during his years as Minister not only improved the care of the cemetery and the indigent, but provided important forums for Americans to socialize and refresh their American patriotism.

During his residence in Mexico City Foster also worked hard to improve relations between the American and Mexican social communities. Although Foster never became confident in his conversational Spanish, he had his speeches translated so that he could deliver them in Spanish himself. He welcomed Mexicans to American community gatherings on Thanksgiving, Washington's Birthday, and other holidays, and encouraged Americans to attend Mexican celebrations as well. Mary Parke Foster shared in this work by opening the legation to Tuesday evening receptions, carefully limited to tea and "light refreshments." Foster was careful to preserve his own customs in the Mexican capital. The Minister considered the Mexican habit of exchanging social calls on Sunday unacceptable for a day devoted to worship. Mrs. Foster's weekly receptions, pointed out her husband, provided an acceptable social alternative, without "unnecessary extravagance, ostentation, or strong spirits." While many in the capital may have found their religious prohibitions on alcohol, tobacco or Sunday socializing "a little odd," Foster felt the Mexicans grew to respect their beliefs.

By the time Foster departed Mexico in 1880 he proudly noted that he had succeeded in breaching the social barrier between the elite Mexican and American communities. Relations certainly did change over the course of Foster's tenure, but Foster's comments revealed more about his aspirations than reality. Foster had certainly set out to provide an example of decorous American behavior in his own household, yet accounts of banquets and balls during the ensuing years suggest that his practices hardly set the standards for all American social life in Mexico. More importantly, although the American population was expanding, the comments of later residents suggest that contact with Mexican society actually decreased (see Chapter 5). Foster's most important social legacy was not breaching the divide between the two communities, but in forging an American community among the disparate American residents of the southern capital. Adaptation and compromise in social relations, Foster's overall behavior suggested, should come from the Mexican, not the American side.

Foster did not confine himself to social diplomacy, but set out to promote trade as well. Upon arrival he had been shocked by the state of American commerce in Mexico City. Despite Mexico's proximity to the U.S., Americans were vastly outnumbered by Spanish and British merchants. Just that spring, departing U.S. Minister Thomas Nelson had lamented that in Mexico City, the largest city of Spanish America, there were no more than two or three mercantile houses run by Americans. Nelson compared U.S. merchants with their European counterparts and concluded that Americans simply had not made serious efforts to enter the market. Americans charged higher interest for credit, ignored Mexican preferences, packaged their goods poorly (a significant complaint in a region where the vast majority of transport was by mule) and responded rudely to Mexican complaints. Nelson also noted the absence of American bank branches in the capital, crucial for providing credit in a region with generally scarce banking facilities. Finally, Nelson condemned the poor quality of U.S. consular agents, who showed little interest in surveying opportunities for American traders, seldom spoke Spanish, and were generally considered useless by both the American and Mexican business communities. U.S.-Mexican commerce, the former Minister had concluded, was in a state of "the utmost prostration and decay."[7]

Foster found little to dispute in Nelson's assessment, and also faulted both the American business sector and the U.S. government for the dearth of commerce. He was embarrassed to report that his own nation showed no interest in promoting regular exchange with its neighbor, while Mexico, a much poorer nation, subsidized steamship service between New York and

Veracruz to assure regular communication with the outside world.[8] In Foster's view irregular communication and the lack of reliable information were key impediments to bi-national commerce, and the Minister took personal responsibility for improving U.S. knowledge of Mexican commercial opportunities. As Minister, Foster enjoyed making investigative visits to factories, mines and plantations. He used these excursions to gather information on Mexican industry and pressed his consuls to collect data on coffee production, wheat prices, local regulations, judicial practices, and other useful topics. Foster summarized his research in formal reports to the State Department, published data in trade and popular periodicals, and shared his opinions with individuals investigating investment opportunities. "The Cultivation of Coffee in Mexico," published by Foster in the *Monthly Report of the Department of Agriculture*, exemplified his methodical style. He not only described the techniques and technology of Mexican coffee farmers, but reported on the economics of the coffee plantation and the coffee trade, the extent of coffee cultivation in Mexico, and the opportunities for investment and trade.[9]

Like Nelson before him, Foster found fault with the consular agents he supervised. At the time there were no standards for selecting or training consuls, and few financial incentives for seeking the post. Consuls were frequently appointed simply because they were Americans living abroad, a situation which usually implied business or family connections with the region. It was hard for consuls so connected to preserve the Washington-centered perspective expected in the commission of their duties. Foster soon dedicated himself to retraining his consuls to his own specifications and he issued a stream of recommendations to Washington on the need to apply uniform standards, training and procedures throughout U.S. missions abroad.

Foster's interest in rationalizing the work of America's agents abroad reflected both his own preference for order and a broader American transformation as increasingly complex organizations demanded improved attention to management methods and standardization of practices. The State Department, like other public and private entities of the era, was in the throes of reinvention occasioned by expansion and integration.[10] The new sciences of time management, quality control, and resource management that were emerging in corporate organization and city planning practices appeared in federal government reorganization as well. Foster, like other managers of his era, joined in the search for order in his field.

When Foster was not inventorying Mexican production or lecturing his consuls he attended to the specific tasks the Department of State had set for him. Secretary Hamilton Fish had instructed the new Minister to support the efforts of the U.S.-Mexican Claims Commission of 1868 and to promote the general security of American persons and property in Mexico.[11] The simple phrases masked an array of intractable problems that had plagued U.S. – Mexican relations for decades. The staggering caseload of the Claims Commission, which investigated legal suits that had arisen since the conclusion of the U.S.-Mexican War in 1848, was an indication of the difficulties Foster would face in safeguarding Americans and their possessions, and a political challenge in itself. Years of civil strife had left a legacy of legal cases involving forced loans, wrongful imprisonment, seized and destroyed property, and personal death and injury among residents of Mexico and the border region. Although a portion of the suits investigated by the commission involved Mexicans demanding compensation for American-inflicted damages, the overwhelming majority of the cases handled were Americans suing for payment from the Mexican government. The investigation and prosecution of these cases was limited by Mexico City's limited control over outlying regions and its frequent refusal to pay compensation for damage inflicted by rival factions. In addition, the Lerdo government had little interest in the claims process; the payment of claims to distant Americans did nothing to raise the government's stature before its own citizens, especially when there were seldom funds or mechanisms to redress the suffering Mexicans had endured during the same turbulent years.

The border region presented other headaches for Foster. Frontier issues had been a constant source of conflict between the nations throughout the previous century, but the American and Mexican civil wars had aggravated conditions in the thinly populated region. While government troops were distracted by domestic military campaigns, the undermanned border region had become a battleground of armed factions profiting from smuggling and extortion. The Free Trade Zone, established in the Northern Mexican states by Mexico City in 1851 to stimulate settlement and commercial growth in the sparsely populated north, was criticized on both sides of the border as an inducement to illegal trade, while the expansion of the Mexican and American populations at mid-century created new problems by displacing Native Americans tribes. By the 1870s the poorly patrolled frontier had become the home of refugee and outlaw populations who lashed out at settlers on both sides of the border. They took advantage of the lack of coordination between U.S. and Mexican border patrols and eluded capture by slipping across the international boundary in either direction. Each side accused the other of tolerating the miscreants and by 1873 the situation had induced both nations to appoint commissions to investigate the frontier situation.[12]

This sudden flurry of official preoccupation with border problems did not necessarily mean that the situation had deteriorated further, but rather that the level of regional crime and disorder was no longer acceptable. The expanding Mexican and American populations along the frontier lands and the growth of economic links across the border were creating new demands for security.[13] Nor can military assessments of a frontier 'crisis' be regarded as wholly impartial; both the U.S. and Mexican militaries were affected by post-war malaise resulting from the declining level of public interest in their actions and a weakened sense of mission. In the absence of civil or foreign war, frontier conflicts provided the only podium for winning additional funding, modernized equipment, or career promotions, and these institutional politics encouraged exaggeration and drama in accounts.[14] Finally, the same modernization of the state that was motivating Foster to standardize diplomatic practice in Mexico City was affecting the distant frontier as changes in communication, administration, and techniques of statecraft were increasing the reach of national capitals. During the 1870s the shadow of the State fell over the realm of vigilantes, sheriffs and mountain men as the borderlands were integrated into each nation's national territory.

Foster assumed his post in the midst of this transition in the reach and interests of the state and was soon busy investigating suits, drawing up petitions, and requesting restitution for injury and damages. His methodical style served him well through the complex issues he pursued and it was only a matter of time before Foster began to suggest systematic solutions aimed at resolving the underlying sources of disorder. He proposed the abolition of the northern Free Trade Zone and the negotiation of an agreement to permit reciprocal border crossings in pursuit of suspected felons. Foster pressured President Lerdo to rein in autonomous chieftains like the infamous northern General, Juan Cortina, who was reputedly encouraging and profiting from cross-border raids. Foster emphasized the practical advantage of an extradition treaty to the Mexican President, and frequently recommended ways in which the Mexicans could better their military training, custom house management and postal system, and thus improve their management and control of the national territory.

Although Foster never recorded Mexican comments on his proposals, the Mexican response appears unenthusiastic. None of his specific suggestions were adopted by President Lerdo. Extradition treaties and reciprocal troop crossing agreements were wildly unpopular in Mexico, and thus politically infeasible for the insecure Lerdo administration. Nor, in 1873, did the central government have the political power to revoke the northern Free Trade Zone or clamp down on distant military factions. When Lerdo did arrest Cortina, partly in response to intense U.S. pressure, it may have cost him the presidency. Cortina escaped from federal prison, joined his forces to those of Porfirio Díaz, and helped push Lerdo from power.

While Foster's official diplomatic record depicts a Minister busily imposing order on trade patterns, consular methods and Mexico itself, the *Memoirs* also captures another side of the Minister's experience. Lyrical descriptions of the Mexican landscape, social customs and pleasure outings outshine in detail and vibrancy the discussions of diplomatic business. Foster clearly delighted in his new home and in the excursions he and his family made from Mexico City. Accompanied by other residents of the capital they glided among the floating gardens of Xochimilco and picnicked at the foot of the volcanoes guarding the southern side of the city. They crossed the lake to Texcoco, explored pre-Columbian ruins at Teotihuacan's Temple of the Sun, and lunched amid the flowering plazas of San Angel. Foster and his family made rail and road excursions to country houses in Cuernavaca, Pachuca, Puebla and Toluca. The Minister and his wife even ignored the hysterical reports of bandits circulating in the American community and undertook long investigative visits to southern and central Mexico on horseback and by stage. Foster delighted in these sojourns and was "agreeably disappointed" by his failure to encounter hardship in his travels.

A letter Foster wrote in 1875, reprinted in the Memoirs, captures the enthusiasm with which Foster approached his early years in Mexico. Foster and his wife, Mary Parke, set off across one hundred miles of highlands from the town of Cordoba to Jalapa in the state of Veracruz. During the week-long horseback trip they were accompanied only by a private secretary, a guide and a muleteer. "You would have enjoyed seeing us starting out from Cordoba," he wrote his daughter, "all of us with broad-brimmed Mexican hats and riding accoutrements, and our baggage strapped on the pack horses—a novel sight for Americans, and we even attracted much attention from the natives."[15]

Of course the Minister and his wife were not the only scenery; Foster also recorded the visual impact of the lush vegetation, wild orchids, stands of coffee and tropical fruit crops, as well as the existence of a remote mountain pueblo, "beautiful for situation," but disappointingly unattractive in its bamboo and thatch construction. The pattern of description persisted throughout Foster's accounts of trips to Oaxaca and other states. Fruits and flowers received detailed discussion, while the human landscape of Mexico through which Foster and his wife proceeded was barely recorded. Native residents were noted only when they clustered in the streets to watch the progress of the visitors, as if their silent observation of the visitors were their only occupation. In Foster's accounts it was the travelers themselves who monopolize attention, obscuring dramatic vistas as they make perilous ascents and complete grueling rides. Foster, who seemed instinctively to see himself in the third person in his letters and *Memoirs*, cut a dashing figure in his saddle as he descended the rugged hillsides of Mexico.

Superficially, the chatty accounts of picnics and vacations appear to have little to do with the staid and systematic work Foster carried on in his professional capacity, yet their inclusion in the *Memoirs* suggests that Foster saw his social life in the community and his travels in Mexico as an integral aspect of his mission to Mexico. In his early years in Mexico Foster explored not only his host country, but his own professional, social, and backcountry abilities. His account revealed enthusiasm for the southern nation, but even more clearly it revealed enthusiasm for the image that Foster, and the civilization he represented, cast against the backdrop of Mexico.

NOTES

1. Foster, *Diplomatic Memoirs*, 1–17, and Michael Devine *John W. Foster: Politics and Diplomacy in the Imperial Era, 1873–1917* (Athens, OH: Ohio University Press, 1981). On State Department practices of the era, see Robert L. Beisner, *From the Old Diplomacy to the New, 1865–1900* (Arlington Heights: Harlan Davidson, 1975) and Warren Ilchman, *Professional Diplomacy in the United States, 1779–1939: A Study in Administrative History* (Chicago: University of Chicago Press, 1961).

2. U.S. Minister Lewis D. Campbell, as described in Daniel Cosio Villegas, *Historia Moderna de México, El Porfiriato: Vida Politica Exterior* (Mexico: Hermes, 1963), 5–6.

3. "The Inauguration of the Mexican Railway," *Two Republics*, (Mexico City) 4 January 1873.

4. While most Mexicans remain convinced even today that the U.S. ignored their struggle to preserve republican government during the French intervention, the real story is somewhat more complex. See Matías Romero, *Mexican Lobby: Matías Romero in Washington, 1861–1867*, ed. Thomas Schoonover (Lexington: University Press of Kentucky, 1986).

5. Deborah Baldwin, *Protestants and the Mexican Revolution: Missionaries, Ministers and Social Change* (Urbana: University of Illinois Press, 1990), 1–23; William Butler, *Mexico in Transition: From the Power of Political Romanism to Civil and Religious Liberty* (New York: Hunt and Easton, 1892); "George W. Clarke," *Two Republics*, 25 December 1880; and Andrew F. Rolle, *The Lost Cause: The Confederate Exodus to Mexico* (Norman: University of Oklahoma Press, 1965).

6. Foster, *Memoirs*, 20–21; "The Fourth of July in Mexico," *Two Republics*, 5, 12 July 1873.

7. Richard J. Salvucci, "The Origins and Progress of U.S.-Mexican trade, 1825–1884: 'hoc opus, hic labor est'," *Hispanic American Historical Review* 71 (November 1991): 697–735. The report of Minister Thomas Nelson to Secretary of State Hamilton Fish was summarized in the *Two Republics*, 8 February 1873.

8. Vicente G. Manero, *Noticias históricas sobre el comercio exterior de México desde la conquista hasta el año de 1878* (México: Tip. de G.A. Esteva, 1879), 57.

9. "The Cultivation of Coffee in Mexico," *Monthly Report of the Department of Agriculture*, 14 (July 1876).

10. The impact of management science on government practices is explored in Stephen Skowronek, *Building an American State: The Expansion of National Administrative Capacities, 1877–1920* (New York: Cambridge University Press, 1982). Also illustrative is John Francis Matthews, "Little Favors from my Government: U.S. Consuls in Mexico, 1821–65" (Ph.D. diss., Texas Christian University, 1993).

11. Secretary of State Hamilton Fish to John W. Foster, 26 April, 25 June 1873, U.S.D.S. Instructions, National Archives, Washington, D.C.

12. U.S. Congress, Senate, "Report of the U.S. Commission to Texas," 42nd Congress, 1st. sess., ser. 1565, Senate Report No. 39, (Washington, 1874) and the United States of Mexico, "Reports of the Committee of Investigation sent in 1873 by the Mexican Government to the Frontier of Texas, English edition," (New York: n.p., 1875). Detailed accounts of frontier disputes can be found in Robert Danforth Gregg, *The Influence of Border Troubles on Relations between the U.S. and Mexico, 1876–1910*, (Baltimore: Johns Hopkins University Press, 1937) and James Morton Callahan, "A Decade of American Foreign Policy Related to Frontier Troubles," in *American Foreign Policy in Mexican Relations* (New York: MacMillan, 1932), 341–68.

13. Mario Cerutti, "Estudio Introductoria" in Mario Cerutti and Miguel A. Gonzalez Quiroga, eds., *Frontera e História Económica: Texas y el Norte de México* (México: Instituto Mora, Universidad Autónoma Metropolitana, 1993), 7–27.

14. Robert Wooster, "The Army and the Politics of Expansion: Texas and the Southwestern Borderlands, 1870–86," *Southwestern Historical Quarterly* 93 (October 1989): 151–67.

15. Foster, *Memoirs*, 35–36.

Chapter Two

Awaiting the Descent into Chaos

The Díaz revolution of 1876 disrupted Foster's plans for Mexico and altered the conditions under which he would finish his mission. General Porfirio Díaz, a Liberal hero of the struggle against the French, had disputed President Lerdo's claim to the presidency since 1872. Over the years Díaz and other critics had continued to decry what they saw as the emergence of a Lerdo dictatorship. In January 1876 revolutionaries in the southern city of Oaxaca accused Lerdo of manipulating the Constitution and pledged allegiance to Díaz, a native son and former governor, in the Plan of Tuxtepec. Lerdo's control quickly unraveled during the following months as reports of new revolts arrived from Puebla, Veracruz, Guerrero, and even distant Yucatán.[1]

The instability of Lerdo's government was obvious to Foster. In April he wrote Secretary of State Hamilton Fish that "the revolution has steadily increased. The railroad between this city and Veracruz has been destroyed and traffic has been practically suspended." Mail communication had become "uncertain and difficult," stagecoaches were "detained and robbed in all directions, and travel throughout the country is greatly interrupted and dangerous." Foster's was not the only voice of concern to reach Washington; relations along the perennially troublesome border had deteriorated also and Texans clamored for the U.S. to impose order on the cross-border region with or without Mexican permission.

The multiplying declarations of martial law helped convince Foster of the wisdom of packing his family off for a long summer visit to the Centennial Exhibit in Philadelphia. One spring evening Foster and his family mounted a heavily garrisoned train and with "great foreboding" threaded their way down the mountains to Veracruz. American flags placed at either end of the train, common practice for diplomatic vehicles, alerted all to the presence of the American Minister and led many to assume that Foster had used his

22

influence with the rebels to secure safe passage for the train, a charge Foster firmly dismissed. The passengers arrived unmolested in Veracruz where Foster escorted his family aboard a waiting steamer before returning to his duties in the capital. In July the Minister also departed for the U.S., ostensibly to consult with colleagues in Washington, but also to resume his work for the Republican Party in anticipation of the upcoming U.S. elections.[2]

In the fall Foster learned of unexpected gains by Díaz and hurriedly returned to Mexico City where the strain of the struggle for the presidency was evident. There was "widespread alarm…and a general fear of an uprising of the lower classes of malcontents," noted Foster in his report to Secretary of State Fish. In Foster's opinion General Díaz's revolt lacked public support and was seen by Mexicans as "unwarranted" and "the work of a professional revolutionary." Despite the disorder, Foster assured Fish that the rumors of Díaz's strength were undoubtedly exaggerated.[3]

The following weeks revealed that Foster had underestimated Díaz, whose supporters won a critical battle against the government troops on the sixteenth of November and forced Lerdo's troops to retreat from the capital on the twentieth. That evening the foreign community, joined by a few apprehensive Mexican Lerdistas, gathered in the halls of the American legation as they awaited the descent into chaos. Despite the air of foreboding that hung over the capital, his guests passed a cheerful evening, recalled Foster, occupied with games of whist, hearty conversation and a late supper. Luckily they were not forced to resort to the armed defense of the legation, for the morning dawned to reveal quiet streets. Lerdo, his cabinet, and the Congress had decamped and the municipal police and federal garrison peacefully transferred their allegiance to Díaz.

The transition to the new regime passed without the turmoil Foster feared, but the Minister must have felt uneasy listening to the thunderous cheers that greeted Díaz and his twelve thousand troops as they entered the city on November 23. As the weeks went on, Foster, like many American observers back home, assumed that Mexico was slipping back into the chaotic despotism believed endemic to tropical nations. After all, the revolutionary government of Díaz had not only overthrown an elected government, it canceled contracts, imposed forced loans, enacted martial law and employed the controversial Juan Cortina among its military chiefs. From Foster's perspective, Díaz assaulted not merely Lerdo, but the fragile scaffolding of civilized government itself.

To complicate matters, Foster's diplomatic accreditation was now unclear; former President Lerdo had fled north but continued his claim to the presidency. Meanwhile, a third presidential contender, Supreme Court Justice José María Iglesias, challenged Díaz from the central Mexican town of Guanajuato.

Without the ability to evaluate each combatant's position, Foster had little way of knowing whether Díaz's strong showing in the capital accurately reflected his control throughout the nation or whether Lerdo or Iglesias would soon unseat him. Given the uncertainties of the situation Foster suggested to Secretary of State Hamilton Fish that the United States should refrain from immediate recognition of the Díaz administration. Fish, preparing to leave office himself following the election of Rutherford B. Hayes in November, agreed, instructing Foster to use his "best judgment" on the matter.[4]

Foster's reasonable response to the Mexican political situation had unexpected consequences as the temporary delay in recognition stretched into an eighteen month hiatus in official relations while relations between the two nations steadily deteriorated. The dispute over recognition reflected a deeper dispute over visions of the emerging international system. Although Foster's concerns over extending recognition in 1876 were practical more than principled, he quickly became tied to an American policy which saw the extension of recognition as a diplomatic tool for influencing the Díaz regime. While Foster later disagreed with the State Department's decision to continue delaying recognition, in general he shared the basic assumption that Americans would set the standards and rules for hemispheric behavior.

Díaz, in contrast, saw the American decision to withhold recognition as unwarranted intervention in the domestic politics of a sovereign nation and evidence of ominous American paternalism in regional relations. The denial of recognition had both practical and psychological repercussions as it cut off the Mexican government's access to international credit and disrupted trade while nervous merchants waited for a climate in which contracts would be more secure. More alarmingly, it signaled to Díaz's opponents that they could continue arming, organizing, and competing for U.S. attention and aid. The absence of U.S. recognition of the Díaz government could even embolden filibusterers along the U.S.-Mexican border, who might attempt to negotiate land transfers with shady officials of their own choosing.

Over time the battle over recognition assumed the character of a bitter personal competition between the new ruler of Mexico and the U.S. Minister in Mexico City. The Díaz administration fought the U.S. policy not only for the sake of Porfirio Díaz's political survival, but for the security of the Mexican nation, which had suffered repeated invasions and annexations from other states who had dismissed Mexico City's authority over Mexican territory. The contest would persist even after diplomatic relations were restored in 1878 as Foster continued to prosecute a policy which assumed the eventual ascendance of an American-inspired global order, while Díaz sought unconditional international recognition for his regime and his nation. During the next three years the bi-national relationship would be marred by these conflicting expectations.

Maintaining the U.S. policy of non-recognition would present the most inconveniences to the U.S. Minister in Mexico City, who continued to be faced with practical problems that required some level of interaction. Foster had barely committed himself to non-recognition when an awkward deadline approached. In January the Mexican government was due to submit the first payment on the settlements awarded by the U.S.-Mexican Claims Commission of 1868. Foster had to weigh his original diplomatic instructions (to facilitate the work of the Commission) with his misgivings over the new administration and his uncertain accreditation status in the capital. Díaz faced a far more difficult choice. Ignoring the payment would probably end his administration's access to future international credit and might even provide the excuse for yet another U.S. annexation, but raising the money would require him to impose a forced loan on the wealthy families of the capital, hardly a way to win them to his side. In the end, Díaz traded the good will of the Mexican elite (who were mostly opposed to him anyway) for the good opinion of a much stronger interest group, the U.S. financial community, and raised the forced "loan" among the capital's residents.

The logistics of the payment were complicated not only by non-recognition and the use of forced loans, but by disrupted telegraph lines, shipwreck, currency exchange disputes and confusions with letters-of-credit, all typical hazards of international finance during the era. The saga concluded with diplomatic pettiness in Washington, where the Mexican government was forced to rely on the former administration's Minister to Washington, Ignacio Mariscal, as Díaz's newly arrived representative, José María Mata, could not be officially received until the Díaz government had been recognized. Mariscal agreed to accompany Mata to see the U.S. Secretary of State, but he left Díaz's representative waiting in an outer officer while the payment was delivered. In his notes Secretary of State Fish noted only that the issue of recognition was not raised at the meeting. Although the payment left the issue of recognition unresolved, it proved a wise investment on Díaz's part; the timely payment helped establish the regime's reputation for fiscal responsibility among international financiers, providing Díaz with a future reserve of financial and political capital abroad.[5]

Unfortunately Washington's attitude toward recognition appeared to be hardening as the incoming administration of Rutherford B. Hayes took shape. In February Foster suggested that the Mexican government officially notify the world community of the change of government through the common diplomatic practice of a government letter to heads of state, but when Díaz issued the letter, Foster indicated no change in U.S. policy. In the early spring, Foster notified Díaz that the newly inaugurated Hayes administration was awaiting the return of an elected constitutional government, yet Díaz's victory in the Mexican elections of April 1877 passed without official comment from Washington. Foster then informed the now constitutionally elected President Díaz that the U.S. government was awaiting proof of stability, but, again, the obvious control of the Díaz administration elicited no change in U.S. policy.

By late spring the Díaz administration was becoming frustrated with the delay. Relations declined precipitously after June 1, 1877, when President Hayes instructed General E.O.C. Ord, commander of the frontier army, to place his forces on alert and pursue suspected criminals across the border into Mexican territory if necessary. Hayes was not really announcing a change in practice for both the U.S. army and the Texan militia had been crossing the border in pursuit of suspects for several years, but Hayes' bald and unilateral statement to the world community implicitly discredited the Díaz administration for failing to control the border region. From the Mexican perspective it appeared as if the Americans were building justifications for invasion and President Díaz responded by placing his own frontier army on alert, directing General Gerónimo Treviño to repel "force with force."[6]

The standoff along the frontier was matched by a diplomatic standoff in Mexico City. Incoming U.S. Secretary of State William Evarts followed the June orders to the military with new instructions for Foster detailing the issues to be resolved before recognition could be considered. One section of the instructions concerned border security, another the restitution (plus interest) of forced loans extracted from American citizens and compensation for damaged property or wrongful imprisonment, a third, the abolition of the Mexican Free Trade Zone, a fourth the extradition of "wild Indians" living in Mexico to U.S. custody, and, not to overlook any pending matters, the negotiation of a reciprocity treaty and new postal conventions.

When Foster communicated the lengthy list to Mexican Foreign Minister Ignacio Vallarta, he was met with an angry denunciation of U.S. policy. Vallarta condemned the American course of action as "utterly without cause or provocation." The Mexican Foreign Minister insisted that his government had met all the conditions of recognition customarily demanded under international practice and that the military order of June 1 "disregarded all the rules of international law and the practices of civilized nations and treated the Mexicans as savages, as Kaffirs of Africa!" Vallarta concluded by declaring that, "an absolute declaration of war would have been more considerate." In his official report of the interview Foster wryly noted that the written account fell "far short of conveying the intensity of [Vallarta's] feelings."[7] Foster was so impressed by the atmosphere of hostility in the capital that he even cancelled his annual 4th of July celebration.

Foster was not the only observer to fear that war was imminent. Newspapers across the U.S. watched the standoff between Mexico City and Washington with varying degrees of enthusiasm. Most disturbing to Mexican readers of American papers must have been the common assumption, shared by papers from New York to California, that a plan was afoot to annex the northern states of Mexico to settle American damage claims. On 24 June the *San Francisco Chronicle* quoted their Washington correspondent as saying that it was well known that Secretary Evarts and the Administration "are promoting by all means at command the annexation of the five northern states of Mexico." The *San Francisco Chronicle* found nothing surprising in this news, and, in fact, thought a "weak" nation should take advantage of the opportunity to settle its debts and "part with a slice of territory" to avoid continuing chaos and mismanagement. While the advantages to the U.S. were clear, the editors worried that it would be hard to convince Mexicans of the case, as there is "a strong prejudice against the Americans there, an unyielding Spanish pride of nationality, and a pervading fear that the native population would be forced into the background by Yankee energy and tact." A few days later the paper followed up by noting that perhaps a more limited annexation of the river valleys of the Rio Grande and the Gulf of Mexico, for which Mexico has "no sort of use," would satisfy U.S. claims without "serious offense to Mexican pride."[8]

Other newspapers echoed the themes. The New York *Herald* interviewed Texan Congressman Gustav Schleicher who, dissatisfied with the work of the Claims Commission, was overseeing the preparation of a new statement of damages to be presented to the government of Mexico. Schleicher, the paper reported, supported the possibility of trading land in lieu of claims payments for the land in question remains "comparatively desolate, and will remain so until some energetic people again develop its resources."[9] The St. Louis *Globe Democrat* sarcastically agreed that there was "no more able bodied race of claimants in the world" than the Americans living along the Mexican border. Despite his reservations regarding the reliability of the American claimants, the author concluded that "the country [Mexico] is one of marvelous wealth; it is a shame to see it going to ruin in the hands of the present natives and there seems to be no salvation for it unless we take it." *The Democratic Statesman* of Austin, Texas, also supported Evarts' policy to "bring Mexico to a proper sense of international obligations." The paper added to the insult by arguing that Texas did not desire outright annexation because it had no interest in the voting population "Mexico would furnish," but merely sought to secure rail corridors to Monterrey and Mazatlán.[10]

Although later studies of the Hayes and Evarts papers suggest that the annexationist plots received no serious attention in the White House, the administration may have found the rumors a convenient distraction from matters closer to home, namely the ongoing investigations of irregularities in the 1876 election. The simultaneous appearance of several nearly identical newspaper editorials encouraging an American protectorate over northern Mexico on March 4, Hayes' inauguration day, is certainly suggestive of coordination.[11] In addition, Hayes was heavily dependent on the Texan wing of the Republican Party and may even have encouraged the tales of annexation to strengthen his domestic political position in the Southwest.[12]

Hayes policy showed little concern for the uncomfortable position of Minister Foster in Mexico. From Mexico City it was easy to believe that American troops would soon be pouring across the border and the frustration with Washington focused increasingly on the American representative in their midst. From the Mexican perspective it appeared that Foster exercised masterful control over U.S. policy. When, in June, Foster submitted the petitions dictated by the Secretary of State's office in Washington to the office of Vallarta detailing the "pending issues" obstructing recognition, the Mexicans could not help but notice how closely the concerns outlined matched Foster's earlier objectives in Mexico. From Vallarta's perspective the consistency in the American concerns proved Foster's ruthless determination to force Mexican compliance with the American Minister's long-range goals for reorganizing Mexico.

In reality, Mexican anger against Foster was misdirected. Despite the apparent evidence against him, Foster's communications with Washington reveal that he was not nearly as masterful as the Mexicans believed. Although it was Foster who decided not to grant recognition at the moment of the revolution, his influence on U.S. policy toward Mexico declined steadily as the new cabinet of incoming President Rutherford B. Hayes took shape, and appeared to disappear entirely after Hayes' inauguration. As early as January 20 Foster questioned the wisdom of withholding recognition from a government with which the U.S. had many outstanding concerns; but he received no permission to change policy. On February 19 Foster suggested he proceed to recognize Diaz, and two weeks later he argued that the upcoming Mexican election and Hayes inauguration in Washington would provide a convenient occasion for justifying a shift in relations. Initially the incoming Secretary of State, Evarts, approved Foster's suggestion, but three days later he reversed his position and issued a blistering critique of the depravity along the border and a thinly veiled threat that the U.S. might soon consider unilateral action along the frontier.[13]

Foster conveyed the brusque message to Vallarta but confidentially informed Evarts that he felt it would be better to first recognize Mexico and then negotiate for reciprocal crossings and other means of addressing border insecurity. He followed this observation with a personal letter to Evarts on April 28th that presented arguments in favor of recognition, including his growing belief that Diaz, now sanctioned by elections, represented the best hope for avoiding general turmoil in the nation. After Diaz's inauguration in May, Foster again reminded his government that he was awaiting "specific instructions," but what followed was an ugly warning from acting Secretary of State William Seward that the U.S. government, which normally did not "scrutinize closely the regularity or irregularity of the methods by which presidents are inaugurated," was awaiting "some guarantee" of Mexico's commitment to enforcing order and resolving outstanding issues. Foster was further surprised by the military order of June 1st that was reported in Mexican newspapers even before official notice reached the U.S. Legation in Mexico City.[14]

To contribute to his misery, Foster narrowly escaped the personal insult of losing his diplomatic post to another political appointee during the presidential transition in Washington. Only frantic letters and the intervention of his original sponsor, Senator Morton of Indiana, saved his appointment. Even with his post assured, however, Foster was rapidly losing his predominant position as dean of the diplomatic corps in Mexico City. Emperor Wilhelm of Germany was the first to officially recognize the new Mexican regime and the leaders of El Salvador, Guatemala, Italy, and Spain soon extended recognition as well. Even France, still bitter over Mexico's defeat of and assassination of Emperor Maximilian, made tentative overtures towards Díaz. By the end of July Foster lamented that the U.S. would soon be the only power without formal relations with the Mexican republic.[15]

Contrary to the Mexican belief that Foster was the masterful architect of U.S. policy, the American Minister was in an unenviable position, alienated from Mexican political circles and ignored by the Department of State in Washington. During the summer of 1877 Foster pursued the frustrating and unproductive negotiations Evarts had assigned him with Mexican Foreign Minister Vallarta, yet his efforts were apparently irrelevant to U.S. policy. In July President Hayes noted in his diary that he saw no further reason to delay recognition, he only wondered whether they should extend recognition immediately or "let Mexico hang by the eyelids" through August. In deciding to ignore Mexico for another year the Hayes administration left Foster hanging as well. Months later an uncharacteristically despondent Foster plaintively questioned his State Department superiors about the rationale of Hayes' June 1 order, which he assumed was "based upon the recommendations of military officers in command in Texas, not upon my dispatches to your department." Even thirty years later the frustrations of the era were evident in Foster's

Memoirs. While Foster normally described his career in terms of challenges met and mastered, the account of the recognition crisis portrays him as a man trapped within levels of intrigue and ignorance, hindered by scheming politicians and amateur diplomats.[16]

Foster's perception of policy derailed by machinations at the highest level was partly accurate, yet also conveniently self-serving. While the Hayes administration never made any serious preparation for war with Mexico, it cultivated public indignation with Mexico to mollify the Texan delegation and distract public attention from the scandal-ridden election of 1876. Ironically, in his *Memoirs* Foster used the Mexican crisis in an identical way to distract the reader from these less flattering events. Foster hinted at Washington "war schemes" to divert attention from the irregularities of the U.S. election, but he failed to mention his own role in the electoral controversies of 1876. He did not mention the party work he completed during his home leave in the summer and fall of 1876, nor did he mention his later investigation by the U.S. House Select Committee on Electoral Frauds. Although Foster was never charged with wrongdoing, the congressional committee cited him as being "instrumental" in the secret financial takeover of an opposition newspaper and in the administration of a "sort of side committee" that paid voters to switch parties.[17] Neither Foster nor Hayes was in a strong position to criticize Mexican politics.

Foster also faulted the amateur diplomats, or 'extra official agents,' who began arriving from Washington for derailing negotiations between the two nations. The appearance of Simon Stevens, who arrived flaunting a card from Evarts which he used to misrepresent himself as a State Department emissary, John Frisbie, who arrived bearing a letter of introduction from Evarts, and N.S. Renau, entrusted with dispatches from Evarts, disheartened the Minister, whose authority as the chief U.S. spokesman in Mexico was undermined with every new guest.[18]

While the political troubles of the Hayes administration and the lack of discretion within the State Department certainly contributed to the complications of the era, they were not the primary causes of Foster's diminished role in Mexico City. Underlying the angry rhetoric, the bungling amateurs, and the military alerts was a new age of communication, transportation, and economics that was expanding the international horizons of each nation. The confusion was in many ways a testament to Foster's success in promoting U.S. interests in Mexico in earlier years, as well as a product of improved infrastructure. Travel was improving, mail was more predictable, and telegrams were possible. Those same improvements Foster had once advocated now eroded his monopoly on information and weakened his ability to set the rules for American activity in Mexico. What Foster perceived as distortions of the diplomatic process (new attention to Mexican issues in U.S. Congressional debates and White House policy, the increasingly frequent appearance of potential investors and other private American citizens in Mexico, and a higher profile for Mexico in American newspapers and journals) were merely evidence of new forms of contact outside of Foster's immediate control.

The new era in U.S.-Mexican relations was replete with growing pains and opportunities. President Hayes was only able to exploit Mexican issues in support of his domestic political needs because relations with Mexico were already attracting new attention within both government and private circles. While earlier Mexican coups had attracted little notice in the U.S., changing strategic and commercial concerns led American policymakers and investors to take a dim view of political disorder in 1876. Many feared that Mexican domestic turmoil would once again tempt Europeans to interfere in the southern nation, an outcome that an increasingly assertive U.S. sought to avoid throughout the region. The U.S. business community was also becoming interested in commercial opportunities in Mexico and, more generally, in establishing common international practices in trade and investment. General William S. Rosecrans, a railroad investor and a former military commander of Hayes during the Civil War, exploited his acquaintance with Hayes to repeatedly stress his belief that the U.S. should demand commercial and financial guarantees from Mexico prior to recognition. President Hayes recognized this new chorus of voices in American policy when he spoke before the U.S. Congress in 1877, defending his decision to break with traditional practice and withhold recognition from a de facto government. The approval of the domestic population was no longer sufficient grounds for American recognition of a regime, Hayes implied, now it was necessary for the new government to address U.S. concerns as well.[19]

The increased American attention to U.S.-Mexican affairs was matched by new notice from Mexico itself; even if invasion were unlikely, the Porfirian administration could not ignore the American political debates. The Lerdista movement was still actively fundraising in New York and Washington and Lerdista milita continued to train on the Texan border. The Diaz administration had already noted that former U.S. consul turned railroad promoter, Edward Lee Plumb, was promoting the Lerdista cause in Washington, and they worried that other opposition movements might also find allies among American investors who sought contracts and concessions.[20]

More immediately, Mexican officials wondered how to handle Americans like John B. Frisbie, the Californian entrepreneur who appeared in Mexico City in the early spring of 1877 bearing dispatches from Evarts. Frisbie's lack of discretion (tremendously annoying to Foster) soon allowed all to know that he hoped to arrange the sale of northern Mexican states to the U.S. as a means of settling the border issue. Frisbie had called upon Evarts in Washington and convinced the Secretary that his Spanish-Californian father-in-law could gain him a sympathetic audience with Diaz. Evarts, showing a tremendous lack of discretion himself, did not directly endorse Frisbie but instructed Foster to assist him in all his inquiries.[21]

The Diaz administration not only avoided an embarrassing overture from Frisbie by making known its adamant refusal to discuss territorial sales, it actually converted Frisbie and sent him back to Washington and New York to promote the Diaz administration. Diaz offered Frisbie the railroad concession previously granted to Edward Plumb, cementing Frisbie's interest in Diaz's success, and sending a clear message to other investors. James Stillman and William Palmer, who held rail concessions granted by earlier administrations, took careful note and moved from confrontation to accommodation with the new regime. In his conversion of Frisbie, Diaz signaled his own diplomatic offensive and the effective end of Foster's control over the American community.[22]

Foster's experience with Frisbie was emblematic of the Minister's confrontations with the inconveniences of the new era. Increased contact and U.S. activity abroad required competent and informed diplomatic representatives, yet the same growth of communications permitted international contact on an increasing variety of levels. Foster could not control the activity of private U.S. citizens with an interest in Mexico, and the still underdeveloped State Department worsened the situation by confusing the lines of authority in Mexico City. From Foster's perspective Frisbie's amateur diplomacy only aggravated an already volatile situation. The Minister dismissed Frisbie's father-in-law as a "garrulous old man" and described both as too "greatly elated with the importance of their mission" to preserve a low profile.[23] In the memoirs the portrait of Frisbie as bumbling amateur provided the perfect counterpoint to Foster's self-depiction as the skilled diplomat.

Foster's hostility toward Frisbie was more than professional, however for Frisbie, with his fluent Spanish, family connections, and freedom from diplomatic mandates, was at ease in the society in a way that Foster could never hope to duplicate, yet obviously envied. In his *Memoirs* Foster stressed his social role in the capital, describing an intimate relationship with the Mexican President in which Foster offered welcome advice to "the inexperienced statesman" and played matchmaker between Díaz and his future wife, Carmen Romero, in the salons of the capital. Yet Foster's portrait is not supported by other accounts of the era. Díaz's contemporary biographers mention Foster only in passing as "the U.S. Minister," and describe contact as minimal and Foster's advice as unwelcome. Justo Sierra, a leading intellectual in the Díaz circle, recalled that Foster "assumed the attitude of a haughty and disapproving tutor" in his interviews with Díaz. Even Foster's claim to Díaz's later marriage appears oddly exaggerated. Even if Díaz did first meet Romero at a legation tea, as Foster implies, the Mexican President was not yet widowed and it is highly unlikely Foster would have encouraged a romance between a married, middle aged "professional revolutionary" and the teenaged Miss Romero.[24]

In reality, it was not Foster but Frisbie who prospered in Porfirian circles. Frisbie remained in Mexico long after Foster left and several of his children married into the Mexican elite. In his memoirs, however, Foster dismissed the Frisbie episode only as an embarrassing failure, completely ignoring the way in which both Diaz and Frisbie turned the awkward situation into a profitable and long-lasting alliance.

During the summer and fall of 1877 Foster was mired in tedious written negotiations and conferences with the Mexican Foreign Minister over the punitive instructions Evarts dictated to Foster as terms for recognition. It cannot have been a satisfying experience. Vallarta was a skilled jurist and distinguished legal scholar, and Mexican historian Daniel Cosío Villegas observed that Foster "made the mistake of his life" in trying to negotiate a written agreement with him.[25] Foster's frustration was compounded by his belief that withholding recognition was unjustified, and his sense of humiliation as Washington ignored his advice and populated his post with itinerant, self-styled diplomats. Finally, Foster must have sensed that the Mexican Minister was only stalling in the unproductive meetings. Unbeknownst to Foster, Mexico had already moved ahead to initiate a strategy that would shift the U.S.-Mexican struggle from Mexico City to Washington, D.C., leaving Foster's negotiations empty exercises in policymaking.

Foster certainly shared the ethnocentric assumptions of his compatriots that the U.S. would set regional standards for nation-state behavior, but he was truly one of the more conscientious diplomats of his era, and the distressing circumstances he found himself in after 1876 in Mexico were no reflection on his talents, but merely his situation. He was serving as Minister at a crucial moment in the transformation of the international system and the mechanics of foreign relations. Above Foster, the foreign ministries of each nation dedicated greater attention to imposing order and interests on international relationships and Presidents were increasingly conscious of the impact of the bilateral relations on the domestic political scene. Below Foster, American and Mexican entrepreneurs had begun to take advantage of the new forms of communication and commerce and appraise each other's qualifications, leaving their former chaperone behind at the gates of the American legation. Foster was no longer the central and decisive link between the two nations; his days as solitary trailblazer were over.

In retrospect it is appropriate that Foster devoted such detail to the description of his personal experiences on the eve of the Diaz revolution in 1876. While Foster was steaming down the mountain, flags flying and pistols drawn as he guided his family from the chaos of the capital, the forces that would undermine his role in U.S.-Mexican relations were rolling into power in the commercial and political centers of both nations. In the *Memoirs*, however, Foster ignored the emergence of new patterns of contact and interests and portrayed the difficulties of 1876–80 as a series of professional hurdles rather than a fundamental decline in the role of Minister as policymaker. In his memoir Foster reveled in his role as guardian of the American community during the revolutionary transition with descriptions of himself sheltering compatriots in the legation and escorting refugees through the disorder. During the difficult months of the recognition crisis the Minister recalled battling annexationists and amateurs who threatened to derail the diplomatic process. In the *Memoirs* Foster remained the rational (if unheeded) authority, the trained professional and the unquestioned leader of the American community. Foster translated his personal experience of alienation and marginalization into a testimonial to his indispensable role at the heart of American diplomacy in Mexico. In Foster's memoir it is the political realm that descends into chaos about him, yet in looking back it is obvious that it was only Foster's control over the bi-national relationship that was crumbling; the relationship would go on growing without him.

NOTES

1. Porfirio Díaz remains an enigmatic figure. Paul Garner provides a concise political history of the regime in *Porfirio Díaz: Profiles in Power* (London: Longman, 2001); while Enrique Krauze captures the social flavor of the era in *Porfirio* (Mexico: Clio, 1993). More important for this work are the early biographies based on interviews with the President that reveal how Díaz wished to be memorialized. See James Creelman, *Díaz: Master of Mexico* (New York, Appleton, 1911) and José Godoy, *Porfirio Díaz: President of Mexico: The Master Builder of a Great Commonwealth* (New York: Putnam, 1910). On the events of 1876 and 1877, see John Mason Hart, "The Seizure of Power: Porfirio Díaz, American Expansion and the Revolution of Tuxtepec," in *Revolutionary Mexico: The Coming and Process of the Mexican Revolution* (Berkeley: University of California Press, 1987), 105–129.

2. Foster to Fish, *DDM*, 22 April 1876; Foster, *Memoirs,* 77–81; Devine, *John W. Foster,* 18–25.

3. Foster to Fish, *DDM*, 11 November 1876.

4. Foster to Fish, *DDM*, 18, 28 November 1876, 20 January 1877; Fish to Foster, 19 January 1877, *U.S.D.S. Instructions.*

5. Charles W. Hackett, "Recognition of the Díaz Government by the United States," *Southwestern Historical Quarterly Online*, 28 (2006), *http://www.tsha.utexas .edu/publications/journals/shq/online/v028/n1/contrib_DIVL424.html*

6. Rippy, *The U.S. and Mexico*, 282–95; Shelley Ann Bowen Hatfield, *Chasing Shadows: Indians along the U.S.-Mexico Border* (Albuquerque: University of New Mexico, 1998).

7. Foster, *Memoirs,* 91–2; Foster to Evarts, *DDM,* 20, 23 June 1877; Cosío Villegas, *Historia Moderna*, 106–7.

8. *San Francisco Chronicle*, 24, 28 June, 5 July 1877. Also see the *New York Herald*, 18, 19 June; 6 July; 15 August; 5 September 1877.

9. *New York Herald*, 18 June 1877.

10. *St. Louis Globe Democrat*, 4 July 1877; cited in Gibbs, 63–93; *The Democratic Statesman* (Austin, Texas) reprinted in the *New York Herald,* 18 June 1877.

11. See editorials in the *New York Times*, the *Herald Tribune*, the *World*, the *Republican* and the *Press* (Philadelphia) 4 March 1877.

12. Both Americans and Mexicans commented upon the opposition of the Texan delegation to recognition, see John Frisbie to Diaz, 7 December 1877; *Archivos del General Porfirio Díaz (APD)*, 28: 73–74; Manuel Zamacona to Diaz, 5 March 1878, *APD*, 27: 260–61; also see Ari A. Hoogenboom, *The Presidency of Rutherford B. Hayes*, (Lawrence: University Press of Kansas, 1988), 174–5; and Gibbs, 63–93.

13. Foster to Fish, *DDM*, 20 January, 19 February, 3 March 1877; Evarts to Foster, U.S.D.S. Instructions, 27 and 31 March 1877; Callahan, 374; Cosio Villegas, *Historia Moderna*, 56–59.

14. Foster to Evarts, *DDM*, confidential, 28 April 1877; Seward to Foster, *U.S.D.S. Instructions*, 16 May 1877; Callahan, *American Foreign Policy*, 371–4; Cosio Villegas, *Historia Moderna*, 65; Kaiser, 160.

15. Gibbs, *Spadework Diplomacy*, 33; Foster to Evarts, *DDM*, 30 July 1877; Cosio Villegas, *Historia Moderna*, 34, 61.

16. Rutherford Birchard Hayes, *Hayes: The Diary of a President, 1875–1881*, ed. T. Harry Williams (New York: McKay, 1964), 92; Foster to Evarts, *DDM*, 14 December 1877; Foster, *Memoirs*, 92.

17. U.S. Congress, House, *House Select Committee on Alleged Frauds in the Late Presidential Election*, 45th Congress, 3rd Sess., Misc. doc. 31, vol. 2, (Washington, 1878), 98–108; cited in Devine, 25.

18. Callahan, 378–83; Foster to Evarts, *DDM*, 30 July 1877.

19. Hoogenboom, 174–77; President Rutherford B. Hayes, *Congressional Record* 7 (3 December 1877): 1, 4.

20. See the correspondence between Plumb and Secretary of State Hamilton Fish in the Plumb Papers, Library of Congress, Manuscript Division; cited in David Jules, "American Political and Economic Penetration of Mexico, 1877–1920" (Ph.D. diss., Georgetown University, 1947), 153–6.

21. Railroad investor William Rosecrans had already made the same proposal to Evarts, see Hoogenboom, 174–5.

22. On Frisbie's long relationship with Díaz, and Díaz's savvy use of American businessmen to further his own objectives, see William Schell, *Integral Outsiders:*

The American Colony in Mexico City, 1876–1911, (Wilmington, DE: Scholarly Resources, 2001). Also see Hart, *Revolutionary Mexico*, 119–128.

23. Letters exchanged between Foster and Frisbie suggest the dislike was mutual. See, Diaz y de Ovando, 547–9.

24. Foster, *Memoirs*, 87, 106–7; Justo Sierra Mendez, *The Political Evolution of the Mexican People* (Mexico: Ballesca, 1910; reprint, Mexico: Fondo de Cultura Económica, 1940) 441.

25. Cosio Villegas, *Historia Moderna*, 106–7.

Chapter Three

The "Inconvenient"
Mr. Foster

In the summer of 1877 the Mexican government initiated a diplomatic strategy that circumvented the American representative in Mexico. In the months following the disastrous June interview between Vallarta and Foster, the Mexicans embarked upon a campaign that reached beyond the U.S. State Department with direct appeals to American public opinion and business interests, and through these, to the U.S. Congress and President Rutherford B. Hayes himself. While Foster's control of the Mexican situation foundered, the Díaz administration pursued an increasingly coherent strategy toward the United States and Foster soon found himself facing an unexpected challenge. The disorder accompanying the recent political transition had threatened his program for reforming Mexico, but the new actions of the Mexican government subverted his entire vision of international order. The Díaz administration competed directly with Foster in the struggle to control both the bi-national relationship and the American interpretation of events in Mexico.

The Mexican campaign reflected a combination of domestic and foreign policy objectives. The *Puro* faction of the Liberal party surrounding Díaz assumed that foreign investment was the only means for creating the modern economy and infrastructure necessary to ensure the survival of the Mexican nation. Mexican Liberals were haunted by the memories of the tortuous mid-century years when Mexico, mired in civil strife, had proven vulnerable to invasion and dismemberment by more powerful nations. Now they wanted the roads, rails and modern communications that would unite the nation, promote economic expansion and strengthen the power of the government to defend the country. While some Mexicans feared creating ties to the U.S., *Puro* leaders pointed out that the American investors, restrained by Mexican law, could serve as a counterweight to the Spanish and British merchants already entrenched in the national economy. During the early Porfiriato the

Puro vision triumphed. After all, the specter of U.S. influence over the Mexican economy was a hypothetical problem, while the memories of civil war, military vulnerability and European interference were recent and concrete.[1]

From the very beginning the Díaz administration took an interest in courting the attention of international investors. Díaz had certainly hoped that delivering the first claims payment to Washington before the deadline would impress Washington policymakers but he also sought to capture the attention of American businesses and banks which could provide the investment Mexico sought and serve as useful allies. During his earlier exile in Texas Díaz had come to appreciate the advantages of preserving cordial relationships with influential groups in the U.S. Now, locked in a dispute with Foster and the administration of Hayes, Díaz set out to pursue foreign investors as a means of strengthening Mexico City's domestic and international bargaining position.

The administration's quest for foreign investment was complicated by increasing popular Mexican nationalism. In the years preceding Díaz's revolution the government had reduced the emphasis on the Spanish colonial heritage and cultivated alternative icons of national identity drawn from the pre-Columbian past and the wars for independence. The reinvention of national identity, evident most publicly in the street monuments adorning the newly renovated capital streets, both responded to and spurred the new nationalism.[2] Díaz certainly followed in this practice of state-led nationalism, exploiting in particular those sentiments most convenient to his own career. His defiance of Foster and the American State Department during the crisis of 1877 provided him with an easy means of draping himself in patriotic colors and discrediting opponents. His de-legitimization of political rival and former president Lerdo for seeking refuge and allies in the U.S. conveniently overlooked his own exile in Texas. Emphasizing his role as defender of the nation also gained Díaz the political capital he needed to extend the reach of the federal government from Mexico to the distant provinces. The border dispute that led Díaz to send troops under General Gerónimo Treviño to the distant North also gave Díaz the opportunity to remind northern Mexican residents of the long reach of the new administration in Mexico City.

Yet the new patriotism was not merely a complacent creation of the state and Díaz was also limited by the public's embrace of nationalism in the era. New means of communication and printing enabled the rapid reproduction of arguments and images throughout the republic and spurred public discussion of government actions. While Díaz felt he needed to attract foreign investment and credit to assure the survival of the nation, he could not afford the appearance of compromise with the United States. The only politically feasible solution was to secure both American recognition and investment without appearing to have pursued either.

The appearance of U.S. business agents John B. Frisbie and N.S. Renau (discussed in the previous chapter), whom Foster dismissed as inept and meddlesome fools, may have suggested the solution the Mexican government needed. These amateur diplomats infuriated Foster, but for the Díaz administration they hinted at the possibility of building a relationship with private American citizens and using them to lobby the Hayes administration. The conversion of Frisbie from menacing annexationist to Mexican lobbyist proved the first success for the new Mexican foreign policy strategy. Díaz also freed John Jay Smith, an American who had been imprisoned by former President Lerdo for selling arms to the opposition. Once released, Smith returned to the U.S. and gave favorable interviews to American papers urging the immediate and unconditional recognition of Mexico.[3]

The Mexican administration quickly realized it need not depend upon converting and exploiting the few business investors who appeared on Díaz's doorstep; instead, Mexico could pursue a public relations offensive within the United States itself. The departure of Díaz's personal emissary, José Maria Mata, for Washington, announced by Secretary Vallarta to a stunned Foster in the early summer of 1877, made it clear that the Mexicans had seized the initiative in cultural and diplomatic relations.

Foster quickly wrote Secretary of State Evarts to remind him that negotiations were already underway in Mexico City and urged him not to complicate the issue (or undermine Foster's authority) by conducting simultaneous talks in Washington.[4] Evarts never did offer Mata an official audience, but that did not derail the Mexican campaign. Mata quickly hired Caleb Cushing, a respected diplomatic and legal consultant who had served in several administrations, to draw attention to the Mexican question in Washington. Cushing knew the Washington system well, but unfortunately the seventy-seven year old had outlived many of his influential contacts and was not particularly helpful to Mata.

The Mexican campaign moved into high gear under the direction of Manuel Maria de Zamacona y Murphy. Zamacona was fifty years old when Díaz took power in 1876 and had acquired the skills now desperately needed by the Porfirian administration during a varied career as editor, jurist and diplomat. After studying law in his hometown of Puebla, Zamacona moved to Mexico City and edited the prestigious newspaper, *Siglo XIX*. He served briefly as Foreign Minister in 1861–62, but resigned as the nation slipped into civil war. Zamacona worked for Mexico's Minister to the U.S., Matias Romero, during the following years and observed first-hand Romero's use of social gatherings, press coverage and "confidential agents" in promoting Mexican policy in Washington. During the 1870s, Zamacona spent another three years in Washington as a member of the committee negotiating claims settlements, an experience which allowed him to further his understanding of the policy-making process in the northern capital. Zamacona's varied professional life had provided the perfect preparation for his new role in cultural diplomacy.[5]

Zamacona had not been a supporter of Díaz's revolution, yet he was moved to write the new President during the tense summer of 1877. The lawyer, still residing in the U.S. in connection with his Claims Commission work, had followed the inflammatory American newspaper coverage of U.S.-Mexican relations closely. Despite the hostile rhetoric against Mexico in the U.S. and the fears of his compatriots in Mexico, Zamacona told Díaz he did not expect war to break out along the border. He suspected that the bulk of the anti-Díaz press in the U.S. was generated by a few international investors and border residents, and that apart from these few parties there was little serious interest in annexation among the general American population. Zamacona informed Díaz that he did not even intend to investigate the rumors of war while in Washington because he did not want the Hayes administration to conclude that Mexico might be vulnerable to intimidation.[6] Even without the possibility of war, however, Zamacona was disturbed by the ability of these few interested groups to control the coverage of Mexican issues. They were able to do so, he argued, because of the overwhelming ignorance of and disdain for Mexico among the U.S. public. The prejudice of Americans against their neighbor, suggested Zamacona, left Mexico vulnerable to dangerous misrepresentation.

Evidence of the prejudice Zamacona cited abounded. In 1876 the American magazine the *Nation* criticized U.S. election irregularities as symptoms of "Mexicanization" in American politics. Editor E.L. Godkin questioned whether a "Mexican poison" had infected American citizens as he noted the abandonment of rational discourse, the criminalization of political opposition, and the declining respect for the franchise surrounding the contentious election of President Hayes. Godkin later expanded upon his comments by noting that he felt any who would speak of political revolt spoke "Mexican talk," not "Anglo-Saxon talk," and might as well put on "embroidered breeches, silver spurs and a sombrero, and go cockfighting on Sundays." Godkin's readers echoed his tone; one correspondent decried those in the U.S. who embittered politics through factionalism as suffering from the "true Mexican spirit." As the comments suggested, 'Mexican' was synonymous with vanity, irrationality, corruption and revolution in the American syntax.[7]

Zamacona was insulted by the tone of American discussion of Mexico, but he also saw opportunity. In his July 1877 letter to Díaz he outlined a new foreign policy strategy that would target American images of Mexico and convince Americans that they had more to gain from recognition than war. Zamacona suggested that appeals to civil organizations, churches, working-class audiences and business groups would create a groundswell of interest in bettering relations and effectively counter the news monopoly enjoyed by investors and border representatives.[8]

Zamacona's analysis of the continuing conflicts between the two nations was fundamentally different from that of Foster and other American policymakers. While Foster concerned himself with hammering out written agreements on specific categories of contact (damage claims, extradition regulations, border patrols, etc.) as a means of bringing order to hemispheric relations, Zamacona assumed that the fundamental problem was the lack of U.S. respect for Mexican autonomy. Zamacona pleaded with President Díaz to terminate the piecemeal negotiations between Foster and Vallarta. While he agreed that there were significant "pending issues" and common security concerns along the frontier, Zamacona's past experience negotiating the 1868 Claims Agreement had led him to believe that the negotiation process only bred contempt for Mexico by feeding into the image of lawlessness and encouraging the exploitation of complaints against the Mexican nation. Zamacona encouraged Díaz to address not just the specific complaints, but the underlying American assumption that all disorder flowed from Mexico. On the topic of border crime, for example, Díaz could begin by documenting and publicizing cases involving U.S.-based bandits and displaced tribes from the American territory. Zamacona soon followed up on his letter and traveled to Mexico City to promote his strategy in person.

Díaz was quick to adopt Zamacona's suggestions perhaps in part because Zamacona's strategy accorded well with Diaz's own political goals. On the topic of the border, for example, Díaz had already recognized the liability frontier chaos presented. Even before the U.S. June 1 order authorizing American troops to pursue suspects into Mexican territory, Díaz had sent General Geronimo Treviño to police the frontier and remove the basis for American complaints against Mexico. In July, on the same day Díaz received Zamacona's suggestions, the Mexican President wrote Treviño again and reminded him that it was vital to record his campaign against "barbaric tribes" and criminals as the documentation was needed by the Foreign Minister himself. Six months later Treviño proudly noted that his documentation of cases involving Mexican pursuit of U.S.-based bandits could serve as a counterweight to charges brought by Minister Foster, who "so liked" to cite statistics in his own arguments.[9]

Of course, Zamacona's strategy had other advantages for Díaz. Treviño's frontier mission, for example, helped Díaz guard against domestic challenges as well as foreign dangers. The frontier had often provided political opponents (like Díaz himself only a few years before) with access to arms, money and territory for mounting a challenge against Mexico City. Treviño's troop deployment and his later consultations with American officers across the border helped Díaz stay abreast of any suspicious activity in the distant north. In addition, Zamacona's emphasis on maintaining a proud and uncompromising stance before the U.S. meshed with Díaz's domestic use of nationalist rhetoric; Díaz bolstered his political legitimacy at home and abroad by grooming his image as guardian of the nation.

Díaz was quick to place Zamacona in charge of the new public relations offensive in the United States. When José Maria Mata returned from his mission to Washington he was replaced by Zamacona, who assumed the newly created role of commercial agent for the Mexican republic in Washington in October, 1877. Before departing Mexico City, Zamacona paid a courtesy call on the American Minister. Foster was the first American to be dazzled by the winning personality of Mexico's new commercial agent and in the afterglow of the meeting he wrote Evarts of his positive impressions. Foster, who had no idea that Zamacona was at least partly responsible for the abrupt standoff in negotiations, asked the Mexican agent to use his influence with the Mexican Foreign Minister and help Vallarta "rise above the prejudices entertained in Mexico" and "cut himself loose from the restraints of public opinion." Zamacona encouraged him, Foster wrote Evarts, to go to Díaz and speak frankly of his concerns, promising him that this would have a "happy effect upon our negotiations."[10] Of course, Zamacona had his own interest in a Foster-Díaz encounter; Foster's comments provided a perfect illustration of Zamacona's argument that the Americans had little respect for the Mexican point of view.

Although Foster did not go to see Díaz, he did take advantage of Zamacona's intercession to mend relations with Vallarta and the two continued their ineffective talks in Mexico City. However it quickly became apparent that the center of action had followed the Mexican confidential agent to the U.S. arena. As Foster gradually realized the extent of Zamacona's ambitions in the U.S. his early warmth for the man evaporated and he predicted disaster for the Mexican campaign. Once again Foster seriously miscalculated the strength of Díaz's position; Zamacona's skilled promotion of the Republic of Mexico took the U.S. by storm.

Upon arriving in the U.S. Zamacona quickly hired 'confidential agents' to circulate in the United States, write editorials supporting Mexico, and promote Mexican business potential.[11] Zamacona employed British journalists G.S. Pritchard and George del Byron and the New York writer Charles Lester, all of whom questioned the American policy of non-recognition and lamented the loss for American business. Pritchard contributed to U.S. newspapers and wrote a lengthy article on Mexican history and resources for the *International Review*, a leading American journal of world affairs. Pritchard also served as an unofficial emissary to the New York banking community and spoke on Mexico before the highly respected Cooper Institute and the Society of Geographers in New York City.[12]

The two other journalists, del Byron and Lester, focused their attention on convincing the powerful New York congressional delegation to push for Mexican recognition. In 1878 Zamacona paid Lester two thousand dollars for compiling a book, *The Mexican Republic: An Historic Study*, that was mailed to leading bankers and industrialists as well as members of the U.S. House and Senate in Washington. The book typified Díaz's campaign for respectability by devoting equal time to the President's political pedigree (it likened him to Abraham Lincoln and George Washington) and his financial responsibility. The book also illustrated Zamacona's other argument for U.S. recognition; it enticed readers with descriptions of Mexico's rich natural resources and potential for investors.[13]

Zamacona also utilized John Frisbie, the Californian entrepreneur whom Díaz had converted to ally, and Julius Skilton, a former U.S. consul in Mexico, to help reach influential contacts in Washington. While Frisbie's loyalty was somewhat assured by the offer of a railroad contract, Zamacona had reservations about Skilton, and noted in a letter to Díaz that he thought the former consul was motivated primarily by anger with his former supervisors at the U.S. Department of State.[14]

Zamacona did not depend entirely upon his assistants but also disseminated his arguments for Mexican recognition in press conferences and speeches before religious audiences, business groups, schools, and other community audiences. He ceaselessly reiterated the theme that Americans had more to gain from peace with Mexico than from war, and adapted his descriptions of potential "benefits" to his different audiences. Before commercial groups he stressed the profit to be made from trade; before religious groups he enthused over the potential for Protestant missions in Mexico. Peaceful contact, concluded Zamacona, would not only result in increased prosperity for both, but would instill the "christian spirit" so sadly lacking between the nations and gradually eliminate the need for wasteful spending along the border.[15]

In Chicago Zamacona informed the Chamber of Commerce that Mexico currently purchased less than one-tenth of her imports from the United States, and that, should relations improve, Chicago was optimally situated to supply Mexico's future needs. While speaking before the Newark Chamber of Commerce in New Jersey he lamented the paucity of American merchandise in Mexico and voiced his hope that new rail and canal lines would soon carry American products south. At every opportunity Zamacona combated American misunderstandings of Mexico that led many to regard the country as a dangerous and lawless land. He gently reminded Americans that Mexicans were not savages, and noted that the Díaz administration enjoyed both popular support and political stability.[16]

Zamacona's campaign showed instantaneous results. Within weeks the U.S. Congress was besieged by inquiries wondering why Mexico had not been recognized. The New York delegation initiated a motion that urged recognition and demanded an explanation from President Hayes for the long delay. A December editorial in the *National Republican* of Washington supported the motion and argued that the time had come to abandon punishment of Díaz and take advantage of the commercial opportunities in Mexico. Zamacona's winning strategy even earned him an opportunity to address the U.S. Congressional Military Committee. Arriving at the U.S. Capitol grounds Zamacona encountered General Ord, who had been recalled from the border to address the Foreign Relations Committee on the topic of Mexico. The American General cordially invited the visiting Mexican to join him before that committee as well. As an envoy from a still unrecognized administration Zamacona was expected to limit his remarks to the topic of private business potential in Mexico but the invitations were a clear coup for Mexico and a snub to the Hayes administration.[17]

Both Foster and the Hayes administration were placed on the defensive. The U.S. Minister informed Evarts that he suspected the sudden onslaught of favorable coverage of Mexico in the U.S. was coordinated by the Mexican government, but that Díaz denied the existence of any campaign to influence American opinion. In Washington President Hayes could not ignore the multiplying challenges to his policy and launched his own public relations campaign by addressing the House of Representatives on December 3. The Díaz government, charged Hayes, had been unwilling to assume responsibility for controlling its northern frontier and had not clearly stated its intention to honor existing trade concessions. Hayes justified his policy of withholding recognition until Mexico should "manifest a disposition to adhere to the obligations of treaties and international friendship." But the administration's defense of American policy was weak and the alleged infractions of the Mexicans appeared paltry when contrasted with the lucrative opportunities painted by Zamacona.[18]

Zamacona's success in Washington contrasted with Foster's dispirited reports from Mexico City. In November Foster noted that the Mexican negotiating position appeared to be "stiffening" and that Díaz appeared "increasingly hostile" to the Minister. Foster could see no advantage in prolonging the situation and urged Evarts to recognize the Díaz government immediately. His recommendation was apparently ignored. Foster then requested permission to visit Washington and review American policy on Mexico, but Evarts denied the request.[19] Just a few weeks later, however, Congress recalled Foster to Washington to explain the administration's policy on Mexican recognition. Foster found himself traveling north not as the result of his own request, but as the result of Zamacona's campaign.

Secretary of State Evarts and Minister Foster were both called to testify at congressional hearings in early 1878. The Secretary defended the non-recognition policy and insisted that only the threat of unilateral U.S. action had succeeded in motivating Mexico to take responsibility for policing the northern border. When Foster's turn arrived he found himself in an unenviable position; he could either publicly disagree with the Secretary and violate his code of political loyalty, or defend a policy of which he firmly disapproved. When finally called before the hostile audience Foster turned aside direct questions about his opinion of Evarts' policy by warning Congress that a public breach with the administration would only weaken the U.S. abroad.[20]

Foster's testimony before Congress showed both his strengths and weaknesses as a diplomat. His broad knowledge of the domestic condition of Mexico was evident in his detailed discussion of the challenges facing the Diaz administration, but his patronizing tone was galling to the Mexicans, who followed the hearings closely in their own press. Foster also encountered hostility from his fellow Americans, both those persuaded by the commercial arguments of Zamacona, and others, like Representative Roscoe Conkling, who carried private grudges against President Hayes and sought to obstruct the president's policy for domestic political reasons. Altogether it was an uncomfortable experience with few options for Foster to exercise any influence on the debate. At the conclusion of the hearings Foster was called before Evarts and instructed to return to Mexico and recognize Díaz. Foster had been attempting for an entire year to persuade Evarts to recognize Díaz, but now the circumstances of the decision made it appear as though the change in policy was a personal rebuke to the U.S. Minister.

During the final days of Foster's stay in the U.S. the American Minister and the Mexican commercial agent, Zamacona, crossed paths in New York. Though cordial, the meeting could only highlight their contrasting professional situations. Foster's high-profile testimony had damaged his standing at home and in Mexico City. He had been forced to defend his record and deny that he had demeaned his office or abused the trust of the U.S. government. The *New York Herald* printed rumors of the Minister's removal and a newspaper in Mexico City termed the U.S. Minister an enemy lying in ambush. Foster had reached the nadir of his career, scorned both by the nation he represented and the nation to which he was accredited.[21]

In contrast, Zamacona was enjoying a season of homage. His appearances delighted American audiences and his speeches were recounted in newspapers, legislatures, and commercial centers. When Zamacona met Foster the

Mexican was in New York to deliver a speech before an enthusiastic audience at the Chamber of Commerce. One week later his speech would be quoted in the halls of the U.S. Congress itself when New York Representative Washington Whitthorne described Zamacona as the "bearer of a commercial olive branch." Whitthorne informed his colleagues that

> Mr. de Zamacona said that in the shop windows of the avenues of New York he saw many articles of commerce that are unknown but needed in Mexico, and that many products of Mexico are needed in the United States. The latter, for instance, go to Messina for oranges, while choice fruit grows at their very doors. A fiber is grown in Mexico, too, out of which better paper may be made than from any other known product. The two countries' commercial interests are identical and should be made one.[22]

Zamacona had succeeded completely in displacing Foster as the authority on Mexico in the U.S. The Mexican commercial agent had become the star witness on Mexico in Congress, while Foster had been reduced to the role of an untrustworthy defendant.

While Zamacona's commercial arguments had gained widespread popularity, his larger campaign to increase American respect for Mexico was far from finished. Congressman Whitthorne, like other Americans, was tempted by the vision of Mexico's commercial potential, and cited the need for a trade treaty as the first step in the establishment of a new Monroe Doctrine. This was hardly the egalitarian vision of hemispheric order Zamacona desired. In addition, Foster had returned to Mexico with instructions to recognize Diaz, but also to continue pressing for concessions in negotiations. Zamacona, now the official Mexican Minister in Washington, urged President Díaz and Foreign Minister Vallarta to remain vigilant in dealings with the U.S. The central tension in the U.S.-Mexican relationship, he reiterated, lay not in disagreements over legal particularities, but in the fundamental inability of the Americans to accept the existence of an autonomous Mexico. Zamacona forwarded newspaper clippings from American papers as evidence of persistent American condescension and defended the need to continue the broader cultural strategy. He observed that, "It is tiring to cut across wave after wave if one can turn aside the current from which they arise." During the summer Zamacona encouraged Díaz to continue to publicize his campaign against "savages" on the northern frontier and to document and protest crimes committed by Americans. A few weeks later, as the social season swept Washington, Zamacona suggested that the Mexican legation in Washington could benefit from a more stately and imposing residence in keeping with its new profile.[23]

Once again Díaz rapidly adopted Zamacona's suggestions. The Mexican President halted the new Foster-Vallarta talks and adopted Zamacona's position that the June 1 military order to U.S. troops must be withdrawn and border crossings suspended before negotiations could resume. Reports of continuing U.S. troop incursions provoked indignation in the Mexican capital and in September the anger erupted when the U.S. Minister was publicly insulted at the Independence Day celebrations in the capital. Minister Foster had become the focal point for Mexican frustrations with the Hayes administration and the arrogant American policy toward Mexico.[24]

Not surprisingly, Foster's dispatches from Mexico City during the summer and fall of 1878 paint a grim portrait of the Minister's frame of mind. In October a frustrated Foster observed that he had achieved not a single "satisfactory adjustment" in the disputes he pursued, while the Mexican government had waged a spectacular campaign to reach its own diplomatic objectives. Mexican newspapers joyfully documented Zamacona's appearances in Newark, Washington, Pittsburgh and Chicago, and Zamacona himself boasted that invitations "fell like rain" about him. The Mexican Minister was invited out on steamboats and fire trucks and to visit theaters, parks and schools. Foster, who led an increasingly lonely life in Mexico, read about his Mexican counterpart with exasperation. He wrote Evarts to denounce the Mexican Minister for distorting diplomacy with "his pilgrimages around the country, haranguing businessmen" with "glittering generalities." Foster's discontent was not solely with the Mexicans however, he mournfully questioned the Secretary over his continuation of the June 1 order and claimed that his ignorance of the rationale behind American policy left him in an "embarrassing and uninformed position." The Minister felt ignored by the Americans, frustrated in his interactions with the Mexicans, and increasingly bitter toward his counterpart in Washington.[25]

The competition between Foster and Zamacona to influence the American image of Mexico culminated during the winter of 1878–79. Zamacona's earlier promotional tour to Chicago had encouraged local businessmen to investigate commercial opportunities in Mexico for themselves and they wrote the American Minister to solicit his views on the topic of American-Mexican trade. Foster, once an ardent advocate of the potential for American trade with Mexico, was no longer encouraging. He answered the brief inquiry with a forty-four page history of American troubles in Mexico, dwelling largely on the insufficient Mexican protection of American persons, property and capital.[26] There was nothing inaccurate about Foster's report, but its pessimistic prognosis revealed Foster's disenchantment with Mexico. Many of the cases Foster recounted dated from the pre-Díaz era when Foster had been an enthusiastic supporter of trade despite the imperfect environment. Now those same difficulties were portrayed as insurmountable barriers to commerce.

Foster's tone was uncharacteristically confessional and explicitly critical of Zamacona. He recalled that he too once possessed "the same exalted ideas of the development of this commerce and have omitted no proper opportunity to express my hopes both at home and in Mexico." Trade, he once felt, would have been a "potent" method of "cementing and making lasting our political and social friendship." Now, however, Foster dismissed Zamacona's promises of commercial wealth as the products of overblown optimism. The Mexican Minister, he noted, stressed only the potential for unalloyed prosperity and left Foster to point out the "embarrassments and dangers." He apologized that his "facts and details may appear to the general reader somewhat dull and prolix" but defended their ability to offer "practical" information, as opposed to the "entertainment" offered by Zamacona.[27] In the American Minister's description Zamacona appeared not as a mature diplomat and jurist, but a dreamy novice, called to account by the staid realism of Foster.

Foster's report was cleared first through the State Department, then forwarded to the Manufacturers Association of Chicago, where it was published in pamphlet form and then reprinted in newspapers in the U.S. and Mexico. It was also published as a separate report by the U.S. Congress.[28] The brief infuriated Mexicans who responded angrily to the implication that Mexico was a land of banditry and corruption. One Mexican resident of the U.S. retorted that Americans had little to gloat about since "in no part of the world was life and property as insecure as New York...where one must go out armed even in the light" and "even cadavers are stolen for ransom."[29] Zamacona quickly denounced Foster, who "heads up this campaign of defamation," and lamented that Evarts had dug out "antique" documents from his archives to corroborate Foster's pessimistic pronouncements."[30]

The Secretary of Finance, Matías Romero, countered Foster's forty-four page report with more than two hundred pages of his own. Romero was no stranger to American opinions of Mexico; he had spent most of the previous 20 years representing Mexico in Washington and in the Claims Commission negotiations, and was married to an American. Years of working with the American press and American civic groups had given him a clear vision of how to defend Mexico against Foster's complaints. Romero's report, which was also widely published (first in the government newspaper, *El Diario Oficial*, and then reprinted in English for distribution abroad) offered an alternative vision of the past that stressed the Díaz administration's cooperation with the U.S. in resolving the sources and consequences of past problems.[31] The Díaz administration, Romero assured Americans, was committed to safeguarding the property of investors and securing the political and economic stability needed for trade. Another Mexico City newspaper, *El Mensajero*, published a five part refutation of Foster's report during February and March, 1879.[32] In regard to Foster's complaints about the lengthy duration of legal suits in Mexico, it admitted that justice was often slow, but reminded Foster that there were few advocates of lynch law ("La ley Lynch") in Mexico. The series concluded by challenging the American Minister to explain why German, British and Spanish merchants had so little trouble maintaining lucrative business operations in Mexico if conditions were as poor as Foster suggested.

Despite the controversy surrounding Foster's tract, the winter of 1879 witnessed an undeniable thaw in U.S.-Mexican relations. Chicago merchants and investors had accepted Zamacona's invitation to explore Mexican potential for themselves and, despite Foster's misgivings, had survived and even enjoyed their three week visit to Mexico City (see Chapter 4). As Díaz's political situation improved he was able to devote more money and manpower to policing the border region, where surprisingly amiable cooperation had emerged between the supposed antagonists, General Treviño and General Ord. In February Zamacona gleefully reported to Díaz that while the American merchants and manufacturers were paying tribute to Díaz in Mexico City, "in Texas they do the same with General Treviño and in Washington they drown the humble representative of our republic with flattery." Even the tone of Congressional debate on Mexico had softened as discussion turned from troops to trade.[33]

Both Mexicans and Americans saw the change in national sentiments as a personal rebuff to the dour attitude of the U.S. Minister. Mexican Minister Zamacona summed up the Washington mood with the assertion that one could "claim without fear of erring that Mr. Foster would result humiliated" in his attempt to dam cooperation between the two republics. In the U.S. the *Nation* praised the upcoming trade mission to Mexico and commented that "even Mr. Foster...seems excited." Journalist Henry Brooks later recalled that the merchants departing for Mexico felt Foster's letter was "calculated" to dishearten them all and they were determined to prove him wrong.[34]

In the U.S. capital Zamacona wasted little time in capitalizing on the Mexican vogue. He issued invitations for a grand reception to honor Secretary of State Evarts at the Mexican legation and close out the Washington social season. Zamacona, who was described in society pages as one of the "social leaders' of Washington, did not disappoint his guests. The Mexican Minister rented the vacant house adjoining his own and had new doorways cut through and the rooms furnished for the party. The decorations provided a sea of symbolism. The exteriors were illuminated and above the door the Mexican national seal of an eagle on a cactus was crowned with the word "Mexico," all blazing in colored gas jets. The flags of the two nations were in profuse evidence, twined together in one vignette by "mercury's rod," symbolizing commercial relations, while the rooms were garlanded alternately in evergreens from the north and tropical orchids and lush ferns from the south. Wreaths inscribed "Mexico," "Welcome," "Trade," "Peace." "America" and "Amity" dictated the themes.

The reception was a resounding success. Guests praised the luxurious silver tea set, gold lined punch bowl, fountains of perfume, and the exquisite dinner. Secretary of State Evarts himself assisted Zamacona in receiving the guests and the society pages detailed the decorations, guest list and even the apparel of the evening. Zamacona was quick to forward the "delirious judgments of the press" to Mexico City, although he insisted that the praise flattered his "patriotic soul," and not merely his personal vanity.[35]

Zamacona's social campaign was the most public manifestation of Mexico's new image before the American public, but he was not entirely responsible for the change in relations between the two nations. Díaz's growing political and military control over the Mexican nation was gradually eliminating armed opposition and thus most complaints of forced loans and seized property. In addition, as Díaz proved his staying power, aspiring U.S. speculators found it more advantageous to cultivate a friendly relationship with the new regime rather than oppose it. Even the border conflict had cooled and the showdown between U.S. General E. O.C. Ord and Mexican General Geronimo Treviño had come to an unexpectedly romantic conclusion. The two commanders had moved from confrontation to cooperation as they first exchanged respectful visits and, later, intelligence across the border. Their collaboration in bringing order to the region was evident in the use of joint patrols, and symbolized in the surprising marriage between Treviño and Roberta Augusta Ord, the American general's daughter, in August 1880. By the time General Ord visited Mexico City in 1881 he was hailed as a hero and welcomed as a relative, hardly the reception Mexicans had envisioned in 1877.[36]

Foster remained in Mexico another long year after the success of the commercial mission he had opposed, seemingly forgotten by both the Hayes and Díaz administrations. Although he had not been responsible for prolonging the punitive U.S. policy towards Díaz and had often attempted to alter Evart's stance in private communications, he had publicly supported his Secretary's decisions on Mexico. In return he had been subjected to a humiliating audience before the U.S. Congress, constant insult in the Mexican and American press, and creeping alienation from the expatriate and local social circles in Mexico City. In seven years Foster had fallen from a position of centrality in U.S.-Mexican relations to one of irrelevance. He was left with few matters for negotiation and fewer fields to organize, and, in contrast to his early years in Mexico, he appeared both adrift and unoccupied. While the lack of work must have been stressful for Foster, more difficult still was his position as captive witness to a new age of bilateral relations over which he seemed to have no control or influence.

Understandably, Foster spent considerable time outside the capital during his final year in Mexico. From the end of September until December of 1879 Foster traveled three thousand miles through the Pacific states and along the northern frontier in an extended reenactment of his earlier investigative visits. The journey provided Foster with the chance to renew his spirit through exploration, although the wilderness he sought was perhaps not so much the unspoiled vistas of the mountainous north as the unreformed Mexican soul, which could restore his faith in the American mission abroad. Foster noted that his travels in the north were "giving me more insight than I have ever had before into the wretched state of society and morals in these secluded parts of the country." He praised "Mr. M.," an American resident in the remote north, for his "consistent Christian life in this land where all the influences tend to neglect of duty or to the Catholic Church." Traveling allowed Foster to slip back into his earlier relationship with Mexico and once again assume the persona of courageous frontiersman, braving danger while dispensing the blessings of civilization.[37]

The journey also allowed Foster to relive his role as leader of the American community. Once again he undertook a duty that "afforded so much gratification to the American residents. No Minister has ever before visited their localities, and besides forming my personal acquaintance, it has been a source of pride to them to see their country so heartily recognized by the authorities." Foster traveled through Guanajuato, Guadalajara, San Luis Potosí, Mazatlán, and Monterrey as he sought out the missionaries and their wives, who "have a very lonesome time, with very little sympathy on the part of the other American residents." He was greeted by crowds, musical bands, and church bells, sometimes even in towns in which he merely paused briefly to change stagecoaches. When he arrived in Guadalajara near midnight, he found the entire plaza illuminated with lanterns, a long row of carriages waiting and the American residents and the state and federal authorities gathered to meet him. Although he appreciated the compliment, Foster thought them "a great set of fools to be engaged in that kind of business at that time of the night" and he would really have preferred to meet them all for breakfast after a bath and a good night's sleep.[38] Despite his sour response, the *Memoirs*' detailed treatment of his official receptions suggests that the cheers of the crowd soothed, at least partially, the insults of the preceding year.

Foster's final pilgrimage through Mexico did allow him to relive his heroic memories of earlier travel, but there was a subtle difference. Foster was no longer bearing the fruits of civilization to Mexico as he carried the American standard into increasingly remote regions. Instead, whether he realized it or not, he now offered the Diaz administration a conduit to the American public. Although his journey was undeniably adventurous (the Minister traveled by stagecoach, mule and foot through some of the most rugged and scarcely populated regions of Mexico), it was not the dangerous escapade it initially appeared. The Mexican government took care to monitor Foster's travels and guarantee the Minister's safety through constant communication with regional governments; it knew that any accident would damage Mexico's image before the American public.[39] While Americans may have had little interest in Foster's awkward diplomatic situation, they would be certain to blame Mexico should any harm befall the American Minister on his travels. Regional leaders, both civic and military, were also interested in reminding the Díaz administration of their existence and loyalty through respectful execution of the President's wishes. Now it was the Díaz network, not Foster's fame, which ensured that he encountered enthusiastic receptions upon arrival in each new city, and the homage was staged less for Foster than for the eyes of the Mexican ruler and the American audience in the United States.

The Díaz administration may have exercised great care to safeguard the physical person of the American Minister during his travels, but it did little to alleviate the hostile social climate that awaited him in Mexico City. Contemporary Mexican news accounts unfairly condemned the "lamentable policy" of Foster, who was "determined to cause all the damage possible for Mexico by converting the immunity and respectability that his character of Minister gave him into an instrument of petty passion." In February George Bowen, the organizer of the Chicago trade mission, accused Foster not only of using his office to promote the war politics of the State Department, but, most unfairly, of profiting financially by prolonging the tension. Bowen's interview with the *New York Herald* was reprinted in Mexico City. Foster, who had always been scrupulously dutiful in carrying out his Secretary's policies, had become the undeserving target of a campaign of defamation that intended to saddle him with the blame for earlier confrontations.[40]

For Mexico City, the decision to focus all blame on Foster provided the means for a rapprochement with Washington: his removal could provide the face-saving explanation for a shift in policy. During the summer of 1879 Díaz wrote Zamacona that the most profitable course of action would be to "lower the esteem in the U.S. of their representative to our nation, making them understand all the difficulties and obstacles that his permanence in Mexico is creating each day for the pursuit of friendly relations and commerce." Diaz noted that an outright rejection of the Minister was inadvisable from Mexico's perspective because it might lead the U.S. to reject Zamacona, whom Díaz considered irreplaceable. Instead, Díaz suggested that Zamacona continue his subtle campaign against Foster, "whose permanence in the country, becomes every day more unbearable." While Díaz acknowledged that the "inconvenient conduct" of Foster reflected Washington policy directives, he also felt that Foster's actions were influenced by the "profound disgust" Foster felt for Mexico's success.[41]

The Hayes administration willingly cooperated in painting Foster as a scapegoat once Washington decided to terminate the standoff and repair relations. On 19 January 1880 Hayes nominated Foster to a new diplomatic post in the Russian mission, a surprise to Foster who had not known "that my promotion to a higher post was contemplated by the Secretary of State or the President." Whether the post was higher or not was debatable, but it was certainly distant and it conveniently removed Foster from Mexico City and Washington circles. Zamacona informed Díaz immediately of Foster's reassignment and connected the transfer, "which appeared to have been made without consulting Foster," with "a modification both obvious and emphatic" in Evarts' attitude toward Mexico. Now, Zamacona noted, "Evarts talks to me of nothing but the commerce and friendship lying before the two republics."[42]

Foster remained in Mexico to preside over the visit of former President Ulysses S. Grant and his party in February 1880, then steamed back to the U.S. upon the same vessel as the Grants, avoiding a potentially lonely and unacknowledged departure. As almost a final insult to the Minister, President Hayes revoked the June 1 order of 1877 authorizing border crossings just as Foster departed the Mexican capital. The Mexican papers were quick to interpret the U.S. action as a victory for Díaz, Treviño and Zamacona, who had "persevered in a dignified and prudent course of action." Even though Foster had always decried the June 1st order as an impediment to bilateral relations, Hayes' untimely action only linked the arrogant military order more firmly to Foster's legacy.[43]

Foster's situation did not improve with his departure from Mexico City. Upon arrival in Washington the former Minister was received coolly and his brief stay, according to Zamacona, was tainted with a general air of "mortification and disdain."[44] Nor did his next post prove more satisfactory. Foster remained in St. Petersburg less than a year. The appointment proved professionally dull, expensive and distant from both friends and Republican Party connections.[45] In August 1881 Foster took leave to return to Washington, and a few months later resigned his post without ever returning to Russia. John Watson Foster's diplomatic career appeared to be finished.

In retrospect Foster's disgrace was hardly the product of personal or professional failings. He was, contrary to most American diplomats of the age, a skilled and methodical professional honestly dedicated to improving U.S. relations with and knowledge of the outside world. Unfortunately his professional abilities were severely handicapped by the indecisive policies and amateurish conduct of the Hayes administration. Foster's greater limitation, however, shared by both his contemporaries and his colleagues, was his profound inability to accept as legitimate the Porfirian perspective on the Mexican state and the international arena.

In Foster's opinion, Díaz's revolt reversed Mexico's march toward evolution and threatened the collapse of order and civilization as he saw it. The Díaz revolution endangered not only Foster's plans for postal regulations, reciprocity agreements and troop crossings; it threatened Foster's fundamental sense of cultural and international hierarchy, especially as Mexico began to actively promote its own policy abroad. Ultimately, the Mexican initiatives even succeeded in disrupting the relationship Foster was establishing with his own government and the expatriate American community in Mexico. The challenge that Porfirian Mexico posed to Foster and his vision of world order was not that of chaos, but the assertion of an alternative order to that envisioned by the U.S. Minister to Mexico.

Foster had set out for Mexico as if it were an errand into the wilderness. He, like other Americans of his generation, was just beginning to imagine an age of expanded American reach abroad and, not surprisingly, Foster approached the new era armed with the mythology of the heroic frontiersman before the ever pliable, ever submissive frontier. What Foster and his companions failed to recognize was that the wilderness might have its own plans for the future.

NOTES

1. David Pletcher, "Mexico Opens the Door to American Capital," *Americas* 16 (July 1959): 1–14; Leopoldo Zea, *Positivism in Mexico* (Austin: University of Texas Press, 1974); and Charles Hale, *The Transformation of Liberalism in late Nineteenth Century Mexico*, (Princeton: Princeton University Press, 1989).

2. Barbara Tenenbaum, "Streetwise History: The Paseo de la Reforma and the Porfirian State, 1876–1910," *Rituals of Rule, Rituals of Resistance*, eds. William Beezley and Cheryl Martin and William French, (Wilmington: Scholarly Resources, 1994), 127–150.

3. William E. Gibbs, "Díaz Executive Agents and U.S. Foreign Policy," *Journal of Inter-American Studies and World Affairs* 20 (May 1978): 165–90; Kaiser, 201.

4. Foster to Evarts, *DDM*, 30 June, 8 July 1877; Cosío Villegas, *Historia Moderna*, 113–4.

5. *Diccionario Porrúa de Historia, Biografía, y Geografía de México*, 1964 ed., s.c. "Manuel Maria de Zamacona y Murphy;" Antonio de la Pena y Reyes, ed. *La Labor Diplomático de D. Manuel Maria de Zamacona como Secretaría de Relaciones Exteriores* (México: Archivo Histórico Diplomático de México, no. 28, 1971).

6. Manuel Zamacona to Porfirio Díaz, 10 July 1877, *APD*, ed. Alberto Maria Carreño, (México: Elede, 1947) 25: 244–47.

7. E.L. Godkin, "What is Mexicanization?" *Nation*, (21 December 1876): 363, 365; "Mexicans in Congress," *Nation*, (8 February 1877): 86; "Mexicanization," *Nation*, (13 June 1878): 383. Americans might have been sobered to learn that Mexicans used the term "Americanize" to describe murder at the hands of a lynch mob. See *Two Republics*, 1 January 1885.

8. Zamacona to Díaz, 10 July 1877, *APD*, 25: 244–47; 19 October, 1 November 1878, *APD*, 29:280–82, 295–6.

9. Díaz to Treviño, 10 July 1877, *APD*, 25: 247–8; Treviño to Díaz, 15 February, 1878, *APD,* 28:199–201.

10. Foster to Evarts, *DDM*, 28 November 1877; Cosío Villegas, *Historia Moderna*, 128–32.

11. Gibbs, "Executive Agents," 165–90; John Frisbie to Díaz, 7 December 1877, *APD*, 28: 73–74.

12. G.S. Pritchard, "The Mexico of the Mexicans," *International Review*, 5 (1878): 170–184; Díaz y de Ovando, *Crónica*, 18.

13. Charles Edwards Lester, *The Mexican Republic: An Historic Study* (New York: American News Company, 1878); publication details in Cosío Villegas, *Historia Moderna*, 147–8.

14. John Frisbie to Díaz, 7 December 1877, *APD*, 28:73–74; Zamacona to Díaz, 14 December 1878, *APD*, 30:7–8.

15. *World* (New York), 8 March 1878.

16. Reprint from the *Commercial Advisor* (Chicago) in *Siglo XIX*, 15 July 1878; cited in Díaz y de Ovando, *Crónica*, 30; Reprint from the *Western Manufacturer* (Chicago) in *Two Republics*, 14 September 1878.

17. "Mexico and the U.S.," *National Republican* (Washington, D.C.), 23 December 1877; Zamacona to Vallarta, 7 December 1877, *Archivo de la Secretaría de Relaciones Exteriores*; cited in Gibbs, 130–31.

18. Gibbs, *Spadework Diplomacy*, 136–37; U.S. Congress, House. 45th Congress, *Congressional Record* (3 December 1877), 7:14; cited in David Jules, "American Political and Economic Penetration of Mexico, 1877–1920" (Ph.D. diss., Georgetown University, 1947), 146.

19. Foster to Evarts, *DDM*, 10 September, 28 November, 3 December 1877.

20. The Evarts-Foster testimony is detailed in Brainard Dyer, *The Public Career of William Evarts* (New York: DaCapo Press, 1969), 199–203. Also see U.S. Congress, "Report of the Remarks of Mr. John W. Foster, the Minister to Mexico, before the Subcommittee of the Committee on Foreign Affairs to Investigate the Mexican Question, on Saturday, February 9, 1878, at the Department of State," in *Report of the Committee of the House of Representatives, Foreign Affairs, Subcommittee on Mexico*, 45th Cong., 1st sess. (Washington, 1878); cited in Kaiser, 278–9.

21. Zamacona to Díaz, 5 March 1878, *APD*, 28:260–61; *New York Herald*, 28 March 1878; Cosío Villegas, *Historia Moderna*, 147.

22. Rep. Washington C. Whitthorne, *Congressional Record*, (12 March 1877), 1701–3.

23. Zamacona to Díaz, 14 June 1878, *APD*, 29:140–1; Zamacona to Vallarta, 14 June 1878, *APD*, 29:141–46; Zamacona to Díaz, 24 July 1878, *APD*, 29: 211–227, 232–5, 14 December 1878, *APD*, 30:7–8.

24. For discussions of the tense atmosphere, see Zamacona to Díaz, 24 August, 18 September 1878, *APD* 29: 241–3, 268–75; Díaz to Treviño, 27 August 1878, *APD*, 29: 246–9; also Díaz y de Ovando, 31–49.

25. Foster to Evarts, *DDM*, 8, 29 October 1878; 14 December 1878; Díaz y de Ovando, 42–93.

26. John W. Foster, *Trade with Mexico: Correspondence between the Manufacturers Association of the North West, Chicago, and the Hon. John W. Foster, Minister Plenipotentiary of the United States to Mexico* (Chicago: SPI, 1878).

27. Foster, *Trade with Mexico*, 6–7.

28. *Trade with Mexico*, House Executive Document No. 15, 45th Congress, 3 sess., (ser. 1852) (Washington, 1879); publication history recounted in Rippy, 309;

29. Benavides to Díaz, 30 November 1878, *APD* 30:312–4.

30. Zamacona to Díaz, 14, 27 December 1878, *APD*, 30: 7–8, 10–11.

31. Matias Romero, *Report of the Secretary of Finance of the U.S. of Mexico on the 15th of January, 1879 on the actual condition of Mexico, and the increase of commerce with the U.S. Rectifying the report of the Honorable John Foster, Envoy Extraordinary and Minister Plenipotentiary of the U.S. in Mexico* (New York: Ponce de Leon, 1880).

32. "Crónica," *El Mensajero*, 27, 28 February; 1, 4, 6 March 1879.

33. Díaz to Treviño, 24 August 1878; Servando Canales to Díaz, 22 February 1878, *APD*, 28: 226–28. On the improved border security, see David M. Pletcher, "Warner P. Sutton and the American Mexican Border Trade," *South West Historical Quarterly* 79 (1976): 373–99; Zamacona to Díaz, 7 February 1879, *APD*, 30:28–9.

34. Zamacona to Díaz, 10 January, 7 February 1879, *APD*, 30: 14–5, 28–9; *Nation*, (30 January 1879), 76–77; Henry Brooks, "Our Relations with Mexico," *Californian*, 1 (1880): 210–23.

35. *Washington Star*, 21, 25 February 1879; Zamacona to Díaz, 8 March 1879, *APD*, 30:38–9.

36. *Periódico Oficial de Nuevo Laredo*, 7 August 1880; Cosío Villegas, *Historia Moderna*, 222–23; Rangel Frias, *Gerónimo Treviño*, 90; "The Arrival of Gen. Díaz," *New York Times*, 2 March 1883; "Major General Ord, U.S.A.: His Visit to Mexico," *Two Republics*, 13 March 1881.

37. Foster, *Memoirs*, 132–3.

38. Ibid. 125, 127–8, 134.

39. Miguel de la Peña to Díaz, 15 December 1879, *APD*, 30:133–7; Servando Canales to Díaz, 27 December 1879, *APD*, 30:132–3.

40. *La Libertad*, 9 March 1881, cited in Cosío Villegas, *Historia Moderna*, 225; *El Monitor Republicano*, 27 February 1879.

41. Díaz to Zamacona, 2 June 1879, *APD*, 30: 57–8.

42. Foster, *Memoirs*, 137; Zamacona to Díaz, 22 January 1879, *APD*, 30:154–6; Díaz to Zamacona, 22 February 1880, *APD*, 30: 183.

43. "El Honorable Sr. Foster," *El Diario Oficial*, 2 March 1880; En Honor de Sr. Foster," *El Diario Oficial*, 4 March 1880; Banquete de Despedida," *El Diario Oficial*, 10 March 1880; Zamacona to Díaz, 20 February 1880; *APD*, 30:178–9; *El Diario Oficial*, 1 March 1880; "La Orden al General Ord," reprint from *La Libertad* in *El Diario Oficial*, 3 March 1880.

44. Zamacona to Díaz, 2 April 1880, *APD*, 30:231–2.

45. Devine, 29–30.

Conclusion: "Such Intimate Connection to the People"

Despite the humiliating end to his Mexican mission, neither Foster's career nor his relationship with Mexico suffered permanent damage. Foster, who left Mexico City ignominiously in 1880, would overcome the disappointments of 1877–80 and go on to enjoy a notable legal career in international arbitration. He combined a lucrative private practice with short stints in the diplomatic service, and even served briefly as Secretary of State. At the time of his death in 1917 Foster was honored as the 'father' of professional American diplomacy and lauded for his long friendship with Mexico. The conflicts and humiliations of the early Porfiriato had vanished from the story.

Foster's professional renaissance partly explains the new version of Foster's past. When Foster returned from his short posting in Moscow in 1881 he settled in Washington, D.C. and quickly regained his reputation as a thorough and skilled international lawyer. His surprising reconciliation with Mexico and Porfirio Díaz sealed his professional rehabilitation. By the early 1880s the former President and former Minister were both released from the constraints of their earlier roles and free to reinvent their acquaintance. Díaz had adhered to his promises and refused to run for president in the elections of 1881, peacefully leaving the office to his successor, Manuel Gonzalez. In 1882 Foster, now also a private citizen, responded to a highly critical American magazine article on Mexican politics with a letter that specifically credited Díaz with effecting the first lawful presidential succession in Mexican history. The letter was interpreted as a peace offering by Díaz, who responded by calling upon Foster and Mary Parke the following year when he and his new bride, Carmen Romero Rubio, honeymooned in the U.S. The lavish tea and dinner, and the influential individuals Foster arrayed around the table may have encouraged Díaz to rethink his relationship with Foster. By the time Díaz left Washington it was clear that the former adversaries had agreed to overlook the differences of the past and Foster and Mary Parke even joined Díaz's party during a portion of their honeymoon journey through the United States.[1]

For Mexico and Díaz , the benefits of the new alliance were clear: Foster was well-connected in Washington circles and his passion for international law, once so maddening to Foreign Minister Vallarta, would be of great use once Foster became Mexico's legal representative in Washington. Díaz must also have been aware of the publicity potential of the friendship. Although he had left the presidency voluntarily, Díaz continued to cultivate useful allies and positive press coverage as he kept one eye on future reelection. By inviting the former Minister and the press to join his honeymoon he assured a constant stream of media attention. Nor was Foster ever one to shy away from useful connections. He certainly realized that Mexico was becoming an important arena for American commerce, a development that could provide him with interesting clients and raise his own profile in U.S. investment and government circles.

Within a few years the outlines of the truce were fulfilled. Díaz, back in office as Mexico's president, made Foster Mexico's principal legal representative in the U.S. and provided the majority of Foster's legal business during the ensuing years. Foster cultivated his reputation as an expert on Mexican issues with frequent and complimentary articles on Mexico in U.S. journals, and maintained a close relationship with the Mexican legation, built next door to his home in Washington in 1892. Mexico's Minister to the U.S. during the 1880s and 1890s, Matías Romero, who once exchanged sharp letters with Foster during the crisis of 1878, now appeared as a frequent guest in the Foster home. In 1892 the *New York Times* made an understandable mistake when it confidently informed readers that Foster's cozy relationship with the Mexican government stemmed from the close relationship he had formed with President Díaz during his tenure as U.S. Minister.[2]

Foster actively encouraged this interpretation as part of his own reinvention of the past, which was ultimately codified in the pages of his two volume autobiography, *Diplomatic Memoirs*, published in 1909. Some aspects of Foster's experiences in Mexico (the heroic explorations, the social exchanges, and the professional satisfactions of the first four years) transferred easily to the pages of the memoir, while the difficulties of the final years were largely ignored or rewritten. The insult in the theatre, for example, reappeared as a testament to the Minister's cool aplomb in the face of volatile nationalist passions. In looking back over the seven years of his stay in Mexico, Foster commented that his relations with the government had "not always been pleasant. At times there were strong tensions in our friendly intercourse, and open hostility seemed the only outcome, but I never lost the personal esteem of the Mexican authorities." Shortly after completing the *Memoirs*, Foster burned his personal papers.[3]

The *Diplomatic Memoirs* debuted to enthusiastic acclaim. One reviewer recommended the volumes to all those "interested in the influence of the United States in world affairs," and praised the work as a "full and modest record of an extraordinary and most exemplary career." Another commended the *Memoirs* not only for its contribution to a "clear understanding" of events, but because they provided a portrait of one whose "career in the diplomatic service has been perhaps the most notable in the past one or two generations." The *American Historical Review* complimented Foster as the unusual example of a man "by nature thoroughly fitted for" the foreign service.[4]

By the time of his death in 1917 Foster's diplomatic career had achieved the status of legend in American foreign relations. Obituaries lauded him as "Our First Professional Diplomat" and the model "Dean of Diplomats" for the younger generation. Foster's early confrontations with Porfirian Mexico were forgotten and he was credited instead with single-handedly winning the hearts of the Mexican people. The *Dictionary of American Biography* praised Foster for "making himself highly agreeable to the Mexican government," while "under trying circumstances." His sound advice, another biographer asserted, was heeded by Secretary of State William Evarts, who "allowed the Minister considerable initiative in making policy."[5]

Of course it was easy for Americans to credit Foster with success in Mexico because over the years his original goals of security, stability and predictability in relations with Mexico were largely met. During the years of the Porfiriato, U.S. investment in Mexico soared and U.S. property and persons enjoyed increased protection. These changes were not the result of Foster's campaigns, however, but reflected Mexican policy choices as the Díaz administration enacted reforms it felt to be in the Mexican interest. Díaz and Zamacona had resisted negotiating the legal framework Foster originally assumed was a prerequisite to these goals (trade reciprocity, extradition, border crossing agreements, etc.), but in the end there was no need for the formalities of international law. In Mexico's pursuit of the expected national security benefits of American commerce and investment, Mexico policed its own territory to preempt American criticism. Tragically, in their desire to strengthen Mexican autonomy, Díaz and his policymakers created the clientelistic Mexico that Foster had originally envisioned.

The strategy of the early Porfirian leaders plays no role in the Foster legend, however. Instead, the redemption of John W. Foster illustrates a curious process of collective amnesia and reinterpretation among his compatriots. His American audience accepted Foster's final assertions of triumph and recalled the era as one in which the U.S., personified by the talented Minister Foster, led its southern neighbor into the light (or clutches, depending on the perspective of the author) of the American sphere of influence. The nationalistic development objectives of the Mexican Liberals, the creative public relations of Zamacona, and even the incompetence of the U.S. State Department were quickly forgotten, obscured by the glowing reputation of "America's first professional diplomat."

It is not difficult to understand the attraction of Foster's story to his compatriots. Foster's account certainly would have appealed on literary grounds alone as it fit the contemporary conventions of autobiography and travelogue perfectly. Foster's *Memoirs* offered readers a morality play that showcased the virtues of American civilization. In the *Memoirs* Foster was not only a skilled professional, but a traveler, a missionary and a businessman; he was the everyman for the new American age, limited only by the ignorance and inefficiency that surrounded him. He portrayed himself as the innocent abroad, capable of laughing at his provincial morals, but never abandoning his standards. He was the unchallenged and beloved leader of the American community, galvanizing its dormant patriotism and rousing its members from their tropical languor. Although U.S. elections might suffer the stains of political corruption, Americans could turn their gaze upon Foster, the standard-bearer of democracy abroad, as he offered welcome counsel to the inexperienced republic to the south. At home, emancipation and immigration undermined assumptions of racial hierarchy, but in Mexico Foster enjoyed the homage of the 'natives.' Industrialization in the U.S. raised fears of emasculation and standardization, but in Foster readers rediscovered the pioneering frontiersman, dismissing danger as he rides heroically into the Mexican landscape.

The *Memoirs* was more than a culturally appealing literary document however, it exemplified and encouraged the new vision of America on the world stage, and it is this image of Foster, as the prescient forerunner of a new breed of American statesman, which deserves the most attention. The *Memoirs* treatment of U.S.-Mexican relations during Foster's reign provided a perfect case study of America's "rise to globalism," except, unfortunately, that it was a fiction. There was no order in Foster's experience as diplomat, neither in his personal experience, nor in the institutions he represented. However, the petty personality clashes, party politics, and amateurism that characterized his contact with Washington, vanished from the final account of his role in U.S.-Mexican relations, leaving behind the illusion of a smoothly functioning, if still embryonic, foreign policy machine.

The Foster of 1878 would have been surprised to read later accounts about his era that portrayed the U.S. as an increasingly assertive nation, newly invigorated with the explosive force of American business and new technologies of communication, transportation and military transformation. From Foster's perspective at the time he was not the powerful envoy of an expansive and purposeful nation, but more often the ignored pawn of an unsophisticated home government that was physically and intellectually unprepared for the challenges of the new age. Even the American business sector had been quick to abandon the advice of the Minister and the shelter of the American state when tempted with the profits of alliance with Díaz. During his difficult years in Mexico Foster did draw his confidence (and his arrogance) from his American identity, but that identity was founded in his vision of his cultural heritage, not his faith in the long arm of a powerful American state.

Historical studies of the cultural assumptions underlying policy decisions and perspectives are common, and it is not difficult to find examples of ethnocentrism in Foster's outlook, but the challenge of cultural history here is much larger than understanding Foster's world view. Foster's perspective was not just imbued with the cultural assumptions of his own era, his story has been transformed to accord with national fictions, most notably the American memory of U.S. foreign relations history itself. Americans, confronted with an increasingly complex relationship with the world beyond, created in Foster a poster-child for a new age. The retrospective image of Foster as architect of a new U.S.-Mexican relationship over the disorganized reality of Foster's experience provided a comforting narrative of control and progress for an era of tumultuous reinvention. The mythical vision of Foster guiding the nation and the hemisphere into an orderly new era is part of the fictional narrative of triumphant American internationalism.

Foster's legend also resonates with the self-delusions embodied in the traditions of diplomatic history itself. Like other cultural constructs, diplomatic history has narratives and conventions that reinforce assumptions about the actors involved, in this case about relations between the American people and the world outside. While diplomatic history may often be divided between accounts which defend the expansion of American interests and those which condemn nascent imperialism, both perspectives perpetuated the vision of an international world organized by state structures and rent mainly by conflicting state interests and programs. The conventions of diplomatic history encouraged readers to trust that the essence of the international system could be captured in the records of official agreements and communications, a poorly disguised nostalgia for the wise old men, or even the diabolic schemers, of foreign policy's mythic past. In short, the conventions of diplomatic history have helped Americans perpetuate their belief in an orderly, manageable world guided or manipulated by the professionals and institutions of the state. In contrast, Foster's experience with the professionals and institutions of the state was largely a chaotic farce of ignorance and miscalculation. For Foster in 1878, the state actor in the international realm was really only a matter of wishful thinking.

This history of the reality and the legend of Foster's mission to Mexico suggests that the significance of Foster's story cannot be captured in the formalities of official contacts, nor distilled from the glaringly evident cultural assumptions in his rhetoric and behavior. These elements, while essential, still fall short of capturing the broader significance of the Foster legend in American memory. Foster's professional resurrection was not merely a personal or personal achievement; it was made possible by the adaptive ethnocentrism of the American public, which preferred the illusion of American directed transformations over accounts of American disarray. In preferring the *Memoirs'* interpretation of Foster's heroic role in Mexico to the messy reality of Foster's experience, Americans protected their illusion of triumphant American expansion, but it also left them with a tragically misleading model for understanding and acting in the world around them. For Mexico, Foster's ability to take credit for the explosion of American commercial and financial relations with Mexico during the Porfiriato exposed the ultimate failure of Manuel Zamacona's grand strategy to reinvent the cultural relationship between the two nations. Mexico may have won the diplomatic battles of 1877–1880, but, as the later popularity of the Foster legend suggests, Foster and his nation eventually won the cultural war.

NOTES

1. *Evening Post* (New York), 20 September 1882. John Bigelow, "Railway Invasion of Mexico," *Harpers* 65 (1881): 745–7; *New York Times*, 2, 8, 22, 29 March; 4, 5, 29 April 1883; Cosío Villegas, *Historia Moderna*, 226–8; Devine, 23.

2. John W. Foster, "The New Mexico," *National Geographic Magazine* 13 (January 1902): 1–24; and "Porfirio Díaz, Soldier and Statesman," *International Quarterly* 8 (December 1903): 342–353; *New York Times*, 4 July 1892.

3. Foster, *Memoirs*, 142; Devine, 159–60.

4. *Annals of the American Academy* 35 (1910): 470; *Literary Digest* 40 (1 January 1910): 26; *American Historical Review* 15 (April 1910): 638–40; see also *Nation*, 20 January 1910, 62–64; *North American Review* 191 (1910): 695; Dial, 16 May 1910, 650; and Indiana 68 (1910): 650.

5. "Our First Professional Diplomat," *Outlook*, (November 1917), 488; "Foster, Dean of Diplomats Dies," *New York Times*, 16 November 1917; "John Watson Foster," *Evening Star* (Washington), 15 November 1917; Reverend Charles Wood, "General John W. Foster," (Washington, D.C.: Church of the Covenant, 1917); *Dictionary of American Biography*, ed. John Garraty (New York: Scribner, 1957), s.v. "John Watson Foster, 1836–1917; " Devine, 25. Other hagiographic biographies include the previously mentioned works by J. Fred Rippy, James Morton Callahan and Chester Kaiser.

Part II

A WAR OF WORDS: REWRITING THE VOCABULARY OF U.S.-MEXICAN RELATIONS

Introduction: "The True Lifeguard of Our Nationality"

On January 22, 1879, the passenger vessel, *City of Mexico,* steamed into the port of Veracruz with the members of the American Industrial Deputation from Chicago gathered queasily at the rail. They were thankful for having survived the four-day ocean journey from New Orleans with only mild discomfort but were hardly anxious to throw themselves into the disorder and disease they expected from Mexico. Across the harbor the gleaming white walls and tiled domes of Veracruz sparkled in the sun, inviting comparisons with the Holy Land, but the hovering peak of the Orizaba volcano served as an abrupt reminder that they were poised on the rim of the tropics. They were a very long way from Chicago.

Despite their apprehensions, the eighty members of the American Industrial Deputation (AID) were not decimated by disease in Veracruz or shot to ribbons by bandits on the backroads of Mexico. Instead they were greeted effusively by the resident American Consul and the Governor of Veracruz at a lavish breakfast reception organized in their honor in the port city. A specially designated train then carried them up past the coffee fields and tropical orchards of the *tierra caliente* into the tablelands of the Valley of Mexico. They disembarked in the capital, a city centuries older than their own, whose inhabitants surprised them with their cosmopolitan manners and commercial concerns. The three-week visit was marked by pleasant excursions to the surrounding countryside, the opening of the joint American-Mexican Commercial Exposition and the exchange of social calls with gracious Mexican families. Throughout their visit they were treated as the honored guests of the Mexican government with no expense spared in guiding them toward the best that Mexico had to offer.

In retrospect, it is difficult to read about the Mexican courtship of the American deputation in 1879 without linking the visit to the legendary excesses of the later years of the Porfiriato. The lavish hospitality accorded the visitors seems to provide a vivid example of a fawning Mexican government entreating Americans to consume the riches of Mexico, while the visitors themselves appear as portents of the coming economic invasion. Yet the warm welcome extended to the mission did not prove that the Mexicans had abandoned the defiant nationalism evident during the public insult of the U.S. Minister, John W. Foster, only four months before. From the Mexican perspective of 1879, the reception of the mission reflected the same impassioned patriotism as the insult. The hosts paraded the cultural, historical and physical wealth of Mexico before the American visitors not to offer them control, but to overwhelm them with the evidence of Mexico's rich history and future potential.

Díaz, while welcoming the AID at a formal reception in the capital, hinted at the Mexican objectives when he blamed past conflicts on the inaccurate American image of Mexico. The faulty American picture of Mexico, he instructed the visitors, was the product of "a lack of knowledge of the elements composing our social and political condition, differing from your own, and therefore strange to you and difficult to be understood."[1] From the Mexican perspective the AID members were not forerunners of an American economic invasion but the passive targets of a momentous public relations campaign.

Although the Porfirian elite has been stigmatized by its popular reputation for friendship with the foreigner, historians have long recognized that ardent nationalism among Porfirian leaders was too widespread and persistent to be dismissed as a charade.[2] For scholars the difficulty has never been finding evidence of nationalism, but reconciling the evidence with the undisputable rise of American influence in Mexico during the Porfiriato. The AID experience suggests one approach to the problem. Rather than view Mexican nationalism only as if it were a reactive sideshow to the main event of American expansion, as many histories of the period have done, it may be best to shift the focus to an earlier era when it is easier to sympathize with the early Porfirian assumption that a selective alliance with the U.S. would strengthen, not undermine, Mexican national security in a changing world. However, both the ways in which the Mexican leaders sought to promote Mexico and the ways in which promotion was ultimately understood by the American audience, suggest that long before Mexico became enmeshed in an inequitable economic relationship with the U.S., it was affected by the distortions of an inequitable cultural relationship. Mexicans and Americans were cooperating to build a new economic relationship, but they were also competing to define that new relationship according to two distinct national narratives, and ultimately the American narrative would prevail.

In the late 1870s, however, these inequities were less obvious and the Díaz administration's decision to seek an alliance with U.S. investors was understandable. In Mexico, tragic evidence of the recent French intervention served as a daily reminder of the nation's past humiliation by foreign banks and foreign troops and Porfirian leaders hoped that new investment would spur industrialization and modernization and reduce Mexico's vulnerability to more materially developed nations. Despite the bitter memories of 1846, in the 1870s investment from the U.S. appeared to be the best way to pursue development and counterbalance the existing dependence on European trade and finance.

The robust growth of the United States also served as a sobering reminder of Mexico's grim decline during the nineteenth century, making Porfirian leaders uncomfortably conscious of the divergent paths of the two former colonies. In 1800 Mexico City governed a population of six million, easily surpassing the 5.2 million residents of the U.S., and claimed control of territory far greater than that of the fledgling nation to the north. Yet by 1880 Mexico lagged behind the U.S. in every measure of political and economic development. While the Mexican population had increased by only one third, to nine million, the U.S. population had multiplied tenfold to reach fifty million. While Mexico had lost control of nearly half her former territory, U.S. territory had more than tripled. Per capita income in Mexico had never exceeded that of the U.S., but during the half century following independence it actually declined, falling from U.S.$73 in 1800 to U.S.$62 in 1880, while per capita income in the U.S. rose from U.S.$165 to U.S.$430 during the same period.[3]

Other measurements echoed the disparities. In 1884 Mexico registered 1.8 million tons of shipping, handled 212,000 telegraph messages and (in 1884) operated 1,500 miles of railroad.[4] In contrast, in 1880 the U.S. registered 15 million tons of shipping, handled 31 million telegraph messages and operated 89,000 miles of railway.[5] While much of the development gap could be explained by the immense physical disparities between the two nations (the U.S., for example, possessed an abundance of rich and accessible agricultural land, natural harbors and inland waterways, while Mexico had no naturally protected deep-water harbors, few navigable rivers and little potential for canals), Mexico's poor development record also reflected the impact of political instability and civil war. Constant conflict had discouraged immigration, retarded domestic population growth, diverted and destroyed scarce resources and increased Mexican vulnerability to foreign interference. In turning their attention to the U.S. investment community, Porfirian leaders revealed their willingness to tackle the twin challenges of development and security and convert a former adversary to a partner in progress.

Neither the Mexican people nor their leaders had forgotten the past, however, and the controversy surrounding recognition reignited lingering suspicion and anger against the U.S. in Mexico City. Most importantly, it served as a forceful reminder of the historic vulnerability of Mexico before the American people. Porfirian leaders could not afford to ignore the insults that peppered the American press and political speeches; these insinuations that Mexico City was incapable of administering her people or policing her territory endangered Mexico by de-legitimizing the nation-state in American eyes. Clearly a hostile and patronizing neighbor was no asset to the Mexican nation, and the need to reinvent Mexico in the eyes of the American people became not only a prerequisite to winning the trade and investment needed for modernization, but an integral aspect of the national security strategy itself.

Mexican Commercial Agent Manuel Zamacona was not the only one to realize that winning American investment and respect would require an aggressive public relations campaign. A few years before, *Two Republics* Editor George Clarke had tried to interest American mining companies in the resources of his adopted country, only to be bluntly informed that "the existing prejudices in the minds of the people, more especially in the northern cities, present a formidable barrier against business in your republic." Editor George Clarke was certainly familiar with those "existing prejudices," and had long sought to overcome American ignorance of his adopted country. Clarke was incensed by American newspapers that published outrageous articles on Mexico without ever examining the author's credentials. In 1868 Clarke accused the *New York Herald* of inciting pro-annexationist sentiments as he noted that "for several months that periodical has filled its columns with the vilest slanders against Mexico to excite hostility in the hearts of the American people toward this country....The *Herald* is the organ of filibusterers and adventurers and all that class." These "adventurers," he added a few weeks later, arrived in Mexico with the intention of making their fortunes by "furnishing their readers with worthless trash." Clarke urged Americans not to depend upon the limited U.S. coverage of Mexican conditions, but to "resort to correspondence with reliable persons in this country...or look to the papers published in Mexico, where there is a responsibility to the intelligence of the community for the truthfulness of their statements."[6]

Despite his impatience with the inaccuracies in American coverage of Mexico, Clarke realized that American indifference to Mexican issues was equally dangerous. Clarke responded to a competitor's editorial in 1868 by noting that the "*Vera Cruz Correo* is greatly mistaken in its idea that the American Press, as a general thing, is engaged in exciting animosities against Mexico. The majority of the American periodicals exhibit ignorance and indifference on Mexican Affairs." Mexican elections, he complained, passed almost completely unnoticed in the American press. John J. Finerty, a journalist traveling in Mexico a decade later, in 1877, found both Americans and Mexicans who still agreed with Clarke's complaints. One American miner laughed at the newspaper stories back home and told Finerty that "Americans know as little about the interior of Mexico as the interior of Africa."[7]

The comment was perhaps more insightful than intended. Not only were Americans ignorant of Mexico's history or people, but what little attention they did devote to Mexico was often colored with echoes of older narratives of exploration and conquest. The stereotyped incidents that prevailed in American depictions of Mexico reflected both the influence of British literature on colonialist adventures in India and Africa (see Chapter 6) as well as the influences of more specific anti-Latin and anti-Mexican traditions in Anglo-American letters.[8] Together these various traditions of representation exerted a powerful influence on the vocabulary and images employed to describe American-Mexican relations. Americans may have been as ignorant of Mexico as of Africa, but in neither case did Americans begin with a neutral attitude.

Many late-19th century American complaints against Mexico could be traced back to 16th and 17th century English literary depictions of the new world. That era marked the height of imperial rivalry between Spain and England as well as an era of intense domestic English anti-Catholicism, and English readers patronized works that emphasized denigrating imagery of Spanish, Catholic, and Mexican culture. The Englishman Thomas Gage's lectures and writings on the greedy, gambling and lascivious priests of the new world, for example, were immensely popular with the protestant English public, as were reprints of the Spanish priest Bartolomé de las Casas' denunciations of his countrymen's abuse of the new world natives. Few English readers seemed concerned with the politicized publication of these works. Gage, for example, a defrocked Catholic priest of English birth, admitted to amassing a small fortune while ostensibly serving his poor parishioners in Guatemala, apparently through the same extortion he decried in others. Gage's written denunciations of his former religion then provided him with both an income and a means of restoring his social standing in anti-papist England.

The context of Las Casas' publications was similarly complex; the priest had detailed the conquistadors' exploitation of the natives in the Americas in an effort to convince the Spanish Crown that Indians should be protected, not enslaved. The ability of Las Casas' to offer internal criticism of the colonial system and promote the establishment of a system of courts and regulations for Indians did not capture the imagination of English readers; they focused instead on his horrifying portraits of Spanish cruelty. Nor did English readers bother to compare the Spanish record with their own human rights record toward native societies in the new world. At a time when English colonies in the new world were failing with tremendous loss of life and wealth, reports of Latin cruelty and immorality, however compromised in their production, helped alleviate the British sense of inadequacy before Iberian successes.

U.S. discussion of Mexico and other Latin American nations reproduced this religious and racial prejudice against Latin culture in subsequent years, but also incorporated more specific national concerns. Anti-Catholicism, for example, not only remained a consistent theme in American discussion, but intensified in response to changing immigration patterns in the U.S. Americans in the post-Revolutionary era had mainly worried that the Catholic heritage of Latin America would prevent the emergence of republican governments in the southern hemisphere. Thomas Jefferson expressed a typically divided American response to reports of Latin American independence movements when he enthused over the resource potential of Latin America, while mournfully reflecting that no "priest-ridden people" had ever shown an aptitude for democracy." Increasing immigration from Catholic nations to the U.S. in the nineteenth century only exacerbated these arguments; by the mid century explicit condemnation of Mexican religious traditions was also an implicit condemnation of Irish, East European, and other Catholic immigrants to the U.S.[9]

Racial preoccupations also evolved in response to the U.S. context. While the English had targeted racial miscegenation between Spanish and "Moors" on the Iberian peninsula in their early censure of Spain, Americans focused instead on "mestizaje," or racial mixing, within the new world. Americans, who were resolving their own differences with Native and African Americans through systematic legal restrictions, political exclusion, and virtual genocide, were scandalized by the emergence of "Mestizo," or mixed race, nations to the south. Joel Poinsett, the controversial American Minister to Mexico in the 1820s, spoke for many Americans when he asserted that Indians could never be more than a "clog" to democracy. Throughout the century American attitude towards Mexicans mirrored disparaging U.S. visions of their own native populations.[10]

By the 1820–1830s territorial competition and conflict along the U.S.-Mexican frontier further shaped the American discourse on Mexico. The image of the "greaser" (a term which emerged in the 1830s in the context of Anglo emigration to Texas), justified American political control over the region by portraying Mexicans as dishonest, impetuous, childlike and lazy during an age that increasingly lauded the energy, technological facility, and commercial talents of the American character. Americans, entranced by visions of silver and cotton, assumed that Mexico's apparent lack of development reflected congenital failings, and overlooked geographic and demographic differences (most notably the absence of slavery) that had contributed to a different model of economic growth. It was far easier to concur with Richard Henry Dana's assessment in *Two Years before the Mast*, that the Mexican territory was a land with a great future, were it not for the unprogressive Mexicans themselves. These scornful depictions of Mexicans as lazy and autocratic were more than insulting, they were catastrophic for Mexico. American prejudice conveniently asserted that the Mexicans were undeserving of the land and its resources, ideologically paving the way for the mid-century wars and the annexation of Texas and the Western territories.[11]

In the years following the Mexican War of 1846–48 Americans added yet another stereotype to the national vocabulary of images of Mexicans. In the wake of the military conquest American settlers sparred with Mexican inhabitants of the annexed territory, while remnants of displaced and besieged indigenous tribes added to the jurisdictional confusion within the territories and frontier region. The chaos of these early post-conquest years (bluntly classified as banditry in the American press) was blamed overwhelmingly on male Mexicans. Crime was certainly a problem in the region, but the exaggerated reputation of so-called bandits Juan Cortina of Texas, or Joaquin Murieta of California, reflected Anglo fascination with Western outlaws and other iconic figures of disorder more than local realities. Nor did American images admit that banditry may have included guerilla-like resistance to occupation and annexation of property by families with few legal recourses or protections following the transfer of territory. Belief in congenital banditry was more consistent with the prevailing U.S. belief in the Anglo mission of civilizing the frontier.[12]

Ironically, one of the factors that made possible the new era of U.S.-Mexican relations was the increasing cultural and racial anxiety in the U.S. Those same racist images that stigmatized Mexico in the mid-nineteenth century and set the stage for annexation now slowed the spirit of expansion. Domestic tensions in the post-civil war U.S. dampened U.S. enthusiasm for territorial expansion. By the 1870s most Americans were sufficiently concerned with the challenges of incorporating freedmen, Native Americans and recent immigrants into the national mainstream, let alone the culturally alien residents of potential new acquisitions. As early as 1869 George Clarke sardonically noted that even would-be annexationists "Do not propose to take all of the goods of Mexico under charge at once, they say it is too much to digest; and their moral duty does not require of them to injure their own health and welfare by such a gluttonous operation."[13]

These new U.S. anxieties may have offered Mexico some respite from annexationists, but the publicity was hardly complementary. In 1878 the *New York Times* dismissed the Mexican population as "a mongrel crowd of negroes, whites and Indians," and the following year the same paper warned against the establishment of a U.S. protectorate over the region by noting that "Most Mexicans are composed of native Indian, of Negro and of Spanish, and a worse compound it is not easy to discover.... Intelligent men do not willingly annex the smallpox or the yellow fever." In 1881, the *Two Republics* reprinted an unidentified American editorial that also cautioned that "Annexation would bring untold troubles. One fact that many do not realize is that there are nine million Roman Catholics in Mexico, which, with the Roman Catholic population in this country, would produce political and religious effects desirable to avoid." In 1884 the New Orleans *Times Picayune* doubted that the potential gains of purchasing "nine or ten Mexican states" were worth the challenges posed by incorporating two million Mexicans into the U.S. system. American travel writer Solomon Griffin agreed, observing that all "moral and public considerations make against adding new race problems to those which now vex us." In 1888 John Rice explained that U.S. expansion had only ceased at the Rio Grande because the remainder of Mexico was heavily populated with Indians who were not "nomadic" and could therefore not be excluded from the electorate. Although U.S. border communities continued to make sporadic pleas for additional seizures of Mexican territory, by the 1870s American discussion clearly saw more liabilities than lures in the prospect of acquiring additional Mexican territory.

While the cultural concerns of Americans effectively ended the enthusiasm for U.S. annexation of Mexican territory, the emerging interest in trade and investment opportunities beyond the borders of the U.S. also contributed to a new mental framework for U.S. relations abroad. The growing recognition that merchants and manufacturers could take advantage of markets abroad without the prerequisite of annexation or colonization was expressed in the emerging vision of informal empire. Informal empire, in which Washington sought the promotion of American interests abroad without the entanglements of political expansion, reflected a compromise between American interest in and aversion to the outside world. It offered Americans the benefits of commercial and financial expansion without the cultural and political stress of incorporating new populations into the American system.[14]

For Mexico, territorially contiguous with the U.S. and a victim of past annexations, the cultural situation of the late nineteenth century was hardly ideal but could only be seen as an improvement over the tragic pattern of the past. Mexico, long a victim of European imperial intrigues and American "manifest destiny," welcomed the age of commerce as one of potential for more egalitarian relations and Mexican national development. The Liberal leaders of the Porfirian administration struggled to take advantage of this window of opportunity and pursue the foreign investment and, through the reinvention of the cultural relationship, the international political legitimacy Mexican leaders considered crucial to the survival of the Mexican nation. Moving beyond older assumptions of annexation and conflict to new visions of mutually beneficial economic interaction would not be automatic, however, and Porfirian leaders were particularly active in promoting alternative narratives, terminologies and images more appropriate for new patterns of interaction between the "Sister Republics" of the continent.

In crafting their overtures to the U.S. audience the Díaz administration deliberately emphasized Mexico's credentials as a progressive republic, a strategy that held special significance for the bi-national relationship. Not only did Americans define their own national character as "republican" and "progressive," but U.S. depictions of Mexicans consistently dismissed the Mexicans as incapable of modernizing or of administering a representative government. American disparagement of Mexico presented the most immediate challenge to Porfirian goals for the new era, but in a larger sense Mexico's campaign was to win not just American, but rather world recognition of the autonomous and forward-looking Mexican state. Nation-state status was hardly assured in the nineteenth century, especially for nations branded as young or ineffectual from the Western colonial perspective, and the Mexican leaders had only to remember the French intervention of the past decade, or examine the brewing European partition of Africa, to remind them of their precarious position. The Porfirian goal thus became not merely to market the products and investment opportunities of Mexico, but to market the idea of an independent Republic of Mexico itself before the world.

Unfortunately, although American investment in and trade with Mexico did soar in the years following the 1879 visit of the American Industrial Deputation to Mexico, the "mutual march to a still grander civilization" never fulfilled the goals of the early Porfirian planners. The economic and political links forged between the two nations during the Porfiriato neither assured Mexican autonomy nor improved U.S.-Mexican cultural relations. Chapter 4, "The Language of Business," examines the Mexican Liberals ultimately disappointing campaign to win American respect for Mexico's commitment to progress. Nor did the campaign to win respect for the Mexican republican government, evident during the visit of former President U.S. Grant to Mexico in 1880, triumph; Chapter 5 examines the failure to establish a sentiment of respectful 'republican sisterhood" between the neighbors, and the tragic acceptance of authoritarianism on both sides of the border.

In the years following the mid-century civil wars both nations sought a new relationship as they switched from a framework of hostility to one of cooperation, but beneath the superficial common interest in expanding bi-national trade and investment, they held irreconcilable views of the future world system. While Americans of the late nineteenth century no longer wanted to annex Mexico, neither did they come to accept Mexico as an equal in the emerging international system. The new cultural relationship Americans constructed answered their own concerns with furthering American economic and political interests abroad, but fulfilled none of the goals of the Mexican Liberals of the early Profiriato.

NOTES

1. "Americans in Mexico," *New York Times*, 29 January 1879.

2. For a concise discussion, see Josefina Zoraida Vasquez and Lorenzo Meyer, "Towards an Understanding of the Mexican Liberals, 1868–98," in *The United States and Mexico* (Chicago: the University of Chicago Press, 1985), 72–92.

3. John Coatsworth, "Características Generales de la Economía Mexicana en el siglo XIX," in *Ensayos sobre el desarollo económico de México y América Latina, 1500–1975*, compiled by Enrique Florescano, (México: FCE, 1979), 171–186.

4. *Estadísticas históricas de México*, (México: Instituto Nacional de Estadística, Geografía e Informática, INAH, 1985), 569, 575, 557.

5. Maritime and railway figures from the U.S. Department of the Treasury, *Statistical Abstract of the United States, 1880*, Treasury Department Document no. 120, no. 3 (Washington, D.C.: Government Printing Office, 1881): 138, 159; Telegraph figure from the U.S. Department of the Treasury, *U.S. Census, 1880* (Washington, D.C.: Government Printing Office, 1881), 1322.

6. "Mining Enterprise in Mexico," *Two Republics*, 1 July 1871; *Two Republics*, 10 June 1868; "Mexican Affairs-Foreign Correspondent," *Two Republics*, 18 July 1868.

7. *Two Republics*, 1 August, 1868; Finerty, 40.

8. On the origins of U.S. attitudes toward Spanish America, see Raymund Paredes, "The Origins of Anti-Mexican Sentiment in the United States," *New Scholar* VI (1977): 139–165; Philip Wayne Powell, *Tree of Hate: Propaganda and Prejudices Affecting U.S. Relations with the Hispanic World*, (New York: Basic Books, 1971); and Charles Gibson, ed., *The Black Legend: Anti Spanish Attitudes in the Old World and the New* (New York: Knopf, 1971.

9. Richard L. Kagan, "Prescott's Paradigm: American Historical Scholarship and the Decline of Spain," *American Historical Review* 101, no. 2 (1996): 423–46; Jefferson to Alexander Von Humboldt, Montpelier, 6 Dec. 1813, *The Writings of Thomas Jefferson*, ed. A.A. Liscomb, 20 Vols. Washington: Library Edition, 1903–4, p 24, quoted in John J. Johnson, *A Hemisphere Apart: The Foundations of U.S. Policy Toward Latin America, 1815–30* (Baltimore: Johns Hopkins, 1990).

10. See Ronald Takaki, "Foreigners in their Native Land: Manifest Destiny in the Southwest," in *A Different Mirror: A History of Multicultural America* (Boston: Little, Brown, and Co., 1993); Reginald Horsman, *Race and Manifest Destiny: The Origins of American Anglo-Saxonism* (Cambridge: Harvard, 1981); and Matthew Frye Jacobson, *Barbarian Virtues: The U.S. Encounters Foreign Peoples at Home and Abroad, 1876–1917* (New York: Hill and Wang, 2000); Poinsett's views are examined in Brigitte B. de Lameiras, *Indios de México y Viajeros Extranjeros, Siglo XIX* (Mexico: SEP Setentas, 1973); and Frank Sanders, "Mexico Visto por los Diplomáticos del Siglo XIX," *Historia Mexicana* 20 Enero-Marzo 1971): 368–411.

11. On republican/progressive imagery in the context of U.S. expansion, see Thomas R. Hietala, *Manifest Design: Anxious Aggrandizement in Late Jacksonian America* (Ithaca: Cornell University Press, 1985) and Robert Johannsen, *To the Halls of the Montezumas: The Mexican War in the American Imagination* (New York: Oxford, 1985).

12. On post-war stereotypes, see Cecil Robinson, *Mexico and the Hispanic Southwest in American Literature* (Tucson: University of Arizona Press, 1977); and Arnaldo de Leon, *They Called Them Greasers: Anglo Attitudes Toward Mexicans in Texas, 1821–1900* (Austin: University of Texas Press, 1983).

13. *Two Republics*, 3 February 1869; "Mexico Open to the Negroes," *New York Times*, 22 January 1878; "Peace in Mexico," *New York Times,* 15 December 1879; "A New Yorker's Views about Mexico," *Two Republics*, 17 April 1881; "The Purchase of Mexico," *Times Picayune* (New Orleans), 13 December 1884; Solomon B. Griffin, *Mexico of Today* (New York: Harper, 1886), 39; John H. Rice, *Mexico: Our Neighbor* (New York: J.W. Lovell, 1888), 109.

14. On cultural anxiety and informal empire, see Robert L. Beisner, *From the Old Diplomacy to the New* (Arlington Heights: Harlan Davidson, 1975); Michael Hunt, *Ideology and U.S. Foreign Policy* (New Haven: Yale University Press, 1987) and Eric T.L. Love, *Race Over Empire: Racism and U.S. Imperialism, 1865–1900* (Chapel Hill: University of North Carolina, 2004).

Chapter Four

"The Language of Business"

In 1878 the Mexican Minister to the U.S., Manuel Zamacona, toured the U.S. publicizing the commercial potential of Mexico and encouraging American businessmen to consider trade and investment opportunities in the southern nation. In Chicago he momentarily stunned his listeners when he encouraged them to examine Mexico for themselves. It was a daring invitation, extended during a time of tense diplomatic relations fueled by rumors of invasion and civil war. Despite the hazards, businessmen in Chicago and New York planned a trade expedition for the coming winter. The organizers extended the invitation to any American and soon, judging by the number of inquiries received, expected hundreds of traders to descend upon Mexico.[1]

For its Mexican sponsors the AID mission heralded a promising new era in Mexico's history. Zamacona had originally promoted commercial exchange as part of his larger campaign to win recognition for Díaz by painting an enticing vision of economic opportunities in Mexico, but his vision accorded well with the Liberal belief that only investment and development could secure Mexico's survival in a world of rapacious neighbors. Minister of Finance Matías Romero outlined the Porfirian perspective for the visitors when he assured Americans that the "enlightened portion of Mexico" welcomed a new commercial relationship with the U.S. as a means of creating "American interests in the integrity and independence of this country

The Mexican government moved quickly to showcase Mexico's commitment to economic progress. The Díaz administration recruited Mexican manufacturers to exhibit alongside the visitors at the planned Mexican-American Trade Exposition through notices placed in the official government daily publication, the *Diario Oficial*, and reprinted by regional governments. The Mexican Minister of Development, (chief of the Secretaría de Fomento), Vicente Riva Palacio, proposed that the visitors be regarded as guests of the nation and received luxuriously at government expense. Riva Palacio noted that he was fully aware there were many "men of means" among the excursionists, but defended his proposal to host the visitors as consistent with the Mexico's goal of guiding the visitors' experiences and thus improving Mexico's profile abroad. Riva Palacio was also responsible for commissioning the first English language guide to Mexico, the *Guide for Mexico* by Vicente F. Manero, for distribution to the visitors from Chicago. Manero, head of the geographical and statistical division of the Secretaría de Fomento, offered information on Mexican products and geography, postal fees, tourist sites, and even Protestant worship services, clearly reflected the Mexican government's intention to smooth the path for potential American investors.[2]

Mexican newspapers joined in the enthusiasm and looked forward to the "salvation—regeneration—[and] modernization" that the visit would inspire, and printed frequent updates on the coming exposition. Secretary of Finance Matías Romero's two hundred page report on the commercial potential of Mexico was serialized in leading Mexican papers. Earlier *La Libertad* had praised Manuel Zamacona for encouraging U.S. commercial interest in Mexico, which would "be the true lifeguard of our nationality." *El Monitor Republicano* rejoiced at Zamacona's success in preparing Americans to switch from an era of "conquest to one of licit commerce," and reprinted the speeches exchanged between Zamacona and his Chicago hosts, as well as the U.S. news articles describing the upcoming visit. Several papers joyfully reprinted an American editorial that argued that the time had come to abandon punishment of Díaz to take advantage of the commercial opportunities in Mexico. In general, newspapers supported the government plans for the AID mission, with only minor critiques. When *La Libertad* questioned the sums allocated for entertainment when what was truly needed was an exchange of information, *La Patria* responded that fun and games were also important for improving relations. *Siglo XIX* reminded all Mexicans of their responsibility to show "foreign eyes" the many riches of the nation, including "our historic city, this surprising railway, sign of our alliance with the progress of the century, the ancient city of the Spanish, the conquest and the preconquest eras, to study the reforms, the schools, the libraries, to touch our telegraph line...." In the end the proud perspective of *Siglo XIX* prevailed and the residents of the capital joined together to showcase the riches of Mexico for their guests.[3]

Editor George Clarke, who had long championed the potential of Mexico in the columns of the *Two Republics*, took particular care to publicize the tour in both the U.S. and Mexico by writing to American newspapers and urging them to send correspondents. Clarke described the excursions and the banquets that awaited the Americans and hoped that "if they do not find as many channels of profitable commerce as they desire, they will at least realize the delights of a heavenly climate and a munificent hospitality." In the end seven journalists joined the party; Jerome Collins for the New York *Herald*, William Dwyer for the New York *Tribune*, Byron Andrews of the Chicago *Inter Ocean*, and John F. Cahill for the *Commerce of the Valley*. The popular magazine, *Frank Leslie's Illustrated News*, sent both a writer and an artist (N. Robinson and H.A. Agden) to cover the events, while John Finerty of the Chicago *Tribune* traveled separately to Mexico and joined the mission there.[4]

Despite the grand projections of the organizers, at the time of departure the actual participants in the mission were a small but "agreeable party of eighty," including a few women who accompanied fathers, husbands or brothers. Although the majority hailed from Chicago, there were several New Yorkers and a few from St. Louis and Cincinnati. The excursionists enjoyed complimentary rail passes from Chicago to New Orleans, where they embarked for Veracruz. Once united in travel they pronounced themselves the "American Industrial Deputation to Mexico" and chose John F. Fisk as spokesman. By the time they arrived in Veracruz, a "succession of unfriendly 'northers' [tropical stormwinds] had so ground the merchants against the manufacturers and the manufacturers against the merchants, that it was impossible to tell which from which."[5]

The Mexican government spared no effort to impress the American merchants. From the moment the American delegates arrived at the shores of Mexico they were entrusted to government officials. The visitors were guided through customs by the Governor of Veracruz State, the Mayor of Veracruz City and the American Consul. The visitors paid an early visit to the Consulate, where they received a long line of local dignitaries and other well-wishers, then were shepherded away to a working breakfast at the commercial exchange (the *Lonja Mercantil*) hosted by the Mexican government. The Mexican government had appointed subcommittees to organize presentations for the visitors and during their first afternoon the Americans were entertained by lectures on the raw materials, the state of communications, and the climatology of Mexico. In the evening the city was illuminated with hundreds of lights suspended from trees and buildings, and the streets and plazas were thronged with citizens anxious to welcome (and inspect) the American visitors.[6]

Local officials, well aware that one impediment to commerce was the American fear of tropical disease, proudly invited the deputation to visit the new hospital. The invitation was tendered so courteously, noted Finerty, that a majority of the delegates accepted only to find themselves within the very wards housing the dreaded miasma of the yellow fever. The sickness was transmitted by mosquitoes, not proximity, but in 1879 visitors knew only that the mysterious disease could lead even robust individuals to a rapid and agonizing death. The merchants scurried through holding their breath and spent the next few days anxiously peering into each other's eyes for signs of yellowing.[7]

That evening the American visitors began the rail ascent out of Veracruz. During the journey they perused the complimentary guidebook by Vicente Manero with its detailed accounts of the towns and regions along the way. They retraced the steps of Cortés on his historic journey into the heartland of the Aztec empire, and noted the sites of battles between the American forces under Winfield Scott and the Mexican defenders in 1847. They sadly recalled their own Civil War while passing the abandoned colony of American Confederate expatriates near Córdoba and cheered the memory of the French Empire's defeat at the hands of Mexican Republicans on the outskirts of Puebla in 1862.

The landscape proved equally fascinating. The Americans noted the alien features of the terrain as they passed from the rolling sand dunes outside Veracruz to the tropical lowlands of the coast. Manero's comments provided a chatty overview of the route. At the village of La Joya, for example, he noted that "as at all the other depots of La Tierra Caliente, the natives bore you with the parasitical orchids, bananas, pineapples, oranges, etc.; but as a compensation, under an open shed, one may indulge in a cup of coffee."[8]

The merchants were amused, not bored, as they tried to identify the fruits and flowers lining the tracks. The naturalists among them enthused over the brilliant birds that darted in and out among the sugar cane, while others sketched the novel butterflies of Mexico. Occasionally, the vegetation parted and the travelers received a sudden glimpse of thatched roofs, shaded hammocks, or a mother with babe in arms standing in a narrow track through the jungle, before the wild vegetation once again engulfed the view.[9]

All were relieved to leave the heat and humidity behind as the train began to climb through the narrow ravines and frequent tunnels of the sierra. Conversation died away as the merchants contemplated the inspired engineering of the railway with its suspended bridges and switchback curves. The passengers were plunged into the deafening blackness of tunnels only to shoot suddenly into the open sky as the train cut across nearly vertical mountain slopes thousands of feet above the distant valleys below. The air of the heights was not only cooler, but thinner, and many visitors professed to feel the first tingle of altitude sickness as the reached the city altitude of 7300 feet. By the time the train pulled across the final miles of the Valley of Mexico after twenty hours of travel, the Americans were subdued, intoxicated with both the fresh air and new sights of their journey. They were escorted to their various hotels by torchlit carriages and had barely time enough to note the curious stone palaces and gaping arched entries along the deserted city streets before collapsing in cavernous hotel rooms.

A night of rest and a full breakfast restored the booster mentality of the Americans, who, by mid-morning, were prepared to venture out from the shelter of the hotel into the novel scene. The empty streets of the previous evening had been transformed. They were filled with ladies draped in lace mantillas, going and coming from church while plantation owners and ranchers with their broad-brimmed hats, leather jackets and pants, mounted on festively outfitted horses, crossed the streets. Dark-skinned Indians crowded the sidewalks as the men hurried by with open baskets of produce or livestock balanced on their backs. The women, with children bound across the chest or back by long blue shawls and their arms filled with the day's provisions, hastened behind with tiny steps.

The colonnades along the sidewalks had become open markets for fruits, vegetables and sweets as Indian vendors spread their colored serapes on the bricks and laid out their wares. Throughout the multitude loudmouthed drivers steered recalcitrant burros that nearly disappeared beneath towering loads of straw, flowers, or pots. Beggars clad in dirty cotton rags wandered amid the stands seeking to be rewarded with a piece of overripe fruit, a damaged vegetable or perhaps a blessing from one of the passing priests. Piglets squealed, chickens clucked and itinerant musicians coaxed unfamiliar rhythms out of high-pitched violins. Through it all, the Americans in their European dress appeared to journalist Robinson "like so many spots of soot on a brightly colored ball dress, or like a flock of crows mingled with a flight of Mexican parrots and cardinals."[10]

As the first order of business, the American visitors divided themselves into committees that were joined by Mexican professionals who assisted in compiling the statistics so vital to the success of U.S.-Mexican commerce. Some studied the markets, others the resources, while still others inventoried the Mexican press. The merchants were anxious to visit the site of the joint U.S.-Mexican exhibition and pleased to find that the government had reserved the lavish salons of the Palacio de Minería for the use of the exhibitors. The impressive colonial-era edifice was one of the most revered sites of Mexico City, nearly equal in symbolic stature to the National Palace where the Mexican President's offices were located, or the National Cathedral in the central plaza.

During the next few days the delegates prepared their samples of American sewing machines, engravings, plows, ink and maps under the open stone galleries that surrounded the interior courtyard garden. Americans were not the only exhibitors. The sixteen American booths were overwhelmed by more than one hundred Mexican displays that ranged from archaeological treasures to opals to shoes. Culinary delicacies, artisan work and folk art from different regions of Mexico predominated. During the two weeks of exhibition the fair received a continuous stream of visitors who poured through the two floors of displays examining the booths. The exposition provided Mexicans with a chance to take stock of both their neighbor and their own nation as they arranged their wares before the foreign visitors.[11]

The exhibitors spent time inspecting the adjacent displays and courting the throngs of visitors, but not all of the U.S.-Mexican socializing took place at the fair. The Mexican and American communities of Mexico City, anxious to promote the cultural understanding that good relations required, organized a series of excursions to the sights and suburbs of the capital. Americans studied Mexican art in the halls of the Academy of San Carlos and commented on the exotic rituals of Roman Catholicism while visiting the Shrine of Guadelupe and the National Cathedral. Americans climbed the pyramid of the Sun at Teotihuacan and cheered the bullfighters on the outskirts of town. A few hardy hikers ascended the volcano of Popocatépetl; most were content to picnic at its feet.[12]

Many considered the most pleasant outing the day they journeyed down the tree-lined Paseo de la Reforma to the National Military Academy within the hilltop castle of Chapultepec. This volcanic knoll at the center of the Valley of Mexico once housed the palace of Emperor Maximilian and, in the far distant past, the summer palace of the Aztec emperors. It was already familiar to the visitors as the "Halls of Montezuma" besieged by the troops of Winfield Scott during the Mexican American War. Once upon the summit Americans were stunned by the beauty of the Valley of Mexico as they gazed out from the marble balustrades of the academy across the city to the distant villages lining the shores of the lakes and the twin volcanoes whose white peaks floated eerily over the whole. They could imagine the American flag of Scott flying over the hill, but also the standards of the Spanish Viceroys or the banners of the Aztec emperor. The visitors were pleasantly surprised by the attractive terraces of the academy, for after dwelling on the long history of the spot they "rather expected to find the hall covered with skulls and leg bones and teeth and such things."[13]

In the evenings the American merchants were feted at a series of brilliant receptions, where the "beauty, grace and refinement of the Mexican ladies" promised to link the societies of the two nations as the merchants were now linking the economies. The social scene culminated at a grand ball where more than one thousand members of the Mexico City community joined the American deputation at the French Club and danced until three o'clock in the morning. The hall was decorated with the flags of the three nations and filled with luscious tropical plants. The ladies, according to press reports, "represented the chief types of Mexican, American and European beauty and were gorgeously clad in silks, satins and lace, ornamented with diamonds and opals of the rarest kinds." Spokesman Fisk, reeling at the least from the music, was led to propose a grand union between the two nations as he hoped that "A larger number of our noble countrywomen might find favor in the eyes of the noble sons of Mexico; and in return many of my countrymen might find wives among the lovely and bright eyed daughters of this hospitable land—a consummation most devoutly to be desired."[14]

Most symbolic of speeches were those exchanged by Fisk and President Díaz within the regal splendor of the presidential offices in the National Palace. The delegates arrived to pay their respects as emissaries of the new international brotherhood of commerce, confident that economic cooperation would erase the misunderstandings of the past. Fisk stressed that he greeted President Díaz not as a diplomat would, "but in the plain, straight-forward language of business." He voiced the hope that there "may grow up between these Sister Republics an enduring bond of friendship, and that side by side, hand in hand, heart to heart, we may go forward in united prospects, demonstrating to the whole world the power and value of the great principles of liberty." Central to this goal he hoped that "commerce, the friend of all universal peace, and the most important of all agencies to bind nations and people together, may grow up between these Sister Republics." Fisk concluded by assuring Díaz that he spoke for the entire deputation in expressing the hope that "the friendship so happily existing between the people of the two great Republics may be perpetual."[15]

Díaz graciously accepted the delegation's gift of an American flag and held it respectfully while he thanked the Americans and joined them in their optimistic predictions for the future. Yet he did not shy away from either recent or longstanding conflicts. Friendship, he observed, had not traditionally marked relations between the two nations and, although he hoped for warm relations with the "elder sister" of the continent, he could not help but notice recent international tension—tension which had been aggravated by false images held by the American public. "I do not attribute the wrong information that has prevailed in your nation in regard to ours to sinister motives," Díaz assured the Americans, "but to a lack of knowledge of the elements composing our social and political conditions, differing from your own, and therefore strange to you and difficult to be understood." He encouraged the "intelligent and impartial gentlemen" of the Deputation to take the opportunity to correct these images so that American and Mexican flags would blend their colors in a "mutual march to a still grander and more comprehensive civilization." The Americans sat impassively through Díaz's appeal until the interpreter translated his remarks into English, and then the hall erupted in applause as the reception concluded.

As the delegates filed out they encountered a portrait of George Washington hanging in the antechamber, inspiring them to lead a set of robust cheers for the United States, modified in mid-course to include Mexico as well. Díaz appeared slightly taken back by the American behavior, observed journalist William Dwyer of the *Tribune*, who attributed the President's reaction to his inability to understand English. As it were, the Americans spilled through the halls of the National Palace, confident that the universal "language of business" would smooth their path.

The final days of the three-week visit were spent dismantling the Mexican-American exhibit and disposing of the samples. The merchants cemented new commercial friendships with a handshake while their wives paid final social calls. As the train departed back down the mountains for Veracruz, *Two Republics* editor George Clarke noted the sudden void in the society of the capital, yet was optimistic that the excursionists "returned with a much more favorable opinion [of Mexico].....Many prejudices have been entirely removed or greatly modified. They belong to the intelligent classes at home and they will sow among their countrymen the seeds of good will and future friendship." The merchants spent the few days at sea drafting and signing a report on their "favorable impression" of future U.S.-Mexican trade and encouraging government promotion of the same. In Washington, Minister Zamacona, who had issued the original invitation to the Chicago business community the year before, gleefully reported a Mexican vogue in the U.S. capital. And in Mexico the *Secretaría de Fomento* announced a second international trade exposition to take place the following year. Minister Vicente Riva Palacio was convinced that the AID mission had furthered Mexico's goals to promote industrial and commercial development, to develop her wealth of natural resources, and to achieve a new peace at home and abroad. One Mexican journalist proudly reviewed the tours and exhibits as proof of Mexico's "immense" natural wealth and concluded that any visitor would "have to close their eyes to the light" to deny Mexico's potential.[16]

Despite the optimism of the moment, the AID mission proved an eventual disappointment to Zamacona, Díaz and the other Mexican promoters who had hoped that the visitors would return committed to an economic partnership with Mexico and the initiation of a new age of egalitarian relations. The first suggestion of failure came in the American coverage of the commercial mission. The Mexican press quickly reprinted and commented upon the American press coverage of the AID mission, which it found scanty, farcical, and even insulting. Although the Mexicans had hoped to highlight a vision of "progressive Mexico," journalist John F. Finerty recalled that most editors back home considered the AID deputation a "fool's mission" and preferred articles on picturesque Mexico to serious discussion of Mexican potential. American coverage not only did little to challenge stereotypes of Mexico, but it actually exploited them, as the titles ("the Gentle Greaser," "Not in a Hurry for News," and "The Lawless Land") suggest. One author shared his fascination with Mexican boots, constructed in the "height and style of 20 years ago....In this sensible and comfortable footwear the Mexican dandy walks with much the same grace, and very much the same motion, as a chicken over a hot piece of iron." The coverage provoked smiles, but did little to further investment or improve American knowledge of Mexico. In April *El Republicano* angrily reprinted an article from the *Chicago Times* that derided Díaz for linking occasional turmoil in Mexico to the lack of economic opportunities. "The good sons of Mexico," the *Times* stated, "consider it more economic to steal cattle in Texas than to raise their own...more economic to rob than to earn a living through work...[and] more economic to confiscate the property of foreigners to satisfy the exigencies of military factions." *El Republicano* sadly concluded that, despite the hospitality of the Mexican nation, the American guests had preserved the "unjustified hatred" of the "filibusterer" despite the visit.[17]

The biased coverage seemed to disprove the Liberal contention that new contact would override older prejudices. Echoes of the "lazy greaser" stereotype that had justified the American annexations of the 1830s and 1840s remained in depictions of Mexicans as lethargic, tardy and backward. Although the visitors were impressed by the early morning bustle of the markets and the strength of the Indian cargo bearers who shouldered heavy burdens through the city streets and along mountain paths, they looked for and found dozing peasants who suggested an easy explanation for Mexico's lack of development (unless one remembered that those dozing workers might be the same who stocked the market with produce carried from the countryside long before dawn). The visitors criticized the commercial break in the early afternoon and faulted Mexicans for the absence of familiar products they considered essential for a modern market. The gravity-defying route of the Veracruz-Mexico City railway was credited to the British, while the Mexicans were faulted for not having conquered the remainder of their challenging terrain with adequate transport. As the *Two Republics* sadly concluded two years after the exposition, the AID visitors "could not understand or appreciate the people of this country. They haunted the bar-rooms of this city and wrote home bilious letters because they could find no whiskey."[18]

Even compliments were bestowed in telling ways. President Díaz, for example, was described in one press account as a handsome Indian, "'copper colored'-but of such an agreeable shade as to be hardly noticeable." Upon meeting the gracious Mayor and Governor of Veracruz, the merchants agreed that the two were "calculated to make their mark in a more wide-awake country than Mexico." The formalities of Mexican courtesy were described as "a series of pow-wows." Even the abundant hospitality the Mexicans offered the deputation was attributed by visitors to Mrs. Foster, who "by her refined hospitality...has conquered the Mexican distaste for reception, and has thus partly Americanized the society of this historic city."[19]

A less ethnocentric perspective could have led to different conclusions. Rather than critique the mid-day break, mistakenly reduced to a "siesta" by the Americans, visitors could have praised the work schedule for assuring the unity of the family during the main meal of the day. Mexican markets did not carry all the products familiar to the Americans, but vendors in Mexico City routinely carried fresh seafood from the coast and a multitude of agricultural products from the many diverse climates the altitudinal variation in Mexico created. The AID visitors could have acknowledged the lack of navigable rivers and the challenge of the Mexican mountains and marveled that Mexican traders had conquered the terrain with only their feet, pack animals and small carts. Finally, they could have praised the assistance of British engineering and investment in the construction of the railroad but also respected the back-breaking labor contributed by the Mexican workforce whose own engineering feats were in abundant evidence throughout the terraced and irrigated countryside. These visitors were not the first or only outsiders to misjudge their surroundings; throughout the nineteenth century American visitors to Mexico routinely dismissed alternative farming and construction styles, no matter how appropriate to the local climate and resources, as illegitimate according to their U.S. based frame of reference.[20]

The Mexicans had sought to improve relations by countering what Díaz called the American "lack of information" with an introduction to Mexican economics, culture and history. But the American spokesman Fisk had proposed a different understanding of American ignorance. Upon opening the U.S.-Mexican exposition he applauded the AID organizers for providing the opportunity for U.S. manufacturers to "learn what Mexico wishes to purchase, the means of reaching your country, and the manner of trading here." The *Secretaría de Fomento* had organized presentations on Mexican geography, resources and production, but *El Mensajero* denounced the AID delegates for having "eaten their fill without worrying in the least about the explanations and notations of the official committees." The delegates had scattered through the streets of Mexico intent upon their own fact-finding. They were oblivious to the local fruits and wares displayed but enthusiastic in compiling a list of the American scales, clocks and soaps, which they were convinced would find a "large market" in the country. The subtitle of an interview with a returning delegate summed up the limits of the American perspective: "The people are too poor and too ignorant to buy or use American manufactures." The Mexicans offered a broad introduction to the nation of Mexico, but the Americans focused their inquiries on the potential of the Mexican market.[21]

American press coverage incorporated the AID mission into their larger understanding of U.S.-Mexican relations, but it was not the collaborative scenario the Mexican planners had optimistically anticipated. Instead of recognizing Mexican initiative in promoting the trade show, American press coverage treated the AID as a product of U.S. initiative and an example of U.S. national economic acumen. The New York Tribune described the visit as "the outgrowth of that industrial expansion which impels American manufacturers to assert their right to representation in the great markets of the world." The paper applauded the merchants, who were soon to apply the "Monroe Doctrine commercially as well as politically to the continent," and compared the delegates to the "Argonauts of old" or the "British colonizers of India." The paper acknowledged that Mexico's potential was great, but stressed that "she needs the impulse of American skill and capital in every branch of her industrial system." George Bowen, one of the tour organizers, mistakenly credited Chicago merchants with initiating the AID after they invited Minister Zamacona to visit Chicago and witness "our ability to produce for and supply" the needs of the Mexican people. In a similar fashion Henry Brooks specified the ways in which U.S. trade would "save" Mexico; it would "replenish the treasury of Mexico, sustain her chosen Executive, relieve the poor and enrich the rich." But most of all, argued Brooks, it "would open the vast treasures of that wonderful country to the commerce of the world, and furnish a new and inexhaustible field for the young and enterprising of our own race and nation." John Finerty concluded his reports from Mexico with a plea, "In what I have seen of the country of the Montezumas, I can say honestly to the people of the U.S., there is no hope in Mexico but in you—if you will take the trouble of being her saviours." Mexico had succeeded in moving only partially beyond the framework of 1846. Its territory no longer tempted American annexationists, but now it appeared as a new frontier for an American economic invasion.[22]

During the following years the young and enterprising of the U.S. did "discover" Mexico. In 1880 David Strother, U.S. Consul in Mexico City, was one of the first to note a "strikingly evident" shift in U.S. attention to Mexico. "There has been latterly a very considerable interest in the various commercial enterprises of this country," he observed in his annual report. Leonidas Hamilton agreed heartily, noting that his guide to business practices in Mexico (*Hamilton's Mexican Handbook*) passed through four printings between 1881 and 1883. William Bishop, traveling in Mexico in 1880, noted the inescapable chatter of American entrepreneurs who drew him constantly into discussions of electrical lights, coal mines, sugar refineries, shoe factories, and cotton mills. He found his hotel crowded with "archaeologists, constructors of telegraph lines and engineers starting out or returning from surveys." Alden Case, a missionary who arrived in northern Mexico a few years later, recalled his amazement at encountering Americans "everywhere, building railways, dragging out the precious metals, operating great stock ranches, planting immense rubber and coffee plantations, cultivating citrus groves and other fruits,...and prospering." In 1881 the *Two Republics* rejoiced in "the increase in the number of Americans in the country." The editor described the new American onslaught as a commercial invasion, carried forward by steamers crowded with American voyagers. "This is only the commencement of the rush," he cautioned, "A regular Mexican boom is in order."[23]

The prediction proved accurate. During the thirty years of the Porfiriato the size and influence of the American community in Mexico mushroomed beyond all expectations. In 1873 U.S. Minister John Foster had been dismayed to find barely three hundred American residents in Mexico City, far fewer in number and less influential than other expatriate communities. By 1900, however, the Americans comprised the most numerous foreign community in Mexico, with 15,000 of the 57,000 registered foreigners declaring U.S. citizenship. In 1910 the Mexican census recorded 20,000 American residents in Mexico; others estimated the figure to be far higher.[24]

The exact figures of the expatriate community were impossible to come by, even in 1880 Consul Strother had found the Mexican census figures notoriously unreliable due to the "carelessness of the [American] residents themselves, who very generally neglect and often perversely evade" registration rules. All observers agreed, however, that the influx of Americans was concentrated in the federal capital and the states along the northern frontier. Elsewhere, about twenty agricultural emigrant colonies and scores of travelling Protestant missionaries provided smaller, scattered, but still important arenas for American action.[25]

American-Mexican trade flourished as well. In the early 1870s U.S. Minister to Mexico Thomas Nelson had lamented that U.S. citizens played no significant role in Mexican commerce and were vastly overshadowed by the efforts of Spanish, British and German merchants. Yet by 1884, when the international rail lines opened between the two nations, the U.S. had become Mexico's leading foreign trade partner. Americans did not so much take over existing trade as open new areas of commerce made possible by improved foreign relations, transportation and communication between the two nations. Although European residents continued to dominate Mexican trade with Europe, by 1900 the largely U.S.-controlled U.S.-Mexican trade sector exceeded the size of all the Mexican-European nation sectors combined. By 1912 the U.S. supplied fifty percent of Mexican imports and bought more than seventy-five percent of her exports.[26]

Unfortunately, the explosion in commerce and contact fulfilled the American vision of the relationship, but not the Mexican. Most disappointingly, the distorted dependence of the Mexican economy upon American trade by the late Porfiriato endangered rather than strengthened the Mexican national security situation. Nor had trade and contact promoted the improved cultural relations that Zamacona's campaign originally envisioned. Commercial exchange and interdependence had partially reinvented American images of Mexico, but not in the way the early promoters had desired.

Mexican promoters of the early Porfiriato had probably assumed that new American traders and residents would imitate the experience of their predecessors. The Americans who arrived prior to the Díaz revolution were few in number; the three hundred residents Foster encountered in Mexico City represented the largest community. Veracruz and Sonora (with 220 and 200 residents, respectively) were also centers of American activity, while the remainder were scattered thinly throughout the nation. The consular reports estimated that there were perhaps twenty-five Americans in Chihuahua, twelve in Acapulco, and twenty-two in Yucatán.

During the early years this diverse group, which included stage drivers, doctors, farmers and miners, had been unable to rely on each other for political or economic security and had recognized the necessity of preserving cordial relations with local families. They had no separate social circle and, in consequence, had learned to speak Spanish and had adapted to Mexican social, commercial and culinary customs. Even social functions benefiting the American Benevolent Society (a charity established for the aid solely of American citizens in Mexico) included Mexican guests, served Mexican food and reflected Mexican social protocol as much as American. In 1869, visiting Secretary of State William Seward was received at banquets where Mexican military officers and American veterans (both confederate and union) sat side-by-side.[27] The bi-national receptions organized in 1879 for the AID mission and in 1880 for President Ulysses S. Grant (see chapter 5) were not unusual; they illustrated the mixed social world of the early American residents in Mexico.

In contrast, the new generation of expatriates soon lived, shopped, and socialized in American-run establishments. Even in 1880 William Bishop found that in Mexico City the newly arriving American "engineers and employees form settlements in boarding houses of their own; [and] make resorts of certain economical restaurants where little but English is spoken. They associate but little with natives." In 1881 the *Two Republics* noted the novel appearance of American guest houses and American grocery stores in Mexico City. Soon the paper carried advertisements for American-style bars, bowling alleys and restaurants and reported the scores of baseball games played between teams of American railway workers. It recorded the popularity of American community climbing excursions to the Volcano of Popocatépetl and the caverns of Cacamilpa, and bicycle races through the outlying towns of the Valley of Mexico. American settlers in Northern mining communities established mini-colonies as well, with their own stores, hotels, schools and hospitals. By the turn of the century Wallace Gillpatrick could live an entire year in Mexico without acquiring any of the language. There simply was no daily need to master the language or branch out from the worn paths of expatriate life. Whereas the earlier residents had, by necessity, become integrated into Mexican society, later arrivals spent the bulk of their hours in the company, and cultural worldview, of other Americans.[28]

The transformation was partly a response to the demographics of the new community. The American-run boarding houses, social clubs and restaurants that emerged after 1880 hinted at the bachelor lifestyle of the new American community. The construction of rail lines, mines and industries attracted hordes of skilled and hopeful American workers who were invariably male and usually young. Bishop estimated that there were six hundred American engineers in Mexico City in 1880, while travel writer Fanny Gooch put the number at six to eight hundred in 1887.[29]

Single or unaccompanied men would have found few opportunities for entering the traditional social life of Mexico City that revolved around careful rounds of residential social calls and family introductions. Men without a wife, sister, or mother to accompany them would have found it almost impossible to rent a separate residence or hire domestic help, driving them into the rented rooms and cafeterias of their compatriots. In Mexico City public consumption of food and drink was associated with the poorest class, upper class Mexicans had socialized primarily in private homes with extended family. The sudden appearance of pubs and cafe spelled cosmopolitanism to the visitors, but struck the local population as unseemly.

Even if American men had been prepared to endure the carefully chaperoned rituals of Mexican courtship (which required "at least six months of industrious diplomacy," according to Solomon Griffin), few Mexican families would have encouraged a daughter's romance with a Protestant northerner of unknown family. Oil investor Edward Doheny recalled that the Americans flooding Mexico were seen as "young, hardy and impetuous," and their attention to Mexican women was "particularly resented." Not surprisingly perhaps, bicycling, baseball and bowling soared in popularity. Gooch urged the

American community to furnish "reading rooms" that could also help keep the young men profitably occupied.[30]

As the American community matured it ceased to resemble a gold-mining camp. However, the social institutions it developed did little to promote integration with Mexican life but instead preserved the separation between Mexican and American social circles. The growth of the English-language American School in Mexico City reflected the community's evolution as well as this exclusionary trend. In 1884 nine English-speaking students studied an American curriculum in a private home, by the eve of the revolution there were more than five hundred students in the grammar school and an equal number in the high school program. The obvious expansion of family life among expatriates had done little to remove the social barriers between Mexican and American circles however, for the American school educated members of the younger generation to prepare them for their future as American citizens, not residents of Mexico. From the perspective of the classroom the Mexican experience was always the marginal one.[31]

The increasing number of American residents and travelers also raised demand for a proper American-style hospital, especially following the miserable death by yellow fever of the Raymond Excursion tour guide, John Bolton, in 1885 in Mexico City. Tourists and residents could not be cared for in their hotels or boarding house rooms if afflicted with a contagious illness, and no private home would have undertaken the risk of boarding any but a close relative suffering from disease. Over the following years, fundraising dances, lunches and other events supported the construction of an expatriate clinic and played a significant role in the social life of the American community. Tourist James Hale Bates attended a charity benefit performance of the Orrin Brothers Circus in Mexico City in 1886, where he was pleasantly pleased to encounter the leading figures of the American community.[32]

Church congregations offered other alternatives to the bachelor amusements of the early Porfiriato. In 1879 Reverend William Butler abandoned his decade-long effort to convert Mexicans and invited his sons to join him in ministering to the needs of the growing American community. Other ministers followed his lead. During the 1870s the twenty churchgoing American residents shared a single nonsectarian service, by 1900 there were four English-speaking Protestant churches in Mexico City, each of which offered a range of social activities for the largely American congregations.[33]

Americans in Mexico City, like Americans at home, also created formal social clubs. The Shakespeare Club provided a scholarly forum, while the Anglo-American club (originally the Al Fresco Club) invited the "whole English-speaking community" to join them for "croquet, lawn tennis, archery, football and dancing." In 1895 American businessmen established the American Club in recognition of the colony's growing numbers, wealth and social impact. Through the "magnificence and splendor" of its quarters (which included dining rooms, music halls and a bowling alley) the club intended to "do honor" to the foreign community. Within a few years the American club had over six hundred members and more on a waiting list. In 1905 the American community founded the Mexico City Country Club at Churubusco. Other golf and country clubs already existed, but the Churubusco club was informally considered the 'American' country club. Although the social clubs were not limited exclusively to Americans (even one-third of the original members of the American Club were not from the U.S.), the code of behavior was inevitably "yankee." By the 1890s northern mannerisms had become compatible with elite status.[34]

By the turn of the century the large American community no longer found residence in Mexico an experience of exile or alienation, they could remain firmly focused on achieving recognition by U.S., not Mexican standards. Even those who remained thirty years in Mexico identified themselves simply as Americans, their residence abroad an apparent accident of geography. Their educational, social and religious institutions strengthened this identification by encouraging Americans to look to their compatriots for friendship, and social standards. Americans could choose from a number of local and imported English-language daily newspapers, as well as numerous weekly and monthly publications in English. Their children could be educated in American schools and their sick cared for in American hospitals. They worshipped in American churches, attended plays at the local YMCA and borrowed books from community reading rooms, such as the Railroad Library Association. Americans played golf and tennis at the Country Club and planned crew regattas and clambakes with the Lakeside Club. American residents considered the community a testimony to American virtues: "no finer group of high class, honorable, active, efficient men of affairs was ever assembled anywhere."[35]

Not surprisingly, the American community gained a reputation for its isolation from Mexican circles. Marie Robinson Wright, who visited Mexico in 1896 and again in 1910, found the social life of the American community "delightful," although "confined to themselves." Other American observers agreed. In 1886 a visiting American journalist wrote that "In social relations where there is a mixed population, the line of separation is almost as distinctly drawn between Americans and Mexicans as in Ohio between the white and colored people. Marriages between Americans and Mexicans seldom occur." Harry Franck, who stopped over to visit a friend that was managing a mine near Guanajuato in 1915 noted that men who married a Mexican girl, even one of education and 'good character,' were derided as "squawmen" by the other American men and women in the community, while those men who married "any old rounder" from the states enjoyed greater prestige. Wallace Gillpatrick also found that much discussion among his American friends in the northern mining communities centered on "disparagement of Mexico and the Mexicans," and eventually concluded with the discouraging consensus that "Mexicans did not like Americans" either.[36]

Other observers were more critical of the distance between the two communities. American Charles Flandrau, who visited his brother's coffee plantation in Mexico in 1905, was both "enraged and annoyed by what seems not only lack of curiosity, but positive ignorance on the part of Americans who live in Mexico." Flandreau described a community preoccupied with gossip, whose only interest in Mexicans appeared to be in their suitability as servants. Expatriate gossip was preoccupied with discussion of who had stolen away a good cook, inconvenient deaths of servants, and who drank.[37] A common theme in many commentaries was that the American residents were interested only in their own interests in Mexico; Mexican matters or perspectives concerned them little.

Mexicans also commented on the social isolation of Americans in Mexico. A 1910 Mexican-authored guide to the foreign communities in Mexico City was cool in its appraisal of American residents. Although the guide enthused over the contribution of the French and German communities to Mexican life, it was noticeably reticent in its discussion of the largest foreign enclave. The guide limited itself to providing pictures of American institutions (the country club, the American Club, etc.) and perfunctorily acknowledged the skill of the American diplomatic staff. Another Mexican-authored guide (prepared for the 1893 Chicago Columbian Exposition) noted that the typical American resident in Mexico "Mixes very little with the Mexicans, when appointed to a position of some importance, where he has to treat with the natives of the country on equal or officially superior terms, he generally gives himself many airs of superiority and obstinately refuses to adapt himself to the system of courtesy and the usual formality which prevail in Mexico, and the neglect of which determine the degree of sympathy to which a person is entitled." The author, Manuel Caballero, asked his American readers to forgive him for his frankness, but noted that in Mexico "it is necessary to devote a reasonable time to the apparently useless task of making connections, studying the character of the people, and, in a word, making oneself agreeable." Harry Franck was more blunt in describing the kinds of behavior to which Caballero alluded, in Guanajuato he watched in horror as American mine engineers lit their cigarettes from the candles burning in workplace shrines to the Virgin of Guadelupe, oblivious to the chagrin of their employees.[38]

Although many Americans acknowledged that their disdain for Mexican "drawing room manners" embittered social relations, they were hardly apologetic. Americans associated their supposed 'brusqueness' with the 'go-getter mentality' that they credited with American commercial success abroad. Alfred Henry Lewis praised the Mexicans for their courtesy and hospitality, but lamented that they hadn't the American's force, fertility or genius to invent." Bernard Moses, an economics professor who toured Mexico in 1895, suggested that Americans could be more sensitive to Mexican feelings, but took pride in noting that "our national virtues are virtues of frontiersmen recently come to town." What Mexicans perceived as boorish the Americans defended as energetic and egalitarian. Engineer Percy Martin considered the charge that American ascendance in Mexico was a result only of mercantile single-mindedness, not cultural or moral superiority, and concluded that "civilizing by syndicate [as opposed to culture] is not such a bad method to adopt." American missionary Alden Case admitted that "American condescension to Mexicans was undeniable," but he still maintained that Americans had improved Mexico by teaching habits of promptness, diligence and thrift."[39]

This condescension was not only insulting to Mexicans, but costly. Many Mexican entrepreneurs complained that Americans avoided partnerships with Mexicans, limiting their ability to profit from new trade potential with the U.S. market. On one level, the preference of Americans for American partners and employees reflected practical concerns with easing communication and legal arrangements. On a more profound level, it was undeniable evidence of the underlying power dynamics in the relationship. It was American culture and connections that brought in contracts and it was ultimately Mexicans, not Americans, who were obliged to adapt to the cultural practices of the foreigners. In 1886 Solomon Griffin reported increasing numbers of young Mexicans studying English, a sure sign, he assured his readers, of Mexican progress.[40] Griffin might more accurately have noted that studying English was a sure sign that young Mexicans had realized the buying power of English language fluency in the lucrative U.S.-Mexican trade sector.

The powerful connections and financial fluidity wielded by American enterprise not only encouraged Mexicans to adapt linguistically to their requirements, but culturally as well. Mexicans who might wish to benefit, like Americans in Mexico, from connections formed through informal socializing might need to learn golf, baseball or bowling. Even more disturbing was the distortion caused by tenacious racial categorizations and racial tensions in the U.S culture. U.S. visitors and employers deemed only "white" Mexicans capable of modernization, the majority of mestizo and Indian Mexicans were routinely dismissed as bereft of invention or initiative. Larger American concerns like mines and railroads imported not only technology, but Jim Crow segregation practices and wage differentials for groups with different racial appearances as well, subtly encouraging would-be Mexican partners to adopt similar practices or face a commercial cold shoulder.

Even the American willingness to make peace with the virtual slavery of the debt-peonage system grew less out of adaptation to Mexican practices than out of the extension of American visions of race to Mexico. Most Americans seemed to agree with visitor Cora Hayward Crawford's assertion that the paternalistic labor system had proved the salvation of the peon, for 'lazy and irresponsible' as they were, they would never have survived if not cared for and directed by a superior class. The American-written *Ferguson's Guide* of 1876, apparently influenced by U.S. debates on Reconstruction, dated Mexico's economic decline from the "date of the first emancipation of slaves on the Mexican territory, [as] the natives, who are naturally indolent and indifferent, partly abandoned the fields and factories." Even John Kenneth Turner, who exposed the horrors of the debt-peonage system to American readers in 1908, adjusted his defense of the Yaqui nation to accepted U.S. racial stereotypes: "We would not call them Indians, for they are workers. As far back as their history can be traced they have never been savages....they tilled the soil, discovered and developed mines, maintained public schools, had an organized government and their own mint." George Gould, an American rubber planter in the Yucatán, wrote Turner to defend debt peonage with arguments that could have been lifted from the antebellum South, "It is the plantation owners who prevent the peons—obviously worthless humans with no profession—from becoming public charges." Not surprisingly, American expectations for Mexican potential depended greatly on the color of the Mexican.[41]

Although Americans seemed to assume that the Americanization of Mexican culture was an inevitable precursor to American-style development, the Mexican view of both Americanization and development was more complex. In 1904 the *Mexican Investor*, a British and American run paper, asserted that the "thoughtful men" of Mexico had awakening to "a realization of the necessity of becoming 'Americanized,' in order to share in the realization of the untold wealth of their country." Ironically, the *Investor* was writing in response to a recent essay by Mexican author M. Chauves, which decried the 'americanization' of Mexico's youth. What Americans saw as a necessary improvement, Mexicans like Chauves lamented as cultural distortion. Young Mexicans, he feared, were rejecting their own heritage because knowledge of the English language and American mannerisms offered concrete advantages in dealing with American business. Yet what both the *Investor* and Chauves considered 'American style' was seen somewhat differently by Mexican youth, who defended their new practices as an aspect of modern rather than American culture. In their view, Mexicans raced bikes, played golf, learned baseball and spoke English not because they were turning their backs on their Mexican identity, but because they saw themselves as both modern and Mexican. From the American perspective however, Americanization and modernization were synonymous. In 1909 Stanton Kirkham observed that much attention had been paid to Mexican "progress-that is to say, its Americanization." And as Edward Conley stated in 1905, "For the past twenty-five years Mexico had been breaking off her moldy shell of past civilization and getting into modern business clothes. What more natural than that they should be cut American fashion?"[42]

By the end of the Porfiriato it was clear that, despite the increase in economic links, the Mexican Liberals had not succeeded in establishing American respect for Mexico as an independent and forward-looking nation, capable of joining with the U.S. in a mutually beneficial alliance for progress. Instead, Americans assumed their role was to lead Mexico toward American-style evolution, as did New Mexico Governor L.A. Shelden in 1884 when he encouraged Americans to teach Mexicans to "be industrious." "To aid a people to most effectively bring out the material resources that nature has supplied," argued Shelden, in voicing a widely held interpretation of the role of the U.S. abroad, "is labor bestowed in the cause of philanthropy and Christianization." Evidence of Mexican modernization was routinely credited to American influence, not Mexican initiative. Confronted with the sight of a local druggist raising a new, illuminated sign above his shop, Sylvester Baxter confidently concluded that the "spirit of American enterprise" was at work.[43]

More disturbingly, the new commercial links had done little to create American support for the "integrity and autonomy" of the Mexican nation, as Manuel Zamacona had once expected, instead growth in the trade and investment sectors was interpreted as a portent of inevitable American expansion. Despite the examples of Mexican activity around them, Americans continued to agree with writer F.E. Prendergast's 1881 observation that "any rapid progress must come about through colonization by some higher or more progressive race." In 1884 the newly appointed U.S. Minister to Mexico was informed by Secretary of State Thomas Bayard himself that "the overflow of our population and capital into these border states of Mexico, must, sooner or later, saturate these regions with Americans and control their political action, but until they are prepared for our laws and institutions we do not want them." In 1895 Bernard Moses agreed with the vision of inevitable American expansion, assuming that Americans were destined to push the border south as their "commercial sagacity and daring" would ensure an easy victory over the Mexicans. The theme was repeated in 1910 when Otheman Stevens portrayed American investors as the advance guard of "materialistic conquistadors…a dominant race invading commercially and industrially the domain of a comfortably contented, unenergetic race."[44]

In the end, thirty years of commercial alliance did little to raise American respect for Mexico. The trade revolution Zamacona envisioned in 1878 arrived, but not the reinvention of the relationship. Even at the end of the Porfiriato many Americans would have agreed with the American-written pamphlet that insisted that "Mexico is not essentially a nation of commerce, except as developed by Europeans and Americans." Yet the nationalistic goals of the Mexican government remained. In 1909 a *New York Times* journalist, Frederick Palmer, reviewed American investments in mines, railroads and agriculture, and concluded that "the big things of Mexico, then, are ours." The title of his article, "Mexico's work done by Americans," was even more insulting. When the Mexican consul wrote the paper to complain of the insensitive article, Palmer insisted he could not imagine why the Mexicans took offense at his essay, and challenged the consul to find one line that was not truthful.[45]

The dispute between Palmer and the Mexican consul typifies the failure of the Porfirian campaign to rewrite the rhetoric and reality of commercial ties with the U.S. as a means of strengthening Mexican national security. In the years after Díaz assumed power, both the U.S. and Mexico were interested in replacing patterns of conflict with the cooperation that would help each nation fulfill its trade and investment objectives. Yet, as Palmer's boorish comments revealed, the relationship that developed was not only asymmetrical, but dismissive. Americans never saw their role as that of a colleague of Mexico, but as her savior, illustrated by Palmer's 'truth' grounded in an ethnocentric fusion of the concepts of American and 'modern.' The consul objected to Palmer's article not to challenge his statistics of ownership and production, but to challenge Palmer's assumption that only yankee ingenuity was responsible for Mexico's development.

Despite the American mythologizing of 'Yankee know-how' evident in article's like Palmer's, in reality, small scale American entrepreneurs and investors were as likely to suffer financial setbacks as their Mexican counterparts. Ironically, even scholarship critical of the negative impact of large American enterprises in Mexico have tended to preserve this myth by distracting attention from the less successful, but more common experiences of small American businesses in Mexico. While it was flattering for Americans to assume that American commercial success stemmed from unique 'Yankee' virtues or business acumen, in reality it was access to capital, markets, and technology that gave some Americans, and very few Mexicans, an advantage in trade. Nevertheless most Americans, like William Carson in 1909, preferred to believe in a simpler explanation, built upon images of Mexico, "the old, the romantic, the picturesque...," passively awaiting the infusion of "new life through the oncoming host of American invaders."[46]

It was obvious in that in the years after Díaz assumed power Americans moved only marginally beyond the cultural framework of 1846 as they replaced assumptions of territorial annexation with those of commercial empire. The disappointing outcome of the effort to raise Mexico's profile should not have come as a total surprise to the Porfirian Liberals, however. The direction of future development was evident from the day in 1879 when the AID visitors ascended the tree-covered slopes to the Chapultepec Military Academy and Presidential offices. Even while visiting the symbolic heart of the Mexican nation—home to Aztec rulers, Spanish viceroys, and Maximilian's court—the Americans relived only the most painful moment of Mexican history. When halted by the guards at the gates of the Military Academy, they jokingly responded that they were not the first Americans to enter without a pass. As they gazed over the academy grounds, they agreed that "The proudest day that Chapultepec ever saw was when the Stars and Stripes flared over its tower."[47] The strenuous hospitality of the Mexicans had not succeeded in reeducating the American visitors; the Americans saw Mexico not with the Mexican eyes of their hosts, but with the covetous eyes of Winfield Scott transferred to an era of commerce.

NOTES

1. "Mexico," *Chicago Tribune*, 4 September 1878; "Señor Zamacona," *Chicago Tribune*, 6 September 1878; and *New York Herald*, 1 February 1879. The AID mission has received little scholarly attention although it is mentioned briefly in Ralph Roeder, *Hacia el México Moderno: Porfirio Díaz* (México: Fondo de Cultura Económica, 1973); and David Pletcher, "México: Campo de Inversiones Norteamericanas 1867–80," *Historia Mexicana* 2 (1953): 564–574. Clementina Díaz y de Ovando compiled U.S. and Mexican newspaper accounts of Zamacona's mission and the AID excursion in *Crónica de una Quimera: Una Invasión Norteamericana en México, 1879* (México: Universidad Nacional Autónoma de México, 1989).

2. "Trade with Mexico," *New York Times*, 4 December 1878; Vincent G. Manero, *Guide for Mexico* (Mexico City: Tip. de Gonzalo Estévez, 1878); circumstances of publication noted in the *Two Republics*, 14 January 1879.

3. See Díaz y de Ovando, *Crónica*, for press coverage reprints; also Carlos de Olaguibel y Arista, "Un triunfo de la paz y el progreso," *La Libertad*, 11 October 1878; Matías Romero, *Report.* (1880); *La Libertad*, 29 August, 15 November 1878; *La Patria*, 19 November 1879; *El Monitor Republicano*, 1 January 1878; *Inter Ocean* (Chicago), 6 September 1878, reprinted in *El Monitor Republicano*, 10 October 1878; *Chicago Commercial Advertiser*, 31 October 1878, reprinted in *El Monitor Republicano*, 7 December 1878; *Chicago Tribune*, 25 November 1878, reprinted in *El Monitor*

Republicano, 10 January 1879; "Mexico and the U.S.," *National Republican* (Washington, D.C.), 23 December 1877; *Siglo XIX*, 20 January 1879.

4. "The Expected Guests," *Two Republics*, 14 January 1879; Finerty's dispatches were compiled in Wilbert Timmons, ed., *John F. Finerty Reports from Porfirian Mexico*, 1879 (El Paso: Western Press, 1974).

5. Organizer George Bowen blamed Foster for discouraging many with his criticism of the Díaz regime. *New York Herald*, 1 February 1879; list of participants published in "Viajeros Americanos," *Diario Oficial*, 13 January 1879; "The Americans in Mexico," *New York Times*, 13 February 1879; "The Commercial Expedition to Mexico," *Frank Leslie's Illustrated News*, 15 February 1879; 430–1.

6. "For Pleasure and Profit," *New York Times*, 8 December 1878; *Philadelphia Public Ledger*, 24 February, 1880.

7. Finerty, 76–77.

8. Manero, 15.

9. "Scenes in Vera Cruz, Mexico," *Frank Leslie's Illustrated Newspaper*, 22 February 1879, 448–9; The Commercial Expedition to Mexico," *Frank Leslie's Illustrated Newspaper*, 1 March 1879, 465–6.

10. "The Extension of Trade," *Frank Leslie's Illustrated Newspaper*, 15 March 1879, 23.

11. "Lista de las personas que han occurrido con sus manufacturas o productos naturals, para dicha Exposición," *Siglo XIX*, 7 February 1879; "La Exposición," *Siglo XIX*, 24 January 1879; *El Mensajero*, 29 January 1879; *El Monitor*, 30 January 1879; "The Exposition," *Frank Leslie's Illustrated Newspaper*, 5 April 1879, 70; "Pleasure and Business," *New York Tribune*, 14 February 1879.

12. *New York Tribune*, 22 January 1879; "Ascent of Popocatépetl," *Siglo XIX*, 16 April 1879, reprint from *Der Seebote* (Milwaukee); C.F. Noetling, "En Mexico," *Siglo XIX*, 18 April, 1879.

13. "A Day at Chapultepec," *New York Times*, 31 March 1879.

14. *Two Republics*, 1 February 1879; *Le Trait d'Union*, 5 February 1879; *El Republicano*, 5 February 1879; The Merchant's Excursion," *New York Tribune*, 18 February 1879; "Pleasure and Business," *New York Tribune*, 14 February 1879; "American Exhibition in Mexico," *Two Republics*, 1 February 1879.

15. "The U.S. and Mexico," *New York Tribune*, 24 January 1879; "Americans in Mexico," New York Tribune, 29 January 1879; *El Republicano*, 17 January 1879; *El Monitor*, 17 January 1879; La Exposición," *Siglo XIX*, 24 January 1879.

16. "American Excursionists—Results—Expectations," *Two Republics*, 15 February 1879; "Merchants Excursion," *New York Tribune*, 14 February 1879; Crónica," *El Mensajero*, 6 March 1879; Zamacona to Díaz, 7 February 1879, APD, 30: 28–9; *Two Republics*, 15 February 1879; *Siglo XIX*, 26 February 1879; J.M. Vigil, "Crónica," *Monitor Republicano*, 30 January 1879.

17. *La Libertad*, 12 November 1878, reprinted in Díaz y de Ovando, *Crónica*, 96; *El Monitor*, 16 January 1879, reprinted in Díaz y de Ovando, *Crónica*, 200. *Siglo XIX* reprinted all of the articles on the AID from the *New York Herald* on 26 February 1879; Finerty, vi; "Pawnshops and Lotteries," *New York Tribune*, 14 February 1879; *Chicago Tribune*, 15 March 1879, reprinted in *El Republicano*, 23 April 1879.

18. The shift in editorial tone can be partly explained by the death of the elder George Clarke in 1880. George Clarke (the son) then took over as chief editor. "American Excursionists," *Two Republics*, 15 February 1879; "Improvement in Mexican Affairs," *Two Republics*, 2 October 1881.

19. "The Americans in Mexico," *New York Times*, 13 February 1879; "Stage Coach Robbers," *New York Times*, 23 February 1879; "Pleasure and Business," *New York Times*, 14 February 1879.

20. See Daniel David Arreola, "Landscape Images of Eastern Mexico: A Historical Geography of Travel, 1822–75," (Ph.D. diss., University of California at Los Angeles, 1980).

21. "American Exhibition in Mexico," *Two Republics*, 1 February 1879; *El Mensajero*, 18 January 1879; *New York Tribune*, 22 January 1879; "Mexico," *Chicago Tribune*, 20 February 1879.

22. "Merchants Excursion," *New York Tribune*, 8 February 1879; "Mexican Excursion," *New York Tribune*, 13 January 1879; *New York Herald*, 1 February 1879; Henry Brooks, "Our Relations with Mexico," *Californian* 1 (1880): 223; Finerty, vii; originally published as "Matters in Mexico," *Chicago Tribune*, 18 March 1879.

23. David Strother to Assistant Secretary of State Robert Hunter, 6 December 1880, *Annual Report*, Consul, Mexico City, *DDM*; Leonidas Hamilton, *Hamilton's Mexican Handbook* (Boston: D. Lothrop, 1883), 1; William Henry Bishop, *Old Mexico and her Lost Provinces: A Journey in Mexico, Southern California and Arizona, by Way of Cuba* (New York: Harper, 1883). 57–8; Alden Buell Case, *Thirty Years with the Mexicans in Peace and Revolution* (New York: Revell, 1917), 249; "A Comparison, 1867–1881," *Two Republics*, 6 February 1881; *Two Republics*, 1 January 1881.

24. Studies of the American community in Mexico include Schell, *Integral Outsiders*, as well as John Mason Hart, *Empire and Revolution: The Americans in Mexico Since the Civil War* (Berkeley: University of California Press, 2002); Moises Gonzales Navarro, *Los Extranjeros en México y los Mexicanos en el Extranjero, 1821–1970* (México: Colegio de México, Centro de Estudios Históricos, 1993–94); David Pletcher, *Rails, Mines and Progress* (Ithaca: Cornell University, 1958); and Ethelyn Clara Davis, "The American Colony in Mexico City," (Ph.D diss., University of Missouri, 1942). Foster, 20–21; Davis, 61–2; Gonzalez Navarro, 272.

25. Strother to William Hunter, 2 January 1880, *DDM*; Of the sixty immigrant colonies established in Díaz's Mexico, about twenty were populated by North Americans, including eleven by Mormons, one by African Americans and one by Native Americans. See Sergio Ortega Noriega, *El Eden Subvertido: La Colonización de Topolobambo, 1886–1896* (México: Departamento de Investigaciones Históricas, Instituto Nacional de Antropología e Historia, 1978), 42. Deborah Baldwin estimates that by 1900 100 U.S. missionaries supervised 300 Protestant congregations in Mexico. See Deborah Baldwin, *Protestants and the Mexican Revolution: Missionaries, Ministers and Social Change* (Urbana: University of Illinois, 1990), 22–24.

26. Report of Minister Thomas Nelson to U.S. Secretary of State Hamilton Fish, summarized in the *Two Republics*, 8 February 1873; Abdiel Oñate, "El Surgimiento de la supremacia estadounidense en los mercados latinoamericanos: el caso de México,

1870–1914," in *El Dilema de Dos Naciones: Relaciones Económicas entre México y los Estados Unidos*, ed. Thomas Noel Osborn and Miguel S. Wionczek (México: Trillas, 1981), 391–404; Fernando Rosenzweig, "El Comercio Exterior," and Nicolau d'Olwer, "Las Inversiones Extranjeras," in *Historia Moderna de México: El Porfiriato, La Vida Económica* (México: Hermes, 1965), 635–730, 973–1177; Rippy, 319.

27. Albert S. Evans, *Our Sister Republic: A Gala Trip through Tropical Mexico in 1869–70* (Hartford: Columbian, 1870), 278; also see Howard Ryan, "Selected Aspects of American Activities in Mexico, 1876–1910," (Ph.D. diss., University of Chicago, 1964), 45.

28. Bishop, 59; "Visitors," *Two Republics*, 13 February 1881; On sport as an arena of cultural contact between Americans and Mexicans, see William Beezley, "The Porfirian Persuasion: Sport and Recreation in Modern Mexico," in *Judas at the Jockey Club* (Lincoln: University of Nebraska, 1987) and Richard V. McGehee, "Sports and Recreational Activities in Guatemala and Mexico, Late 1800s to 1926," *Studies in Latin American Popular Culture*, 13 (1994):7–32; Case, 250; also see the memoir of investor Grant Shepherd, *The Silver Magnet* (New York: Dutton, 1938). Regional studies of American-Mexican relations reveal local social dynamics, see Gerardo Rénique, "Frontier Capitalism and Revolution in Northwest Mexico, Sonora, 1830–1910," (Ph.D. diss., Columbia University, 1990), 248–300; Ramon Ruiz, *The People of Sonora and Yankee Capitalists* (Tucson: University of Arizona Press, 1988): 85–90; Miguel Tinker Salas, *In the Shadow of the Eagles: Sonora and the Transformation of the Border during the Porfiriato* (Berkeley: University of California Press, 1997), 429–456; and Mark Wasserman, *Capitalists, Caciques and Revolution: The Native Elite and Foreign Enterprise in Chihuahua, Mexico, 1854–1911* (Chapel Hill: University of North Carolina, 1984); Owen Wallace Gillpatrick, *The Man Who Likes Mexico* (New York: Century, 1911).

29. Bishop, 59; Fanny Chambers Gooch, *Face to Face with the Mexicans*, (New York: Howard and Hulbert, 1887), 506.

30. Griffin, 203; E.L. Doheny, "Second Interview with Mr. E.L. Doheny," 20 May 1918; "Supplement to 3rd interview with Mr. E.L. Doheny," 20 May 1918, Occidental College, Los Angeles, Doheny Research Foundation Records; cited in Jonathan C. Brown, "Foreign and Native Born Workers in Porfirian Mexico," *American Historical Review* 98 (June 1993): 790; Gooch, 506.

31. Katherine Castillion and Ruth B. Wright, *Centennial: A History of the American School in Mexico City, 1888–1988* (Mexico City: American School Foundation, 1988); Arlene Patricia Scanlon, *Un Enclave Cultural: Poder y Etnicidad en el contexto de Una Escuela Norteamericana en México*, Editorial de la Casa Chata, no. 18 (México: Secretaría de Educación Pública, 1984).

32. *Two Republics*, 6 January 1885; *Two Republics*, 28, 29 April 1885; "How the American Colony in Mexico takes Care of its Sick," *Mexican Post*, 8 October 1921, Sunday Supplement; James Hale Bates, *Notes of a Tour in Mexico and California* (New York: Burr, 1887), 59.

33. See Butler's memoir, *Mexico in Transition*; also Schell, 60; and Baldwin, 11–29; Francesca Luconi Moroni, "Análisis de dos estudios de caso de la estructura religiosa de la colonia norteamericana residente en el Distrito Federal: Union Evan-

gelical Church y la Lutheran Church of the Good Shepherd," (Tesis, Lic. Antropología Social, Universidad IberoAmericana, 1979), 26–27; and Davis, 47–54, 195.

34. *Two Republics*, 1 January 1881; 17 June 1885; "The American Club," *Two Republics*, 1,2 January 1895; Davis, 54, 224; Davis, 218; also *México y las colonias extranjeras en el centenario de la independencia* (México: Bouligny and Schmidt, 1910), 93–144; See Schell, "Land, Church and Society," in *Integral Outsiders*, 251–78.

35. On the later American expatriate experience, see Carmen Icazuriaga, *El Enclave Sociocultural Norteamericano y el Papel de los Empresarios Norteamericanos en México*, Cuaderno de la Casa Chata, no. 35 (México: Centro de Investigaciones Superiores del INAH, 1980); and Kathy Denman, *La Elite Norteamericana en la Ciudad de México*, Cuaderno de la Casa Chata, no. 34 (México: Centro de Investigaciones Superiores del INAH, 1980; Quote from "Mexico Now and Then: An Old Timer Reviews and Regrets the Changes," *Mexican-American Review*, (7 July 1939), 15; also see Adolfo Prantl and José Groso, *La Ciudad de México* (México: Juan buxo y Cia., 1901), 811–2; and Fanny Gooch, 505–518.

36. Marie Robinson Wright, *Mexico: A History of its Progress and Development in 100 Years* (Philadelphia: George Barrie and Sons, 1911), 206; Robert Horatio Thomas, ed., *Journalists' Letters Descriptive of Texas and Mexico* (Mechanicsburg, Pa: n.p., 1889), 137; Harry Franck, *Tramping through Mexico, Guatemala and Honduras: Being the Random Notes of an Incurable Vagabond* (New York: Century, 1916) 72; Gillpatrick, 7.

37. Charles Macomb Flandrau, *Viva Mexico!* (New York: Appleton, 1908), 12.

38. *México y las colonias extranjeras en el centenario de la independencia* (México: Bouligny and Schmidt, 1910), 93–144; Manuel Caballero, *México en Chicago* (Chicago: Knight, Leonard & Co., 1893), 52; Franck, 77.

39. Alfred Henry Lewis, "The Maligners of Mexico," *Cosmopolitan*, 48 (March 1910): 432b; Bernard Moses, *The Railway Revolution in Mexico* (San Francisco: Berkeley Press, 1895), 39, 25; Percy Martin, *Mexico's Treasure House: An Illustrated and Descriptive Account of the Mines and their Operation in 1906* (New York: Cheltenham Press, 1906); Case, 253.

40. Griffin, 250.

41. Cora Hayward Crawford, *The Land of the Montezumas* (New York: J.B.Alden, 1889); also William English Carson, *Mexico: The Wonderland of the South* (New York, MacMillan, 1909), 187–90; *Ferguson's Anecdotal Guide to Mexico: with a Map of the Railways: Historical, Geological, Archaeological and Critical* (Philadelphia: Claxton, Remsen, and Haffelfinger, 1876), 29; John Kenneth Turner, *Barbarous Mexico* (Chicago: C.H. Kern, 1911; reprint Austin: University of Texas, 1969), 28, 189.

42. "Mexico's National Necessity," *Mexican Investor* (9 January 1904), 2. The source of the essay, "The National Necessity," by M. Chauves, was not identified. On the commercial and professional advantages of adopting American styles, see Lorena Parlee, "Porfirio Díaz, Railroads and Development in Northern Mexico: A Study of Government Policy Toward the Central and National Railroads, 1876–1910," (Ph.D. diss., University of California, San Diego, 1981) and Francisco Valdes-Ugalde, "Janus and the Northern Colossus: Perceptions of the United States in the Building

of the Mexican Nation," *The Journal of American History* 86:2 (September 1999) 568–800; as well as the work of Mark Wasserman, William Schell, and Ramon Ruiz; Stanton Davis Kirkham, *Mexican Trails: A Record of Travel in Mexico, 1904–07, and a glimpse at the life of the Mexican Indian* (New York: G.P. Putnam, 1909) v-vi; Edward Conley, "The Americanization of Mexico," *Review of Reviews* 32 (December 1905): 724–5.

43. L.A. Shelden, *Governor Shelden's Jaunt: A Series of Readable Letters on Old Mexico: Letters of Governor Shelden Written to the Santa Fe New Mexican Review While on a Visit to the City of Mexico* (n.p., 1884), 7; Sylvester Baxter, "A Plunge into Summer," *The Atlantic Monthly*, (March 1885) 312.

44. F.E. Prendergast, "Railroads in Mexico," *Harper's Monthly Magazine*, 63 (July 1881): 276–278; Wilfred Hardy Callcott, *The Caribbean Policy of the United States, 1890–1920* (New York: Octagon, 1966) 52; Moses, 7, 25–27; Otheman Stevens, "Mexico the Progressive," *Cosmopolitan* 48 (March 1910): 44; also see N.H. Barton, "Mexico: Treasure House of the World," *National Geographic Magazine* 18 (August 1907): 493–519.

45. "Our Sister Republic," (pamphlet, n.p., c. 1914), 4; Frederick Palmer, "Mexico's Work done by Americans," *New York Times*, 23 February 1909; C. Romero, "Reply to Mr. Frederick Palmer," *New York Times*, 25 February 1909; Frederick Palmer, "Wants Mexico to Specify," *New York Times*, 26 February 1909.

46. See Daniel R. Miller, "The Frustrations of a Mexican Mine under U.S. Ownership," *Historian* 55 (1993): 483–500; Peter Henderson, "Modernizing and Change in Mexico: La Zacualpa Rubber Plantation, 1890–1920," *Hispanic American Historical Review* 73 (1993): 235–60; and William Schell, "American Investment in Tropical Mexico: Rubber Plantations, Fraud and Dollar Diplomacy, *Business History Review* 64 (Spring 1990): 217–54; Mario Cerrutti, "Estudios Regionales e Historia Empresarial en México, 1840–1920, Quince Años de Historiographía," *Inter American Review of Bibliography* 43 (1993): 375–94; Carson, 427.

47. "A Day at Chapultepec," *New York Times*, 31 March 1879.

Chapter Five

"Sister Republics"

In 1877 Manuel Zamacona, Díaz's commercial agent in the U.S., campaigned not merely to achieve U.S. recognition of a particular Mexican regime, but to ensure that the peoples of the U.S. and other nations recognized the legitimacy of an autonomous Mexican state. Porfirian Liberals have been criticized for distorting and diminishing the Mexican experience in order to adhere to the narrow, culturally homogenous, Western model of the nation-state, but in the late nineteenth-century the risks inherent in not possessing a Western-sanctioned state structure were in abundant evidence in Africa and Asia. Western nations justified aggressive colonial expansion in these regions by dismissing local governments' claims to legitimate authority. With that caution in mind the early information campaign promoted by the Díaz circle in America emphasized Mexico's credentials as a fellow republic with a firm sense of cultural national identity and a clear hierarchy of political power and control.[1]

The Liberal campaign placed special emphasis on tracing parallels between the Mexican and U.S. experiences in struggling against tyrannical European monarchs and in defending republican principles. This focus may appear curious to those most familiar with the authoritarian excesses of Díaz's later political career, but during the early Porfiriato Díaz paid extensive homage to the rights guaranteed within the Mexican constitution. Diaz's early stance may or may not have been inspired by a sincere reverence for republicanism, but it certainly had domestic and external advantages for the new regime. In foreign relations, highlighting the common political heritage of the two nations suggested one means of replacing the old cultural framework of op-position and condescension with a new framework of respectful alliance. Domestically, the focus strengthened the position of Mexico City vis-à-vis the provinces and undermined opposition to Díaz's administration.

The Porfirian campaign to reinvent the Mexican state's image in the U.S. centered on the constantly reiterated phrase "sister republics." Ironically, the phrase had a previous, and unfortunate, record in U.S.-Mexican relations. The phrase dated from the early nineteenth century when the generation of James Madison and James Monroe looked toward the independence struggles of the Spanish colonies and waited to welcome (and to direct) the younger sisters of the continent. Events were hardly promising for future relations, however, not only did the U.S. fail to lend material or even moral support to the Latin American Wars for Independence, but the ill-disguised condescension of American officials quickly embittered relations.[2] Nevertheless, the Liberals of the early Porfiriato hoped to exploit the egalitarian potential of the term in their new campaign to assert equal standing in hemispheric relations.

Throughout the Porfiriato, the "sister republics" motif was in abundant evidence in government-authored and government-sponsored publications aimed at the American public. These not only detailed Mexican positions on trade or recognition issues, but undertook the larger topic of explaining Mexico herself to the northern audience.[3] Brief histories streamlined the long and turbulent history of the nation, highlighting only the Independence era struggles to end colonial status, and the subsequent struggles to preserve republicanism in the face of foreign and domestic assaults. The promoters presented Mexico's experience in terms familiar to an American audience, drawing parallels between the disorderly years following Mexican independence and the era of the New Republic in the U.S. They likened the tumult of the Mexican Reforma to the American Civil War. The writers aimed to transform scorn for Mexican political history into sympathy by portraying civil strife as evidence of Mexico's costly resistance to monarchist intrigues. Promotional literature compared the architects of the Mexican and American nations: Benito Juárez, Miguel Hidalgo and Porfirio Díaz were each described as the George Washington of the South, or the Abraham Lincoln of Mexico.

The Porfirian campaign to realign Mexican history into a new chronicle of troubles and triumph responded to domestic dilemmas as well. As Ignacio Altamirano noted in 1885 in his prologue to a government-sponsored volume of patriotic poetry, the *Romancero Nacional*, the Mexican nation was in desperate need of unifying national symbols like the U.S.'s 'Father of the nation,' George Washington. Certainly Díaz's rehabilitation of his former rival, President Benito Juárez, provided one possible icon for the nation. Honoring the ever-popular Juárez helped Díaz overcome lingering resentment against his military coup in 1876, and partly healed the lingering social wounds of the post-civil war years. Of course, Juárez was dead and Díaz could afford to be both generous and audacious in claiming to be his political heir and defender. During the following years Díaz exploited similarly distant historical figures to adorn public works, creating a unifying iconography for the increasingly centralized Mexican nation.[4]

The campaign to redeem Mexico before an American audience could not ignore American prejudice against tropical latitudes. Americans often assumed that "it is not necessary to work for a living with lemons and oranges and bananas, and all sorts of tropical fruits growing around you;" many doubted that such a climate could produce the energetic population needed for a viable republican state. Rather than confront these questionable but widely held American convictions, publications insisted that Mexico was not primarily a tropical nation. It was impossible to deny that large portions of Mexico lay in tropical coastal zones, but promoters rechristened the heart of the Mexican nation "the Mexican Switzerland." Promotional tracts encouraged Americans to visit the cool mountain climate of central Mexico where pine forests and quaint villages replicated both the scenery and work ethic of the European heartland.[5]

Matías Romero was one of the key architects of the reinvented sister republics theme. Romero, who had served at the Mexican legation in Washington, D.C. during the 1860s, (and would serve again as Díaz's representative to the U.S. for most of his professional life) was familiar with the American mind and tailored his appeals carefully to his new audience. During the 1860s Romero had pioneered the sister republic themes as he unsuccessfully attempted to convince Lincoln's Secretary of State, William Seward to assist Juárez in expelling the French troops of Napoleon III. While Seward was concerned with the French invasion of Mexico and sympathetic to Romero's argument that the confederate revolt and the French intervention reflected related efforts to undermine Republican governments, he felt that the U.S. government could offer no support until the Union had defeated the confederate revolt. Although Romero was unsuccessful in convincing the Lincoln administration to fund the loans Juárez needed, or end the embargo on arms and munitions exports, he had more success in raising sympathy (and funding) for Mexico amid private citizens with public relations campaigns that stressed the common republican ideals of the two nations.[6]

U.S. Minister to Mexico Foster had already encountered Romero's dogged defense of Mexico's image after Foster attempted to dissuade Chicago businessmen from planning an investment trip to Mexico in the fall of 1878. Romero had responded to Foster's pessimistic stance with a blistering refutation of more than two hundred pages that traced both Mexican potential and the two nation's common historical trajectory. A few years later, in 1882, Romero disputed the discouraging conclusions reached by John Bigelow in an article printed in *Harper's Monthly Magazine* on American investment prospects in Mexico.[7] He praised Bigelow for making a "very creditable effort" to comprehend Mexico in "only two or three weeks," but he also inundated readers with figures and charts that countered Bigelow's assertion that railway investment in Mexico was a losing proposition. In response to Bigelow's complaint that the Mexican climate could never support profitable agriculture, Romero detailed the variety of produce already evident in Mexican markets. He questioned Bigelow's rationale for stating that a population living at high altitude could never be considered an "active civilizing force," put in an endorsement for the "docile" and underemployed Indian workers of Mexico, and regaled Americans with tales of Mexican growth potential in mining, agriculture, and industry.

While these comments were directed to specific points in Bigelow's article, Romero also devoted attention to cultivating American sympathy with appeals to similarities between the U.S. and Mexican historical experience. He compared past economic success in the American West with future Mexican success on the northwest frontier, and likened mid-century Mexican chaos to the destructive 'revolution' of the U.S. Civil War. He absolved Americans of responsibility for the U.S. invasion and annexation of Mexican territory in 1846 by insisting that the war had been inspired by the 'slaveocracy' of the American South, and that the "obliteration of the Confederacy" had wiped out Mexican rancor over the past. As he had done in his earlier response to Minister Foster, Romero used the words of the American envoys themselves to promote his argument, quoting from the letters of former Ministers Thomas Nelson (1872) and John Foster (1875), in which the Ministers themselves noted Mexican commitment to the promotion of commerce. Finally, Romero ensured that his responses received adequate publicity. His 1882 essay appeared first in the New Orleans *Times Democrat*, then in the national magazine, *International Review*, and was finally reprinted in Washington, D.C. as an English-language pamphlet for distribution in the U.S.[8]

G.S. Pritchard, the British journalist hired by Manuel Zamacona during the recognition crisis, promoted similar arguments in an 1878 article in the *International Review*.[9] Pritchard tempted Americans with florid descriptions of Mexican "valleys and mountains teeming with hidden treasures, which only await the call of industry to spring forth," but he also threatened them with the specter of restless European competition in the Americas. Like Romero, Pritchard devoted a significant portion of his article to painting a historic portrait of Mexico that exploited the "sister republics" focus and invented a romantic fiction of U.S.-Mexican alliance. Pritchard began his history in 1810, ignoring completely the pre-Columbian past of Mexico and reducing discussion of the colonial era to "that chaotic fifteenth century darkness" under the "crushing sway of a perverted clergy." He asserted that throughout Mexican history, "in Mexico's most populous cities as well as in her Indian

villages, in her refined society as among her toiling populations, at the counters of her bankers as at the humbler stands of her itinerant vendors, in her
council halls, as in her public resorts, the name of an American was respected,
the friendship of the United States was courted, the honor of the republic of
Washington was unimpeachable." Pritchard tactfully ignored the revolt of
Texas and the U.S.-Mexican War.

The visit of former President Ulysses S. Grant to Mexico in early 1880
provided the occasion for an overt celebration of the sister republics motif.
Throughout November and December of 1879 the newspapers of Mexico
City circulated accounts of Grant's rumored visit to Mexico. Finally Minister
Foster received confirmation that Grant did intend to visit Mexico in early
1880, accompanied by his friend and former colleague, General Philip Sheridan, and their wives. The news spread rapidly through the social circles of
the city, fanned by frequent updates in both the English and Spanish language
newspapers of the capital. Leaders of the American community met in the
legation to plan Grant's reception, while the Mexican government readied its
own welcome. The Council of the City of Mexico appropriated funds for a
welcoming reception in the capital and neighboring towns clamored to design
excursions that would lure Grant into the countryside.[10]

The promoters of Mexico were obviously conscious of the publicity potential in Grant's visit, and the potential for disastrous publicity as well, should
things go poorly. Although Grant's presidential administration was hardly
stellar, he was still a popular figure in the U.S. and had been continually
hailed by the press and public as the quintessential symbol of republicanism on his recent world tour. In England workers had thronged the streets of
Manchester to welcome Grant, while Queen Victoria herself hosted him at
Windsor Castle. He traveled the Rhine with Prince Leopold of Belgium and
enjoyed extravagant royal receptions in St. Petersburg, Lisbon and Madrid.
After cruising past Egyptian temples on the Nile, Grant traveled through the
Suez to India, and mingled with more royalty in Siam, Malaysia, and China.
After final meetings with the Emperor of Japan he steamed home to a complete his circumvention with parades and banquets from California to Philadelphia. Papers across the United States and around the world carried vivid
accounts of his travels, which were followed avidly by Americans basking in
the reflected glory of their representative abroad.[11]

In the weeks before Grant's anticipated arrival *El Diario Oficial* succinctly
reviewed the highlights of Grant's recent tour, subtly reminding Mexicans
of the international scrutiny which would follow his footsteps.[12] Securing
Grant's endorsement of the new regime would help Mexico attract investment and help Americans see Mexico in a more benevolent light. Mexican
newspapers followed the official lead and reprinted biographical sketches of

Grant with one common element; they either downplayed his role in the U.S.-Mexican war or stressed Grant's well-known remorse over the "unjust war."

In contrast to the scanty attention to this early episode of his military career, the newspapers traced Grant's role in Civil War campaigns in minute detail. Accounts also praised Grant for having dispatched observation troops to the Mexican border in 1865, while the republican regime of Benito Juárez was still engaged in a desperate struggle for survival with the troops of the French empire. Although many Liberal leaders felt the U.S. could have done more to aid Mexico, the sister republics campaign required a forgiving interpretation of the past. The modest American response to the French aggression was recast as proof of the liberal "alliance" between the American and Mexican states.[13]

This benevolent reading of past history converted Grant from an American military hero to an acceptable international symbol for the new era of U.S.-Mexican relations. Grant, as *La República* saw him, was a "soldier of all humanity." He was lionized for his role in abolishing slavery and promoting the brotherhood of man, causes that were "not just America's but all the world's." Grant's record,insisted the *Siglo XIX*, explained why the General "is beloved by all nations, and has received ovations across the globe." In the pages of Mexican newspapers Grant was no longer merely a U.S. champion, but an international icon of triumphant republicanism.[14]

As the inhabitants of Mexico City drew up guests lists and planned excursions, Grant, Sheridan and their wives were enjoying a leisurely cruise from Cuba, "sacrificing a vast amount of bacon" in a vain attempt to catch a shark. Journalists Byron Andrews of the *Chicago Inter Ocean* and G. Stilsen of the *New York Herald* accompanied the party and regularly reported the curiosities of the trip to their readers at home. *Frank Leslie's Illustrated Newspaper* also published illustrated articles on Grant's visit in the popular periodical. Residents of Mexico followed reprinted reports of Grant's arrival and reception in Havana in their own newspapers, even as they repainted and refurbished the Palacio de Minería for the enjoyment of the former President's party. To add a homelike touch the Mexican government hung a full length portrait of George Washington in the Palace, and then installed gas lighting throughout to make sure the visitors appreciated the redecoration.[15]

By the time Grant's party reached the Mexican coast his hosts were prepared. Grant docked first at the Mexican port of Progreso on the Yucatán where a flotilla of citizens from the inland city of Mérida sailed out to greet the travelers and beg them to visit their colonial city, where a banquet awaited the Americans. Contrary winds forced the trip's cancellation, although the Grants, according to local officials, appeared delighted with the affectionate reception.[16] The following night, as the ship anchored off Campeche, another delegation of citizens sailed out to pay their respects, and the next night yet a third committee joined them off the coast of Tabasco.

This warm welcome barely hinted at the preparations that awaited Grant in Veracruz. The passengers had barely sighted the distinctive volcanic peak of Orizaba above the city towers on the 18th of February before a Mexican gunboat carrying U.S. Minister John W. Foster, Ignacio Mejía (a former Minister of War and veteran of 1846) and Matías Romero greeted them at sea. Romero had first met Grant in 1864 when the Mexican minister visited the Union officers in Richmond, Virginia, and had continued to see Grant during his years as military commander and President. Now Romero and his American wife, Lulu Allen Romero, helped to put the visitors at ease. The party sailed past the walls of the Castle of San Juan de Ullua and festively decorated ships to a dock crowded with cheering residents while cannons boomed a welcome. The guests were guided to a formal breakfast reception hosted by the Mexican government where the Governor of Veracruz assured Grant that "this people desired your coming as that of an old friend." Grant thanked him and replied that "it has long been a wish of mine to come to this country."[17]

Grant had, as the Mexicans knew, come to Mexico before with the invading army of Winfield Scott. Although he regretted the hostilities of that first visit, his memories of the southern nation left an indelible imprint on his mind. In 1848 he had written his future wife of the "beautiful and strange" sights of the tierra caliente, where "All seasons of the year you will find vegetables in full bloom. We passed some of the most beautiful sugar plantations in the world and finest buildings in the world. They beat any in Louisiana. Every one has on it fine coffee fields and orchards of tropical fruits such as oranges and bananas and twenty kinds of fruit I never heard of until I came to Mexico." Grant had also praised the defeated yet orderly Mexican troops, who showed no personal hostility to the conquering Americans, but were "punctilious" in observing the terms of the armistice. Overall Grant's letters from Mexico conveyed a sense of wonder and respect for the land.[18]

Thirty years later, at his welcoming reception in Veracruz, Grant accepted the hospitality of the Mexican government and reflected on the change in affairs. "None can be more gratified than myself at your improvement," he assured the crowds. Since Grant had spent scarcely a few hours in the Mexican Republic when the statement was made, it would be difficult to say what kind of "improvement" he might have witnessed. Yet, the logistics of his welcome banquet certainly illustrated one important shift—the new spirit of cooperation between the neighboring countries. Not only did U.S. and Mexican statesmen share the table with Grant, but the breakfast itself was held in the U.S. consulate, which had been loaned to the government of Veracruz for the occasion.[19]

To emphasize the new international spirit the Mexican band in the court-yard below serenaded them with "Hail Columbia," and other American and Mexican tunes. The music was not coincidental; Mejía and Romero had meticulously organized the music, and indeed all the entertainment, to accord with the wishes of President Díaz. Even from distant Mexico City the President monitored the progress of Grant's visit to Veracruz.[20]

Following the banquet Grant boarded an afternoon train out of Veracruz, speeding across the tropical lowlands, where the "supreme beauty of Mexican scenery flashed voluptuously upon him."[21] Onward they travelled past "creepers clinging amorously to trees," past canyons "so full of splendor, so full of horror, so grandly Dantesque....onwards squirming in and out through mountain gorges" into the final haven of Orizaba, where they spent a pleasant evening admiring the curious contrast between the tropical splendor of the public gardens and the snowy peaks of volcanoes towering beyond.

The following day local social leaders escorted the party through fields of bananas, oranges and coffee to the cataract of Rincón Grande. After Grant examined a working sugar plantation and inspected local Mexican troops, he joined the state employees of the region at a formal "picnic." Hundreds of guests dined at china-laden tables under leafy canopies, while applauding the circus-style performances of gymnasts and cowboys at a 'coleadero,' or 'bull tailing.' While Mexican papers applauded Mejía and Romero for organizing entertainment "so representative of our customs" that left the visiting ladies "pale and agitated," the American account offered a different version of events. *The New York Tribune* reported that Grant chose to retire early from the picnic because he was afraid his continued presence prolonged the "cruelty." The following day in Córdoba the women rested while the men explored a nearby coffee plantation on horseback and that evening the visitors attended a ball hosted by local merchants in their honor.[22]

Grant's welcome in Mexico City was even more spectacular. His train pulled into the Valley of Mexico on the evening of February 21st to a depot crowded with Mexican and American residents. The Grants and the Sheridans stepped from their cars to a platform "brilliantly illuminated and tastefully adorned" with Chinese lanterns and American flags as the Mexican band struck up a march. The had barely absorbed the scene before climbing into carriages that drove out under a triumphal arch in which the word "welcome" blazed in the night. The *Rurales*, Mexico's mounted police force, led the way with lighted torches through the crowds to the apartments prepared at the Palacio de Minería. From their balconies the Grants and Sheridans saluted the crowds that flowed through the streets paying tribute to the "Conqueror of Richmond" while a chorus of three hundred and fifty serenaded the visitors with selections from Strauss, Verdi and Rossini, as well as patriotic hymns of the two nations.[23]

The former American president lost no time in paying a courtesy call on President Díaz the morning following his arrival; President Díaz matched the honor by paying a return call at Grant's hotel only two hours later. The American visitors were soon deluged with visits from leading Mexican citizens who quickly followed Díaz's example, and the social ice was quickly broken.[24]

Grant proved to be an ideal guest. Throughout his visit he enthused over the land and people, enthusiastically undertook all manner of outings, and paid constant deference to Mexican sovereignty. Few of Grant's speeches in Mexico were reprinted, but the accounts and quotes available reveal an unsurprising combination of affection and ethnocentrism. Grant addressed the Mexicans continually with the hope that "the relations between the U.S. and Mexico will grow closer every day. The development of this country will be of great advantage to the U.S." He later added, "I think I speak of the sentiment of the great mass of the people of the U.S. when I say that we wish only that this Republic of Mexico may grow and improve, as she is capable."[25] Grant considered himself a true friend of Mexico, but his remarks reveal his automatic assumption that Mexico needed to "improve" and that improvement could be legitimately measured by its utility to the U.S.

Grant continued to attract crowds throughout his three week visit, both while touring the standard sites of Mexico City and while visiting Pachuca, Real del Monte and Puebla. The *New York Tribune* reporter was astonished by the General's popularity in Pachuca, where it seemed as if every one of the city's 20,000 residents (a large portion of whom seemed to him to be small boys with firecrackers) had taken to the streets to welcome him. A reception for Grant at the American legation in Mexico City attracted more than one thousand guests.[26]

Although the Mexicans apologized that the Lenten season forced them to moderate their welcome, they still managed to coordinate an impressive number of dinners and balls at which the Mexican and American communities united in honoring both Grant and the unity of the sister republics. At a banquet organized in the Tivoli Gardens the guests of honor were seated under portraits of Juárez, Lincoln and Washington. The name cards displayed samples of Mexican featherwork in scenes depicting Mexican volcanoes and the entwined banners of the U.S. and Mexico, while the menus were decorated with scenes of Grant's famous journey around the world. To complete the harmonious picture of U.S.-Mexican relations, the band serenaded the diners with Mexican national hymns, interspersed with the "Star Spangled Banner," "Marching through Georgia," and "Hail Columbia." Grant was visibly impressed by the display of cooperation between the two nations and stated his hope that "it may be emblematical of the perpetual peace that may

exist between them. I trust that we may always be a benefit to each other."
The dinner ended with a flurry of toasts linking Juárez with Lincoln and Díaz
with Grant and heralding a new age of cooperation and friendship.[27]

For the most part, his Mexican hosts avoided allusions to Grant's role in
the Mexican-American War of 1846, but Grant discreetly provided his traveling companions with a travelogue of his own. Julia Dent Grant recalled how
the many "historical and lovely villages" surrounding the capital "brought
to the General some interesting reminiscences of the Mexican War." Grant
pointed out a church tower he had captured for an artillery post, the street
where he found Julia's wounded brother, his quarters at Tacubaya, and the
wall he breached in storming Chapultepec Castle.

Publically the motif of the sister republics reigned supreme throughout
the visit. In Amecameca and Real del Monte, as in Mexico City, the party
dined beneath portraits of Juárez, Lincoln, Washington and Miguel Hidalgo.
La República praised the "triumvirate" of the North (John Brown, Abraham
Lincoln and Ulysses Grant), which it paralleled to the triumvirate of Mexico
(Hidalgo, Juárez, and Díaz). Mexican coverage of Grant and Sheridan's visit
to the Military Academy of Chapultepec made no mention of the *Niños He-*
roes (the 'boy heroes') who died resisting the American invaders in 1847.
When Grant and Sheridan reviewed the Mexican troops from the balcony
of the National Palace, the ghostly memories of the American soldiers who
had drilled in the same square during the U.S. occupation of the city were
politely ignored. Ignacio Mariscal, a leading Liberal intellectual, interpreted
the Mexican reception of Grant as a broad tribute to the American people,
"whose heart was on our side" during the intervention. Mariscal, of course,
referred to the French and not the American intervention.[28]

Mexicans were not just celebrating Grant, of course, but their own ability to mount a munificent welcome for the visiting dignitary. Mexican
pride in this lavish display of hospitality toward Grant was evident in the
detailed descriptions of the quarters and schedules prepared for the visitors. *El Municipio Libre* praised the "gallantry" of the Mexican welcome,
which revealed the "urbanity and courtesy" of the nation. *El Monitor*
Republicano congratulated Mejía and Romero for having orchestrated
characteristic national diversions in Orizaba, and applauded Señor Lan-
dero for his "genteel" hospitality in Pachuca. *La Revista Mexicana* and *El*
Diario Oficial reviewed the welcome Grant had received in other nations,
and assured readers that "no other country had received General Grant in
such a splendid and hospitable manner as Mexico." Articles from regional
newspapers detailing Grant's entertainment were reprinted in the official
state newspaper, *El Diario Oficial*, allowing all Mexicans to bask in the
glory of Grant's visit.[29]

The visit of the Americans provoked a different kind of discussion when the hospitality committee proposed closing off the public garden in the National Plaza during an outdoor concert for the guests. Although the committee insisted that the procedure merely aimed to prevent overcrowding and that the limited number of tickets would be distributed free of charge, few could deny that the poor and illiterate were unlikely to apply to the city offices for passes. Ignacio Altamirano denounced the proposal as "unworthy of a democracy." Altamirano noted that the visitors were famous precisely because they had fought to eradicate slavery and legal barriers between peoples. How ironic it would be, he admonished his readers, if the Mexican Republic, which took pride in having "destroyed all legal castes and privileges at the time of independence," should now tolerate social distinctions in public spaces. Altamirano insisted that the visitors would form a "better idea of our republic" if the "jackets of the monthly worker appeared amidst the shirts of the employees, and the shawl of the humble wife of the day worker appeared alongside the silk coat of a woman of wealth." Altamirano was in the minority, however, most press coverage seemed content to celebrate Grant's encounter with Mexico's elite.[30]

During the final days of the visit, as public and private delegations presented their parting gifts to the Americans, Grant received a written request from his hosts. Vicente Riva Palacio, Matías Romero, José Yves Limantour (a financier and future Minister of Finance), John Frisbie (the Californian who had been converted into an ally of Díaz), and other promoters of Mexico urged Grant to turn his energy to the Mexican "cause of material progress," and communicate to Americans the economic potential of the Southern republic. Grant assured his hosts that his visit had convinced him of the mutual advantages to be gained through investment, and pledged his assistance as "a citizen of the U.S. and friend of Mexico." The exchange of letters was published in *El Diario Oficial* as the Grant party steamed away from Veracruz.[31]

In the wake of Grant's departure the Mexicans could congratulate themselves on the apparent success of the visit. They had asserted their republican bond with the U.S., flaunted their cosmopolitan credentials, and won a public statement endorsing Mexico as an investment site. Newspapers reprinted Grant's praise of Mexico's improvement and Sheridan's compliments on the national troops and mounted national police.[32] Grant's hosts fully expected that American coverage of the visit would emulate the coverage of his previous world travels and thus include Mexico in the grand circle of civilized capitals that had honored the former American President.

Unfortunately for the Mexican promoters, the visit attracted little serious attention from its intended audience. The U.S. press barely noted the Mexican reception of the Grants. Most articles on Grant that did appear during February and March of 1880 discussed rumors of Grant's renewed candidacy for the presidency in the fall election and virtually ignored his sojourn in Mexico. The popular weekly the *Nation*, for example, published two articles on Grant's political prospects while the General toured Mexico, but neither article mentioned the ongoing visit to Mexico. One article commented on Grant's world travels, but only to observe that travel had undeservedly recharged his political career. Coverage of Grant in the *New York Times* relegated discussion of Mexico to brief (one or two paragraph) back page articles, while carrying detailed discussion of Grant's future political chances in one or two column front page stories. *Frank Leslie's Illustrated Newspaper* featured Grant in Mexico on the cover art of one issue, but again, the underlying message stressed American politics, not Mexican. Grant was depicted receiving a visit from the ghost of Maximilian, who had apparently made the supernatural effort only to urge Grant not to reenter U.S. politics in 1880. For the most part, for those few papers that did cover Grant's visit the tour provided occasion for entertaining accounts of "fine weather and strange scenes," but little discussion of contemporary Mexican politics or economics. And even though Grant did attempt to carry out his parting promise and prove himself a "friend of Mexico" by promoting Mexico before the American business community, he carried little credibility in U.S. investor circles where he was known for his infamously poor business judgment.[33]

Subsequent history suggests that the problem was not merely one of inadequate press coverage or a compromised messenger. More significantly, U.S. press disinterest in Grant's Mexican sojourn echoed the more profound disinterest Americans felt for the sister republics campaign. Although American tourists, investors and academics showed an increasing interest in Mexico, and sometimes even employed the vocabulary the Mexicans had introduced, most maintained a patronizing perspective. T.S. Van Dyke, who wrote on Mexico for *Harpers* in 1885, lamented that her "Washingtons and Jeffersons, her Greenes, Schuylers, and Hamiltons, were nearly all captured and shot before their work was half done." In 1883 the *North American Review* praised the "real sisterhood" between the two nations, even though one was "wholly inexperienced" in self government. Praise was continually mixed with condescension. In 1884 Arthur Anderson, an associate of U.S. banker J.P. Morgan, was willing to see Mexico as "Our Sister Republic, friend and ally in international politics," but his other metaphors were more imperial. "Mexico," he noted, "is one magnificent but undeveloped mine—our India in commercial importance—our Cuba and Brazil in tropical products—our complement in general characteristics, resources, supply and demand—our Italy in climate and attractions—our Troy in antiquities and classic history." Howard Conkling embarked upon a pleasure tour of "our sister republic" in 1883 in anticipation of the "early federation of the peoples that now inhabit the North American continent." Conkling looked forward to "The meeting of the gentleman from the Isthmus of Panama with the gentleman from the frozen zone, on the floor of the Capitol at Washington, to exchange congratulations that the government of North America is, and will forever remain, one and indivisible." The threat of forced annexation may have dissipated, but the assumption that the U.S. dictated the future of Mexico remained.[34]

One reason Americans found it possible to preserve their condescension within the framework of sister republics rhetoric was because the Mexican campaign had never directly confronted the American prejudice against Catholic, Native American or Iberian civilizations. Instead it had implicitly exploited them by urging Americans to consider the greater challenges to democracy and development that confronted Mexican leaders after independence. In American discussions, however, the Mexican heritage was more than a handicap, it was fatal. Railroad promoter John Rice was convinced that the "corrupt" priests of the colonial era had ruined Mexican prospects by holding "The poor Indians in blind ignorance, submissive degradation, and virtual slavery, through threats of divine wrath, and superstitious awe, enforced by image worship and stage-rites, but a single step removed from those practiced by their pagan ancestors." Traveler Albion Gray contrasted the "semi-barbaric" Spanish conquest of Mexico with the "enlightened" English colonization of Anglo America. Missionary William Butler blamed Mexican constitutional failures on "the dread control of the darkest Romanism on Earth!" John T. Morgan, writing in the *North American Review*, contrasted the "two hundred and fifty years of absolute and despotic rule" that Mexico suffered with the U.S. experience under "a race of people who were highly enlightened and well equipped with every requisite for founding and governing new states." Explicit and implicit condemnations of non-Anglo-American ways permeated American writing on Mexico throughout the Porfiriato.[35]

The rhetoric of the sister republics campaign appealed to Americans on another level because it offered Americans a benevolent interpretation of their own role in Mexican history, flattering American sensibilities and glossing over unbecoming episodes of past years. John T. Morgan recounted Mexican history and insisted that during "her fourteen years of war for independence, there was not a heart in an American bosom in the United States that did not share in the anguish of that desperate struggle." The article skimmed rapidly over the War of 1846 in the hope that "lingering resentments which had their origins in causes that existed fifty years ago" would not derail current cooperation." Other Americans were quick to follow that nation's lead and blame the War of 1846 and subsequent annexation on the "ruffianly propagandists of slavery." Grant blamed the American South for having incited the "unjust war" of conquest against Mexico, and years later former Minister John W. Foster agreed that the "spirit which brought on the hostility was slavery." Ex-Confederates, like *Two Republics* editor George Clarke, preferred to blame the war on filibusterism (an institution as conveniently dated as slavery), while in 1886 an imaginative U.S. consul held the British monarchy accountable for American aggression. Had the United States not taken action, Consul James Whitney insisted, "the Union Jack, and not the Stars and Stripes, would have floated from the Mexican Gulf to the frontiers of Oregon."[36]

As time went on Americans downplayed all memories of the war. In 1888 an American visitor to Monterrey felt obliged to note that Zachary Taylor lost "some five hundred men killed or wounded" in assaulting the city, but had no desire to recap the highlights of the battle. "Let the youngsters turn to their books, or hunt up some old Mexican soldier, and they will learn more than I have time to tell them." Solomon Griffin was embarrassed to recall the war during his travels in Mexico, and encouraged the U.S. to return Mexico's captured cannon as an act of "sentimental repatriation." Griffin made no mention of the annexed territories of Mexico, but insisted that the return of the cannon would "do more to win the hearts and dispel the fears of the people than reams of diplomatic correspondence, and endless trade commissions, and formal international resolutions." Howard Conkling was the most brutally honest in explaining his decision to skip the 1846 war in his account of Mexican history: "As the reputation of our country [the U.S.] for honor and fair dealing was not increased by the circumstances which led to it, it may be well to pass over its history."[37]

Americans carried the benevolent interpretation of bi-national relations one step further and invented memories of American "rescues" of Mexico to explain the new era of amity. Finerty interpreted Mexico's homage to Grant as "gratitude for Grant's role in discouraging the empire of Napoleon III," although Grant's actual role was limited to a show of moral support. Conkling failed to mention the Mexican armed struggle to expel the French when he asserted that the 1865 U.S. demand that Napoleon III remove his French troops from Mexico was, "of course, promptly complied with." Conkling assumed that the Mexican show of affection for Grant was only a fitting tribute to the nation that "had done so much to uphold the republic when its life was menaced by foreign invasion."[38]

Americans also reinterpreted the independence era in flattering terms. Conkling credited the Monroe Doctrine with dissuading Spain from plans of reconquest and securing the independence of Mexico in 1821, neglecting to mention that Latin American leaders found the Monroe Doctrine both laughable (as the U.S. had no means of enforcing a ban on European activity in the hemisphere in 1823) and contrary to their own foreign policy goals. Certainly the Monroe Doctrine had not prevented European invasions of Mexico in 1838 or 1862. John T. Morgan also sketched out a role for the U.S. in Mexico's struggle for independence by declaring that she "took courage from our example, broke her chains, and, with too absolute trust in our wisdom, adopted almost the entire plan of our government as her own. In 1910 Foster published a history of the Mexican constitution in which he chose to reprint a revealingly distorted description of the meeting between President Juárez and the American Minister Robert McLane during the Mexican War of Reform. "This Indian President of disturbed Mexico," wrote Foster, "cries out to the youngest, freshest, and most powerful free government on earth for sympathy and support. The representative of that free government responds in the name of Christianity and humanity, and acknowledges before all the world the right of this downtrodden and despised people to possess and enjoy that priceless boon to man—civil and religious liberty." The vocabulary of the sister republics campaigns made Americans more comfortable with the history and politics of Mexico, but only by distorting the U.S. role in that history. [39]

By the end of Díaz's regime the rhetoric of the sister republics campaign had experienced a curious evolution. Both Mexicans and Americans continued to praise the principles of democratic republicanism throughout the Porfiriato, yet both governments lived comfortably with widespread, institutionalized disenfranchisement at home. On discussion of Mexico the two states appeared to have reached a curious consensus: the political legitimacy of the Mexican state depended not upon constitutionally guaranteed political rights, but upon the maintenance of social and economic order. Díaz, who had taken such care to promote Mexico's republican reputation during his first administration, returned to the presidency in 1884 to preside over a system that became increasingly and unapologetically authoritarian. During the ensuing twenty-five years the Mexican government continued to pay homage to the principles of the 1857 constitution, but it felt no shame in stating, as it did in 1892, that the implementation of the constitution was "impractical at the present time."[40] American observers, who had coolly received news of Díaz's uprising in 1876 as evidence of his dictatorial tendencies and applauded his withdrawal from office in 1880 as a sign of his commitment to constitutional procedure, fell silent in regard to his later transgressions. In fact, within a few years of Díaz's return to the presidency, most American writers applauded his 'fatherly' tyranny.

Former Minister John W. Foster's conversion from adversary to advocate of Díaz was typical. In 1876 Foster criticized Díaz as a "professional revolutionary," but in 1910 Foster praised Díaz as "one of the most distinguished statesman of the world in his generation." Foster, while serving as legal counsel to the Mexican embassy in Washington, detailed the reasons for his admiration in a 1901 biographical portrait of the Mexican President. Díaz, claimed Foster, had been a reluctant soldier for Mexico, called from his beloved Oaxaca to defend Mexico against the Americans in 1846, the monarchists in the 1860s, and the dictatorship of Sebastián Lerdo de Tejada in the 1870s. Foster, who had described Díaz as a *mestizo* to his superiors in 1876, had lessened the Indian element to a "tincture of Indian blood" by 1901. He urged observers not to judge Díaz by his revolutionary actions or political imperfections, but by the "successes" of the past twenty-five years. Díaz had maintained public order, given security to life and property, restored public credit, promoted commerce, industry and agriculture and brought order to the Mexican government and army.[41]

Foster was not alone in crediting Mexico's stability to Díaz. American journalists, investors and tourists no longer referred to Díaz solely as president, but rather as "ruler" or "maker" of Mexico, and honored him as the "grand old man of the Americas." In 1909 President William Howard Taft was pleased not only "to welcome the President of the great Republic of Mexico [to Texas], but to welcome the present President of the Republic of Mexico, who has made it so great." In 1907 U.S. Secretary of State Elihu Root claimed he could think of no individual more deserving of "poetic eulogies, triumphal marches, or hero worship" than the Mexican President. Díaz, the "copper colored" *mestizo* to the AID visitors of 1879, grew progressively paler in both American and Mexican accounts as his political reputation grew. Charles Lummis reduced Díaz's native heritage to "that single infusion of aboriginal blood" in his 1898 official biography. More commonly, it disappeared altogether. "General Díaz is a fine looking man," reported one journalist, echoing a popular refrain, "being of the pure Castilian blood."[42]

Mini-biographies of Díaz emerged as staple segments of travel and promotional literature during the later Porfiriato. Many summed up the story of the nation's situation through hagiographic examinations of Díaz, as did Lummis in a chapter entitled simply "The Man." Even an "unprepared Indian would know instantly that Somebody was coming," he wrote of listening to the approaching steps of the Mexican president, "stealthy like a puma, yet far more graceful, the creator of a new force in American destiny." Díaz and his legend replaced the once ubiquitous discussions of Cortés and Montezuma. "The life of Porfirio Díaz is fascinating," wrote Nevin Winter in 1907, "It savors of the days of knighthood and romance." There was "not a more romantic or heroic figure in all the world," insisted James Creelman in *Pearson's Magazine*, than Díaz, the "Hero of the Americas." Gradually the figure of Díaz eclipsed Mexico itself in the American mind. Arthur Noll sketched out the history of Mexico merely to help the reader "appreciate the life and character of Porfirio

Díaz." "The history of modern Mexico is his history," asserted Frederick Palmer, while Edward Conley put it even more bluntly: "He is not only a Mexican, but the Mexican. He is Mexico."[43]

Certainly many Americans accepted Díaz and his strong-arm state because it was in their economic self interest to see it continue, but the American adulation of Díaz also suggests several unflattering insights into domestic U.S. culture at the turn of the century. Díaz's conversion from *mestizo* to Spaniard reflected the hardening of racial hierarchies in both nations, just as Americans' easy accommodation to authoritarian politics in Mexico reflected growing misgivings toward democracy at home. The Díaz vogue also marked the cultural distance that Americans had traveled in conceptions of their international role since the 1870s. At the outset of the Porfiriato Americans were only beginning to see themselves as a nation with foreign interests; they were uncertain of the propriety of associating a republican people with politically and racially suspect traditions. However, Foster's early confrontation with Díaz quickly taught Americans that linking diplomatic recognition to the political purity of foreign governments could be both impractical and costly for a trading nation. As U.S. Consul James Porch noted in 1886, it was impossible to "go to any country and find the manners and customs of the inhabitants in exact accord with our own finer feelings." He urged Americans to focus instead on what he considered the essentials, "Do they need our surplus production and can we sell at a profit?....It is not necessary to wait until the eve of the millennium when all the nations of the earth are supposed to be in a right condition to be gathered to their fathers, before we look abroad for a market."[44]

In the years after the confrontation over recognition Americans not only adjusted to the peculiar politics of their sister republic, they defended them. In 1884 visiting governor of New Mexico L.A. Shelden admitted that the Mexican government may seem despotic," but it "has turbulent elements to deal with." The Mexican government was but "nominally a republic" during the Porfiriato, proclaimed an American traveler in 1887, but it was "as good a government as the condition of affairs will permit." In 1898 *The Spectator* excused Díaz's political tactics by noting that "to make an omelette you must break eggs." And in 1908 James Creelman explicitly listed the American assumptions in his admiration for Díaz. "No one," asserted Creelman, "has understood better that President Díaz the futility of attempting to deal with his people as though they were Anglo Saxons developed by ancestry, tradition, racial instinct, education and habit to sustain the individual burdens and responsibilities of citizenship." Henry Ware Allen argued that if Díaz were "Governor of Massachusetts he would adapt himself to conditions prevailing there, exactly as Governor Russell would in Mexico exercise that arbitrary power necessary where so large a part of the population is totally incapable of self-government."[45]

American authors compared Porfirian stability favorably against disorderly conditions in the U.S. The financial crises, labor disputes, and race confrontations of the late nineteenth century challenged American confidence in the U.S. model. In 1890 the *Mexican Financier* contrasted Mexican order with the "anarchy" threatening the U.S.: "Mexico, in the most turbulent period of its history, was never so permeated with revolutionary ideas as is the United States today." In 1904 the *Nation* noted that many American tourists enjoyed the safety of Mexico and even voiced a "preference for benevolent despotism." Alfred Henry Lewis was certain that the U.S. had no right to criticize Mexico, where there were no gouging trusts or manipulative Carnegies and Rockefellers. And John Finerty, who had committed himself to a Mexican life at the opening of the Porfirian age, defended his adopted country in 1910 with glowing praise. It was inconceivable, he felt, that Americans could term "barbarous" a nation

> Whose enormous Indian population, excepting a few wild tribes, is absolutely docile, law abiding and Christian; whose upper classes compare favorably with the aristocracy of any nation in the world in birth, education, character, gentility; whose government is striving its utmost for the uplift of its people; where the education of the masses is being enhanced day by day; where strikes and labor unions are unknown; where cranks and anarchists are not permitted to enter; where divorce is not tolerated; where people of all classes are devoted to their religion.[46]

For many Americans, Díaz's resurrection of the Mexican economy made up for his political transgressions. He led the nation "to the portals of peace and prosperity," wrote traveler Dillon Wallace in 1910. Another traveler agreed, "It is wholly to Díaz that her [Mexico's] splendid prosperity is due." In 1910 Otheman Stevens argued that while Díaz might appear to be a political "conservative," his "progressive," modernizing policies had worked a miracle in establishing a stable government and a thriving economy. Americans, asserted Stevens, only trusted their money in Mexico because of Díaz's authoritarian ways. "These are the men," he argued, "who know full well that President Díaz is Mexico; they know that elections are stage managed, and the votes are stage props. They know that Díaz names every congressman and senator, every judge, every governor, and every *jefe político*—in short, that Díaz is the government; and they rejoice in that fact."[47]

The Díaz portrayed in American commentary not only maintained the order necessary for the American economic invasion, he offered an acceptable solution to the dilemmas facing American expansionists. As long as Díaz maintained Mexican stability, the American people enjoyed the benefits of empire without assuming the burden of governing the racially and culturally distinct people of Mexico. In 1904 the American editors of the *Mexican Investor* advocated an extension of the arrangement to Central America, where Díaz could preserve "order" and provide the "signal for a rush of foreign capital" into the region.[48]

Díaz offered Americans something else that satisfied their own misgivings with the broken promises of American democracy—he provided a flattering illusion of racial and cultural "order" through selective discrimination. In Díaz's Mexico white ruled over black and brown, western-style progress triumphed over native traditions, and political rights were withheld from the unworthy. From the perspective of many Americans, Díaz had not merely 'made' Mexico, he made it into something desirable to Americans. Not only their investments, but their unspoken beliefs in the inherent inequalities of races were safeguarded in the Porfirian system. Rather than dwell on the significant impediments to democracy that did exist, including the problems of illiteracy, economic dependence and fragile national integration, Americans repeated convenient race-based charges of innate 'oriental' despotism, childlike infatuations and aversions, and the 'early maturation of passions' among Latin American populations to forgive Díaz his dictatorial practices at home.

Grant's reception in Mexico illustrated how the Porfirian leaders hoped to secure American respect for an autonomous Mexico by highlighting the similar struggles of the "sister republics," yet even Grant's visit was eventually recast to accord with the new vision of legitimacy based on "order" rather than republican guarantees. At the close of the Porfiriato, Díaz's official biographer, José Godoy, recalled the visit of Grant not as an occasion for a bi-national celebration of the republican tradition, but as a visit from the "greatest military chieftain of the U.S."[49] Grant's transfiguration echoed that of Díaz, who had moved from a position as president to one of "ruler" of Mexico. The two nations had succeeded in creating a working vocabulary of collaboration that was acceptable to both Mexicans and Americans, but only by sacrificing the political ideals of both peoples. In the end it was not the autonomous Republic of Mexico that achieved legitimacy in American eyes, but only the authoritarian rule of Porfirio Díaz.

NOTES

1. On the Mexican state and the cultivation of national identity, see Carlos Monsivais, "La Nacion de unas Cuantos y las Esperanzas Románticas: Notas Sobre la Historia del Término 'Cultura Nacional' en México," in *En Turno a la Cultura Nacional* (Mexico: Fondo de Cultura Económica, 1982); and Claudio Lomnitz-Adler, *Exits*

from the Labrynth: Culture and Ideology in the Mexican National Space (Berkeley: University of California Press, 1992).

2. On the awkward history of the "Sister Republics" theme, see Arthur Whitaker, *The Western Hemisphere Idea: Its Rise and Decline* (Ithaca: Cornell University Press, 1954); and John L. Johnson, *A Hemisphere Apart: The Foundations of U.S. Policy toward Latin America* (Baltimore: Johns Hopkins University Press, 1990).

3. For early examples, see G.S. Pritchard, "The Mexico of the Mexicans," *International Review* 5 (1878): 170–184; Charles Edwards Lester, *The Mexican Republic; An Historic Study* (New York: American News Company, 1878); Matías Romero, *Report*, (1880); and Vincent G. Manero, *Guide for Mexico* (Mexico: Tip. Gonzalez Estevez, 1878). Pritchard and Lester were paid publicists hired during the recognition crisis; Manero was employed by the Secretary of Finance to compile a guide for American visitors.

4. Guillermo Prieto, *Romancero Nacional*, introduction by Ignacio Altamirano (Mexico: Secretaría de Fomento, 1885); also see Charles A. Weeks, *The Juárez Myth in Mexico* (Tuscaloosa: University of Alabama, 1987); and Barbara Tenenbaum, "Streetwise History: The Paseo de la Reforma and the Porfirian State, 1876–1910," in *Rituals of Rule, Rituals of Resistance: Public Celebrations and Popular Culture in Mexico*, (Wilmington, DE: Scholarly Resources, 1994), pp. 127–50.

5. "Country Life in Mexico," *New York Times*, 4 March 1879; F.E. Prendergast, "Railroads in Mexico," *Harper's Monthly* 63 (1881): 276; Antonio Garcia Cubas, *Cuadro geográfico, estadístico, descriptivo e histórico de los Estados Unidos Mexicanos* (México: Secretaría de Fomento, 1885) and *Nueva Galicia: A Subtropical Switzerland: Describing the Regions of the Western Sierra of Mexico Now Being Opened by the Mexican Central Railway* (Crawford, Colorado: Wynkoop and Mallerbach, n.d.).

6. Robert Ryal Miller, "Matías Romero: Mexican Minister to the United States during the Juárez-Maximilian Era," *Hispanic American Historical Review* 45 (May 1965) 228–245; Salvador E. Morales Pérez, "Matías Romero: Artífice y Operador de Primera Línea en la Diplomacia Mexicana," in *Artífices y Operadores de la Diplomacia Mexicana Siglos XIX y XX*. Agustín Sánchez Andrés, et. al. (México: Porrúa, 2004).157–172.

7. John Bigelow, "The Railway Invasion of Mexico," *Harper's Monthly* 65 (1882): 745–7; Matías Romero, *Railways in Mexico: An Article in Answer to the Article of the Hon. John Bigelow entitled 'the Railway Invasion of Mexico' published in Harper's, October 1882* (Washington, D.C.: H.W. Moore, 1882).

8. Matías Romero, "Railways in Mexico," *Times Democrat* (New Orleans), 15 October 1882; Matías Romero, "Railways in Mexico," *International Review* 13 (1882): 477–506.

9. G.S. Pritchard, "The Mexico of the Mexicans," *International Review* 5 (1878): 170–84.

10. "General Grant Coming to Mexico," *Two Republics*, 18 October 1879; "General Grant," *Two Republics*, 11 January 1880; "General Grant," *El Diario Oficial*, 12 January 1880; General Grant and Party," *Two Republics*, 18 January 1880; El General Grant," *El Diario Oficial*, 21 January 1880; *Actas de Cabildo de la Ciudad*

de México, Box 528A (Sesión del 20 de Enero 1880), Archivo Histórico del ex-Ayuntamiento, México, D.F.; "El General Grant," *El Diario Oficial*, 21 January 1880, reviewing planned activities as reported in *La Libertad* and the *Two Republics*. For an overview of Grant's relationship to Mexico, including his investments in Mexican Railways and lobbying for the never-completed U.S.-Mexican reciprocal trade treaty, see David M. Pletcher, *Rails, Mines and Progress: Seven American Promoters in Mexico* (Ithaca: Cornell University Press, 1958), 149–181.

11. John Russell Young, *Around the World with General Grant* (New York: The American News Co., 1879).

12. "Ulises S. Grant," *El Diario Oficial*, 7 February 1880.

13. See Leonard Gordon, "Lincoln and Juárez—A Brief Reassessment of Their Relationship." *Hispanic American Historical Review* 48 (February 1968) 75–80; *La Libertad*, 22 February 1880.

14. *La República*, 17 March 1880; "La Fiesta de Ayer," *El Diario Oficial*, 17 March 1880, reprinted from *Siglo XIX*.

15. "General Grant in Mexico," *New York Tribune*, 27 February 1880; "El Alojamiento del General Grant," *El Diario Oficial*, 23 February 1880; "General Grant en la Habana," *El Diario Oficial*, 14 February 1880, reprinted from *El Diario Comercial* and *El Diario de la Marina*.

16. "Bienvenida," *El Diario Oficial*, 21 February 1880; El General Grant en Progreso," *El Diario Oficial*, 6 March 1880, reprinted from *El Eco del Comercio* (Merida).

17. *New York Tribune*, 27 February 1880; "El General Grant," *El Diario Oficial*, 12 February 1880; "El H. Sr. Foster," *El Diario Oficial*, 17 February 1880; "Llegada del General Grant," *El Diario Oficial*, 18 February 1880.

18. Ulysses Grant to Julia Dent, 7 May 1848, *The Papers of Ulysses S. Grant*, vol.1 (Carbondale, Ill.: Southern Illinois University Press, 1967), 156–7; Ulysses S. Grant, *Memoirs and Selected letters of Ulysses S. Grant* (New York: Library of America, 1990), 125.

19. *New York Tribune*, 27 February 1880.

20. Ignacio Mejía and Matías Romero to Díaz, 14 February 1880, *APD* 30: 171–2; *New York Tribune*, 17, 20, 21 and 27 February 1880; "El General Grant," *El Diario Oficial*, 12 February 1880.

21. "Gen. Grant's Tour in Mexico," *Frank Leslie's Illustrated Newspaper*, 13 March 1880.

22. "El General Grant en Veracruz," *El Diario Oficial*, 24 February 1880; "Obsequio," *El Diario Oficial*, 24 February 1880, reprint from *El Monitor Republicano*; *New York Tribune*, 9 March 1880.

23. "Reception of General Grant at the Capital," *Two Republics*, 29 February 1880; "Mexicans Welcoming Grant," *New York Times*, 25 February 1880; "Grant's Mexican Trip," *New York Times*, 24 February 1880; "Gran Serenata," *El Diario Oficial*, 23 February 1880.

24. *El Monitor Republicano*, 25 and 29 February 1880; *La Libertad*, 22 February 1880; *El Republicano*, 22 February 1880.

25. *New York Tribune*, 27 February 1880; "General Grant in Mexico," *New York Tribune*, 14 March 1880.

26. "General Grant's Travels," *New York Tribune*, 30 March 1880; *Two Republics*, 29 February 1880; *New York Times*, 28 February 1880; "General Grant en Pachuca," *El Diario Oficial*, 10 March 1880, reprint from *Siglo XIX*; "El Señor General Grant en Puebla," *El Diario Oficial*, 17 March 1880, reprint from *El Periódico oficial del estado de Puebla*.

27. "General Grant in Mexico," *New York Tribune*, 14 March 1880; *La República*, 17 March 1880; *La Tribuna*, 18 March 1880.

28. "La Fiesta del Ayer," *El Diario Oficial*, 17 March 1880, reprint from *Siglo XIX*; "General Grant en Pachuca," *El Diario Oficial*, 10 March 1880, reprint from *Siglo XIX*; *La Tribuna*, 18 March 1880; *La República*, 17 March 1880; "Visita de los Generales Grant y Sheridan a la Escuela Militar," *El Diario Oficial*, 4 March 1880, reprint from *El Monitor;* "Gran Parada," *El Diario Oficial*, 2 March 1880; "Carta del Sr. Mariscal," *El Diario Oficial*, 3 March 1880.

29. "El Alojamiento del General Grant," *El Diario Oficial*, 23 February 1880; "Recepción del General Grant Preparada en Puebla," *El Diario Oficial*, 3 March 1880; "El General Grant," *El Diario Oficial*, 15 March 1880; reprint from El Monitor; "Ulises S. Grant," *El Diario Oficial*, 7 February 1880, reprint from *La Revista Mexicana*; "La Comisión nombrada para recibir al General Grant," *El Diario Oficial*, 23 February 1880, reprint from *El Municipio Libre*; "Obsequio," *El Diario Oficial*, 24 February 1880, reprint from *El Monitor Republicano*; "General Grant en Pachuca," *El Diario Oficial*, 11 March 1880, reprint from *El Monitor Republicano*.

30. "El Domingo," *El Diario Oficial*, 2 March 1880, reprint from *La Republica*, 29 February 1880.

31. "El General Grant y los Ferrocarriles en México," *El Diario Oficial*, 25 March 1880.

32. "El General Sheridan," *El Diario Oficial*, 3 March 1880, reprint from *La Libertad*.

33. On Grant's political prospects in 1880, see William B. Hesseltine, *Ulysses S. Grant, Politician* (New York: Dodd, Mead and Co., 1935), 431–6; Pletcher, *Rails, Mines and Progress*, 158–9; also General Grant's Political Prospects," *Nation*, 15 January 1880, 38; "Grant's Political Education Abroad," *Nation*, 19 February 1880, 130–131; "The Empire State's Voice: A Large Majority for Grant," *New York Times*, 24 February 1880; "Grant's Mexican Trip," *New York Times*, 24 February 1880; "Connecticut for Grant," *New York Times*, 25 February 1880; "Mexicans welcoming Grant," *New York Times*, 25 February 1880; "Illinois Favors Grant," *New York Times*, 26 February 1880; "Grant Triumphs in Utica," *New York Times*, 26 February 1880; and "Grant Honored in Mexico," *New York Times*, 28 February 1880; "General Grant's Vision in the Hall of the Montezumas," *Frank Leslie's Illustrated Newspaper,* 20 March 1880; cover art; "General Grant in Mexico," *New York Tribune*, 9 March 1880; "General Grant in the City of the Montezuma's," *El Diario Oficial*, 20 March 1880, reprint from *the Galveston Daily News*.

34. T.S. Van Dyke, "Mexican Politics," *Harpers* 71 (1885): 762; John T. Morgan, "Mexico," *North American Review*, 168 (May 1883): 409–418; Arthur D. Anderson, *Mexico from the Material Standpoint* (New York: Brentano Brothers, 1884), cited in Pletcher, *Rails Mines and Progress*, 1; Howard Conkling, *Mexico and the Mexicans:*

Notes of Travel in the Winter and Spring of 1883 (New York: Taintor Brothers, Merrill and Co., 1883), vi–viii, 52.

35. John H. Rice, *Mexico, our Neighbor* (New York: J.W. Lovell, 1888), 8. Also see Robert B. Gorsuch, *The Republic of Mexico and Railroads* (New York: Hosford and Sons, 1881); Albion Z. Gray, *Mexico as It Is* (New York: E.P. Dutton, 1878), 127–8; Butler, 97–99; Morgan, 410.

36. Conkling, 105; "Grant's Speech on Mexico," *Two Republics*, 31 October 1880; Foster, *Diplomatic Memoirs*, 70; "Yankee Diplomacy—Filibusterism," *Two Republics*, 4 January 1880; James A. Whitney, *An Address on the Relations of the U.S. and Mexico*, 18 March 1886 (n.p.), 6.

37. Editorial, *Free Press* (Carbondale, Ill.), 16 December 1888, reprinted in Thomas, 38; Griffin, 239; Conkling, 56.

38. Finerty, 52; Conkling, 55–56, 61–2, 104, 200–201.

39. Morgan, 409; Edward E. Dunbar, *Mexican Papers* (New York: J.A.H. Hasbrouck, 1860), 7, quoted in John W. Foster, "The Contest for the Laws of Reform in Mexico," *American Historical Review* 15 (April 1910): 545.

40. Manuel Caballero, 22.

41. John W. Foster to Hamilton Fish, 11 November 1876, *DDM*; Godoy, *Porfirio Díaz*, 149–50; John W. Foster, "Porfirio Díaz: Soldier and Statesman," *International Quarterly* 12 (1901): 341–353, 253; John W. Foster, "The New Mexico," *National Geographic Magazine* 13 (1902): 1–24; and John W. Foster, "Latin American Constitutions—Revolutions," *National Geographic Magazine* 12 (1901): 173–4.

42. Marie Robinson Wright, *Picturesque Mexico* (Philadelphia: Lippincott, 1897), 14; Fanny Chambers Gooch, *Face to Face with the Mexicans* (New York: Howard and Hulburt, 1887), 366–373; P.F. Martin, "Porfirio Díaz, Soldier and Statesman," *Quarterly Journal of Economics* 211 (October 1909): 526–49; Arthur Howard Noll, "Porfirio Díaz," *Sewanee Review* 144 (October 1906): 436–8; Henry Ware Allen, "President Díaz and the Mexico of Today," *Review of Reviews* 6 (January 1893): 676–96; José Godoy *Porfirio Díaz: President of Mexico: The Master Builder of a Great Commonwealth* (New York: Putnam, 1910) and David P. Thomas, "Porfirio Díaz in the Opinion of his North American Contemporaries," *Revista de Historia Americana* 63 (1967): 79–116; "Taft and Díaz meet, talk of friendship," *New York Times*, 17 October 1909; James Creelman, "Porfirio Díaz: Hero of the Americas," *Pearson's Magazine* 19 (March 1908): 277; Vicente Morales and Manuel Caballero, El Señor Root en México: crónica de la visita hecha en Octubre de 1907 al pueblo y al gobierno de la República Mexicana, por su excelencia el Honorable Señor Root (México: Imprenta de Arte y Letras, 1908); Lummis, *The Awakening of a Nation: Mexico* (London: Harper and Bros., 1898) 103; Thomas, *Journalists Letters*, 97.

43. Lummis, 103; Nevin O. Winter, *Mexico and her People To-Day* (Boston: L.C. Page, 1907), 307.; Creelman, "President Díaz," 231; also Mrs. Alec Tweedie, "Díaz: The Maker of Modern Mexico," *Fortune*, July 1911, 65–74; "Mexico and its Maker," *World's Work*, July 1911, 1431–3; P.F. Martin, "Porfirio Díaz: Soldier and Statesman," Living Age, 1 January 1910, 3–18; Arthur Howard Noll, "Porfirio Díaz," *Sewanee Review* 122 (October 1906): 436. Also see William E. Curtis, *The Capitals of Spanish America* (New York: Praeger, 1969, reprint of 1886 edition), 1–60;

Comisión para los E.U.M. para la Expo Pan Americana, *A Few Facts about Mexico* (Buffalo: White Evans, Penford, 1901); Frederick Palmer, "Díaz, the one Benevolent Dictator: The Man who has made Mexico called most Olympian Figure of Modern History," *New York Times*, 22 February 1909; Edward Conley, "The Americanization of Mexico," *Review of Reviews* 32 (December 1905): 724–5. Also see Frederick Palmer, "After Díaz, What?" *New York Times*, 25 February 1909.

44. James Porch, Consular Dispatch, 24 April 1886, *DDM*.

45. Shelden, 7, 9; Bates, 107–9; "The Progress of Mexico," *The Spectator*, 19 February 1898, 264; Creelman, *Díaz*, 397; Henry Ware Allen, "President Díaz and the Mexico of Today," *Review of Reviews* 6 (June 1893):679.

46. *Mexican Financier*, 14 March 1890, 381, quoted in Pletcher, *Rails Mines and Progress*, 29; "Form and Substance in the Mexican Republic," *Nation*, 22 December 1904, 497; Alfred Henry Lewis, "The Maligners of Mexico," *Cosmopolitan* 48 (March 1910): 432b-c; John B. Frisbie, "Mexico of Today," *Catholic World* 91 (1910): 39.

47. Dillon Wallace, *Beyond the Mexican Sierra* (Chicago: McClurg, 1910), xii-xiv, cited in Pletcher, *Rails, Mines and Progress*, 30; Carson, 206; Otheman Stevens, "Mexico the Progressive," *Cosmopolitan* 48 (March 1910): 434, 444.

48. "Worthless White Nations," *The Mexican Investor*, 12 March 1904, 2.

49. Godoy, 32–3.

Conclusion:
"Order and Progress"

U.S.-Mexican relations underwent a dramatic change during the early years of the Porfiriato. The bitter exchanges that had characterized communication during most of the nineteenth century were replaced by declarations of shared interests and friendship. Economic links blossomed and the belligerent exercises of troops crowding the border were replaced by the bustle of freight forwarders and the greetings of travelers and traders. Superficially, the change suggests that the Díaz campaign to improve Mexico's international reputation succeeded. On closer inspection, however, it becomes clear that Mexico had established a working relationship with the U.S. that incorporated new terminology, but it had not won the unquestioned recognition of the "autonomous Mexican state" that Mexican promoters originally desired. Instead, the Americans incorporated interaction with Mexico into their evolving vision of expanding U.S. political and economic might. What appeared as an alliance between the nations during the Porfiriato was in reality a fragile and superficial truce between two very different visions of the future international system.

The most obvious and eventually most conflict-ridden compromise was reached in economic relations. Both the U.S. vision of international expansion and the Mexican vision of national development included expectations of increased trade and investment. However, even though the two nations were speaking in the universal "language of business," as AID spokesman John Fisk had observed in 1879, they had dramatically different understandings of the words. The Mexicans had envisioned a partnership for development, yet Americans saw the Mexicans as disciples, not partners, in the new religion of progress. In 1909 traveler William Carson unwittingly highlighted the chasm between the high Mexican expectations and the disappointing outcomes of the economic alliance when he praised Mexican progress and predicted that "within twenty-five to thirty years Mexico might become peacefully annexed to the United States." The Mexican, he assured his readers, "would hardly object as the Mexican is not born to be a businessman."[1]

The two nations also reached a superficial, but ultimately untenable compromise in politics. In 1877 the Díaz administration encouraged the sister republics interpretation of relations in order to gain domestic and international political legitimacy for the Mexican government. Yet the uneven aftermath of President Ulysses S. Grant's 1880 visit revealed a fatal miscalculation in the Mexican strategy. The Mexicans attempted to use Grant's visit to highlight mutual respect for republicanism as a base for future cooperation, yet over the years it became clear that the American audience had little sympathized with the Mexican vision of a republican alliance nor concerned themselves with the quality of Mexican internal affairs. Americans grew to prefer, in fact, an orderly Mexico to a democratic one, not merely for the health of their investments, but for the good of their own nation that quailed at the prospect of Mexican disorder.

Nor did later Americans appear devoted to the ideals of republican democracy in their own country. By the end of the Porfiriato, Americans had grown to accept not just widespread disenfranchisement of Mexicans in Mexico, but disenfranchisement of many communities, such as the African American and Native people, in the United States as well. By the close of the Porfiriato it was clear that the Mexican state had achieved respect from many within the U.S. not through its assertion of republican sisterhood, but through the maintenance of a reassuring pattern of "order and progress," which seemed to some Americans to offer a model of governance that their own nation might wish to emulate. Ultimately, it was not the Mexican nation that won American praise or American imitation, but merely the dependable administration of Porfirio Díaz.

Although Mexican efforts to convince Americans of their republican and progressive national character failed in the end, the vocabulary introduced by the Liberal promoters remained in use by both nations because it offered an attractive veneer to a pragmatic and inequitable association. By 1909, however, only the vaguest generalities could preserve the pretense of common cause. In October of that year the two presidents, William Howard Taft and Porfirio Díaz, exchanged historic calls across the El Paso-Ciudad Juárez border. President Taft expressed the hope that the "identical aims and ideals" of the two nations would assure peace for all. President Díaz seconded the sentiment as he also hoped that friendship would "cultivate the common interests which bind the two neighboring countries whose respective elements of life and progress are reciprocally completed and magnified by association."[2] Neither Díaz nor Taft dared define the common interests they hailed; elaborating the terms would have exposed the inherent conflict between the longstanding Mexican quest for increased sovereignty and the American expectations of controlled, informal expansion of U.S. influence.

Despite the vacuous Taft-Díaz exchange of pleasantries, there were signs of serious friction in the relationship. During the mid-1890s the Díaz administration had begun an aggressive effort to pursue trade and investment links with Latin America, Europe, and Asia in order to diversify foreign relations and dilute the influence of U.S. interests in Mexico. Porfirian leaders viewed the aggressive U.S. response to the Venezuela Crisis of 1895 with considerable alarm, and, three years later the U.S. occupation of Puerto Rico and Cuba during the Spanish-American War only confirmed their suspicions of U.S. intentions in the region. The Díaz administration countered the new American assertiveness abroad by redoubling its own foreign policy activism, strengthening independent links to neighboring governments in the region and working behind the scenes to head off potential disputes.[3]

Even before the Revolution of 1910, Díaz's long-playing role as Mexico's patriarch had begun to come under scrutiny in the U.S. Just months after the two republican representatives, Taft and Díaz, shook hands along the U.S. border, a series of articles in the *American Magazine* exposed the horrific labor conditions enforced by the Porfirian government and set off a furor in the U.S. and Mexico between the defenders and critics of Mexico's system of "order and progress." Muckraking journalist John Kenneth Turner, who had infiltrated the infamous "Valle Nacional" by presenting himself as a potential investor, presented chilling accounts of the deportation of Yaqui Indian tribes to labor camps, the persistence of debt peonage arrangements, and other barbaric treatment of the Mexican peasant. Turner condemned not only the Mexican government, but the foreign investors who took advantage of this legal morass to increase profits. By the time the articles were re-released as a book, *Barbarous Mexico*, one year later, Mexico's descent into revolution had begun.[4]

Díaz's downfall in the Revolution of 1910 exposed the total failure of the original nationalist strategy. In the end the Porfirian Liberals won neither international nor domestic security for their nation. As "order and progress," disappeared in the maelstrom of the Revolution, so too did American regard for the autonomy of the Mexican state. "Can the Mexican progress?" wondered journalist A.W. Warwick in the pages of *Forum* as he witnessed the rapid descent into revolutionary chaos. "Shall we annex northern Mexico?" wondered another, while a third journalist questioned American "duty" in the face of "Mexican disorder." "Were the Mexicans ripe for self-government on Anglo-Saxon lines?" queried visitor John Fyfe as he contemplated the chaos of 1914. "Were they, in truth, a nation at all," he continued, "or merely a group of racial elements not yet fused into a coherent whole?" Fyfe's musings were more than insulting, they were dangerous and blatantly exposed the failure of the Porfirian Liberals to secure national legitimacy in American eyes.[5]

At the outset of the Porfiriato Americans had rejected further annexations of Mexican territory because they would bring in unwelcome populations who could never be assimilated into the political or cultural life of the U.S. Yet, in the years since 1876 Americans had accustomed themselves to political compromises in their new colonies, and even more vividly, in the maturation of the Jim Crow system at home. Wilson's decision to land U.S. troops in Tampico and Veracruz in 1914, and to police northern Mexico in the fruitless pursuit of Pancho Villa two years later, proved that Americans had not given up the interventionist spirit. The combination of military activism with reduced reservations regarding political and social apartheid left Mexico in a dangerous position indeed. As stability eroded after 1910, Mexico once again faced the prospect of dismemberment.

Although the campaign to strengthen Mexico's international position through a strategic alliance with the U.S. failed, it marked an important chapter in Mexican nationalism and in the evolution of the international system. Ignoring the initiatives of the early Porfirian promoters to exploit American interest and establish a place for Mexico in the emerging system distorts the history of the era and flatters Americans with a false portrait of American initiated expansion. It causes Mexico and other nations to appear as passive agents in the construction of an American informal empire and, by omitting their own objectives, implicitly blames them for their naïve victimization. Finally it makes Mexican nationalism of the 1920s and later appear as a revolutionary era innovation, rather than the next chapter in the Mexican quest for national security. The tragedy of the Porfirian vision was not that it was not sufficiently nationalistic, but that its strategy only papered over the increasing inequities of the relationship.

NOTES

1. Carson, 176.

2. "Taft and Díaz meet, talk of friendship," *New York Times*, 17 October 1909.

3. Lorenzo Meyer, "The U.S. and Mexico: The Historical Status of their Conflict," *Journal of International Affairs* 43 (Winter 1990): 251–70; Cosio Villegas, *Historia Moderna; Vida Politica Exterior*; and Laura Muñoz, "'El más experto de nuestros diplomáticos.' Ignacio Mariscal, artifice de la diplomacia mexicana," in *Artífices y Operadores de la Diplomacia Mexicana, Siglos XIX y XX*, Agustín Sánchez Andrés, et al. (México: Porrúa, 2004); 125–130.

4. On the furor created by the series, see the introduction by Sinclair Snow in John Kenneth Turner, *Barbarous Mexico* (Chicago: C.H. Kern, 1911); reprint, Austin: University of Texas Press, 1969), ix–xxiii.

5. A.W. Warwick, "Can the Mexican Progress?" Forum 51 (January 1914): 38–49; A.R. Hinton, "Shall We Annex Northern Mexico?" *Independent* 79 (27 July 1914): 124–5; Our Duty in Mexican Disorder," *Literary Digest* 45 (21 September 1912): 455–6; Henry Hamilton Fyfe, *The Real Mexico: A Study on the Spot* (New York: McBride, 1914) 5.

John Watson Foster in uniform, c. 1865. (Library of Congress, Prints and Photographs Division)

General Porfirio Díaz c. 1870. (Library of Congress, Prints and Photographs Division)

John Watson Foster, Secretary of State, c. 1890. (Library of Congress, Prints and Photographs Division)

President Porfirio Díaz, c. 1910. (Library of Congress, Prints and Photographs Division) U.S. Minister John Foster and Mexican President Porfirio Díaz clashed in their early careers, but later formed a mutually beneficial alliance that required them to ignore their hostile past.

The Opening of the AID Exhibit in the Palace of Mines, 1878. In 1878 the leading families of Mexico welcomed the American Industrial Deputation in the prestigious Palace of Mines. Source: Frank Leslie's Illustrated Weekly, (March 15, 1879): 24-25. (Courtesy of Boston Public Library)

The Hotel Iturbide. The Americans of the Industrial Deputation awoke to find themselves in a city older than any city in the U.S., and they were fascinated by the parade of city life outside their hotel. Source: Thomas Brocklehurst, Mexico To-Day: A Country with a Great Future and a Glance at the Prehistoric Remains and Antiquities of the Montezumas. *(London: John Murray, 1883): 22.*

General Grant's Arrival in Mexico City. Former President Ulysses S. Grant was greeted in Mexico City with fireworks, a choral concert, and a torch carrying cavalry escort. The Mexican government intended to match the honors shown to Grant on his recent world tour, and thus raise American regard for their nation. Source: Frank Leslie's Illustrated Weekly, (March 13, 1880): 21. (Courtesy of Boston Public Library)

Orizaba Vista. Early American travelers viewed the Mexican landscape through the conventions of European landscape painters, with the picturesque locals in the foreground, the lessons of history crumbling in the middle, and the sublime mystery of the mountains in the distance. Source: Frederick Ober, Travels in Mexico, Boston: Ester and Lauriat, 1884, 211. (Courtesy of Slippery Rock University)

A Village Church. Source: Nevin O. Winter, Mexico and Her People Today, *Boston: L.C. Page, 1907, 364. (Courtesy Slippery Rock University) Initially American tourists to Mexico contemplated the same architectural, geographic and historic sites that they would visit in Europe, but within a few years they began to slip away from their educational itineraries to focus on the "quaint" mules and market vendors nearby.*

American Railway Tourists in the Tamosopo Canyon. Source: Campbells New Revised Complete Guide and Descriptive Book of Mexico, Chicago, Rogers and Smith, 1907) 279. (Courtesy of Slippery Rock University)

"A Picturesque Pulque Shop." Nevin O. Winter, Mexico and Her People Today, Boston: L.C. Page, 1907, 66. Many American tourists found their vision of 'primitive' Mexico in a visit to a pulqueria. (Courtesy of Slippery Rock University)

"Unexplainable Gringo." Cartoons lauding the American occupation of Veracruz had clearly abandoned the *"Sister Republics"* theme. *Review of Reviews 49 (May 1914): 644 (Courtesy of Dakota State University)*

NOT GOING TO BE ANY WAR—BUT THERE'S GOING TO
BE A FINE HOUSE-CLEANING
—Rogers in N. Y. *Herald*

"Not going to be any war, but there's going to be a fine housecleaning,"
Reprint from NY Herald, Current Opinion 56 (June 1914): 411. (Courtesy
of Dakota State University)

Part III

"MEXICO, THE WONDERLAND OF THE SOUTH!"

Introduction:
Pilgrims to the Past

In March 1884 a spirited crowd of investors, engineers and laborers gathered in Zacatecas to celebrate the completion of the international rail line that now stretched twelve hundred miles from Mexico City to the Texas border. During the previous ten years steady advances in steamship travel, and telegraph and mail communication had increased contact, but the completion of the railroad literally threw the U.S. and Mexico into a new phase of intimacy. In the capital the *Two Republics* applauded the achievement and celebrated the fact that "Mexico is no longer isolated." During the following years new rail lines would open to Sonora, Cuernavaca, Guanajuato, Oaxaca and distant Tehuantepec, spiriting both people and objects across the arid plains of the north and the mountain ranges of the Sierra. Instead of obstructing communication between the two nations, the northern desert now hosted the caravan routes of the new generation.[1]

Unfortunately, the railroad age would not prove a blessing for all and the logistics of the opening celebration of the Sonora Railway foreshadowed the coming inequities. The engineers responsible for the inaugural run between Guaymas and Hermosillo belatedly realized that the only engine available was incapable of pulling all the cars crowded with guests along the planned route. While the state representatives, visiting investors and other dignitaries steamed off to enjoy a scenic lunch and festive ball in Hermosillo, several cars were uncoupled and abandoned miles from their destination. The unlucky passengers left behind dismounted and followed as best they could. The humiliating scene presaged the course of the next twenty-five years as the uneven modernization of the Mexican economy swept a minority of Mexicans into new positions of wealth and power, while the majority struggled along in the dust.

The impact of the railroad on U.S.-Mexican economic relations has received ample attention, but the new ease in transportation had a dramatic impact on U.S.-Mexican cultural relations as well. The railroad accelerated the Mexican confrontation with the U.S. as it flooded Mexican streets with visitors and products from the north.[2] For Americans also the completion of the railroad pushed relations with Mexico into new physical and mental itineraries. Contact with Mexico was no longer reserved for the hardy few who were prepared to brave the terrors of the Caribbean crossing; it was possible for all who were willing to board a train, read a travel account or examine Mexican products in the American marketplace. The railroad thrust Mexico into the realm of American leisure and consumption, and, in doing so, opened new categories of cultural relations between the two nations.

Chapters 6 and 7 examine two arenas of leisure interaction transformed by the railroad: tourism (or travel for pleasure and education as opposed to necessity) and the virtual tourism made possible by Mexican participation in American expositions. Both the increase in international tourism and the rising popularity of the international exposition were reflections of the broadening mental horizons of the late nineteenth century world. For Americans, expansion of U.S. economic and diplomatic vistas made it increasingly easy to visit, read about or sample merchandise from the outside world. The Díaz administration was conscious of these new categories of communication and strove to shape U.S.-Mexican contact in the tourist and fair environments. Once again, however, the zones of contact became occasions of cultural competition as Mexican promoters competed with American travelers and fairgoers to determine the interpretation of new scenes and material.

In many ways the cultural competition surrounding tourism and fairs was similar to that surrounding the Zamacona-Foster exchanges and the visits of the AID mission and former President Ulysses S. Grant to Mexico. In each case, the Mexicans approached contact as a means of enhancing Mexican international standing while the American response incorporated the experience of contact into their own vision of expanding American horizons. Yet there was one significant difference in the American leisure response. In diplomatic and commercial contacts Americans had tended to emphasize negative depictions of perceived Mexican "underdevelopment" and contrast it with positive visions of American initiative, industry and progress. In contrast, travelers elaborated an equally stereotyped, romantic vision of Mexico as a desirable primitive paradise. This portrait was hardly new; it drew upon long-standing stereotypes that cast Latins as childlike innocents in a tropical Eden. Throughout the nineteenth century these clichés had allowed Americans to dismiss the Mexicans as racially dissimilar idlers through backhanded compliments of their simple, unhurried ways.[3]

The cultural interactions that characterized American leisure interactions with Mexico during the Porfiriato, however, revealed not only traditional romantic condescension, but new preoccupations within U.S. life. In particular, it revealed growing ambivalence toward the American path of industrial development. In the end, American leisure infatuation with Mexico's "primitive soul" never undermined American national confidence, but it did provide Americans with an arena for harmless flirtation with alternatives to the U.S. model of modernization. On vacation or engrossed in the pages of a travel memoir, Americans could safely indulge their nostalgia for a bygone world they never knew.

Eventually, even the Mexican Revolution of 1910 was experienced by most Americans through the perspective and vocabulary of the leisure relationship, as is described in Chapter 8. Press coverage of the Revolution channeled discussion of events in Mexico into the familiar conventions of travel literature, safely removing the rebellion from serious consideration as a movement for political transformation. The rhetoric of the leisure tradition exploited the exotic aspects of the revolution and underlined its foreignness in the American mind. Most Americans, untouched by the destruction of the wars to their south, could take comfort in reframing what was a profound rejection of the American model of progress into another series of colorful incidents in the life of their Southern neighbor. The Revolution was portrayed as chaotic, savage, and comic by turn, but ultimately, filtered through the wonderland perspective of the Victorian travel account, it appeared to have as little relevance to American life as a *Harper's Magazine* depiction of family life along the Ganges River.

NOTES

1. *Two Republics*, 8, 12 March 1884. Also see Sandra Kuntz Ficker, *El Ferrocarril Central Mexicano, 1880–1907* (México: El Colegio de México, Centro de Estudios Históricos, 1993); *Two Republics*, 8 March 1884; "Ferrocarril de Sonora," 4 November 1888, c. 442, Archivo Histórico de Sonora, cited in Reñique, 261.

2. The best discussion of Mexican cultural responses to these new forms of contact remains William H. Beezley, *Judas at the Jockey Club and Other Episodes of Porfirian Mexico* (Lincoln: University of Nebraska Press, 1987; 2nd ed., 2004).

3. A clear overview of the dichotomy in stereotypes is Charles Gibson, *The Black Legend: Anti Spanish Attitudes in the Old World and the New* (New York: Knopf, 1971); and Carlos Monsivais, "Travellers in Mexico: A Brief Anthology of Selected Myths," *Diogenes* 125 (1984):48–74.

Chapter Six

From Education to Escape: American Tourism in Porfirian Mexico

During the first administration of President Porfirio Díaz (1876–80), travel to Mexico was undertaken only by would-be investors and missionaries and portrayed in journals in terms of discomfort and danger. Yet by the mid-1880s improvements in communication and the mechanics of travel and lodging lured a new class of tourist south. Travelers began to expect a tour in Mexico to improve their health, not shatter it. They looked forward to a vacation in a land of ancient civilizations and curious customs, and even those who were unable to participate in firsthand explorations could share in the enthusiasm and the observations of others through the sudden plethora of published travel writing. Between 1877 and 1910 nearly one hundred accounts of travel in Mexico were published in the United States. Accounts were serialized in popular magazines and local newspapers, presented as lectures in community forums, or converted into fiction, ensuring broad exposure to the American audience. Porfirian Mexico not only succeeded in capturing the investments of Americans, but in capturing the imagination of Americans as well.[1]

Like the rise in investment and trade, the rise of American tourism in Mexico appeared to prove the success of the early Porfirian public relations campaign. American travelers would hardly have come to Mexico if they still accepted older stereotypes of Mexico as a wilderness of unchecked banditry, pestilence and revolution. Many were apparently willing to trust the Díaz administration to safeguard their persons and property while they explored the nation. Unfortunately, the successful expansion of tourism presented a problem the early promoters never anticipated. The Mexican hosts' careful orchestration of the visits of the AID mission and former President Ulysses S. Grant had presaged the Díaz administration's similar hopes to use travel to introduce Americans to its vision of progressive Mexico. Yet the stream of travelers that followed the completion of the railroads overwhelmed the original itineraries developed by Mexican planners as Americans sought not enlightenment, but merely a pleasant respite from the climate and responsibilities of their normal lives. Most vacationing Americans preferred not to study Mexico but to escape into what they saw as a primitive and timeless refuge from modern civilization.

During the twentieth century the practice of travel for pleasure and relaxation has become common, and contemporary American tourists may find it unremarkable that their predecessors preferred the sunny scenery to the museums of Mexico. Yet, the emergence of a leisure travel tradition in Mexico reflected two transformations; it revealed not only a marked improvement in the safety and ease of travel in Mexico, but more significantly for the future of American-Mexican cultural relations, a wholesale shift in U.S. attitudes toward travel. Ultimately it would be this shift in U.S. attitudes rather than Mexican initiatives to shape travel itineraries or the improvement of travel logistics that would influence the American travel experiences in Mexico and thwart Mexican hopes for improving understanding through the increase in contact.

Prior to this era there was no pleasure travel tradition among Americans heading to Mexico—or anywhere else. Journeys were undertaken out of necessity, health, or, for the fortunate few, intellectual enrichment. Both Mexicans and Americans were familiar with the eighteenth century grand tour model which provided an educational framework for young men during their European travels and led them to seek out opportunities to study and compare different governmental, esthetic and economic systems. These journeys often led travelers far afield from museums and lecture halls, but even in the brothels of Europe travelers preserved the illusion that they were merely completing their education. It was not surprising that both early Mexican and American travel promoters assumed that American tourism in Mexico would imitate a sanitized version of the European model, with an emphasis on exposure to history and art. Yet after an initial experimentation with the European grand tour model in Mexico, Americans quickly developed their own itineraries which led them out of the art galleries and other shrines to high culture and down the back alleys of 'real' Mexico. The emergence of a vision of travel as an escapist respite from modern life soon replaced the educational model among American travelers in Mexico.[2]

The U.S. pleasure travel model appeared first among American travelers in Mexico, but had less to do with the exquisite scenery and climate of Mexico than with the emergence of a progressively more delineated leisure realm in domestic American cultural life. During the mid and late nineteenth century the increasing complexity of American communities and economies led to shifts in the physical and mental geography of human activity. The physical places, hours and behaviors of the work world became increasingly differentiated from the venues and expectations of the leisure sphere. Over the years Americans internalized social codes that called for one set of dress and deportment in the office or shop, and another in the home or club. Victorian America witnessed the full blown demarcation of human activities, with its almost fetishistic preoccupation with the segregation of space (front parlors, back staircases, and breakfast nooks, for example), gender roles, fashion and behavior. Ironically, the emergence of compartmentalized work and leisure spheres did not create dissonance so much as relieve it by allowing Americans to pursue contradictory standards of behavior and identities in different venues. In their work life Americans might pursue the benefits of the new economy, but in their leisure they could safely escape into a realm of alternative standards and values. American pleasure travel in Mexico developed within the context of this work/leisure divide, and despite Porfirian efforts to influence the new industry it was this domestic U.S. cultural debate that ultimately set the tone for the American tourist experience in Mexico. For Americans with money, pleasure travel became one of the key forms of leisure that complemented rather than contradicted modern life by encouraging travelers to seek escape through carefully circumscribed dramas of dissent from civilization.

The changing conventions of travel writing reflected the shifting mental framework through which Americans were approaching the newly expanded world. Although Americans had written narrative accounts of Mexico earlier in the century, the travel literature that emerged after 1880 differed in tone and distribution. The early and mid-nineteenth century romantic narratives produced by writers like William H. Prescott, Francis Berriman, Washington Irving and James Fenimore Cooper were, not surprisingly, riddled with prejudice and factual mistakes, but they placed the mystery of Mexico and her people at the center of the work. In contrast, the writing that emerged in the final decades of the century reflected an almost schizophrenic division between empirical evaluation (the realm of work) and impressionistic portraits of adventure (the realm of leisure). Although the first accounts of the new era attempted to combine the two approaches, describing both business opportunities and scenery in a single volume or article, the two kinds of writing soon divided into different stylistic approaches and different publishing outlets. In both formats however, the historic and living Mexico that fascinated the earlier writers faded from prominence. The new focus highlighted instead the energetic American as investor or traveler against the backdrop of Mexico. The structure of travelogues and commercial brochures were both organized around American action and American judgments, while Mexico remained merely a passive setting for the performance. They were literally accounts not of Mexico itself, but of American entrepreneurs and tourists in Mexico. Not surprisingly, these accounts tell us more about the ambivalence Americans felt toward their own culture than they tell us about Mexico as commercial tracts portrayed Americans comfortably as agents of modern civilization, while travelers increasingly saw themselves as refugees, however temporarily, from the stress of northern 'progress.'

The Mexican travel boom of the 1880s would have been impossible without improvements in the mechanics of travel. Prior to the opening of the intercontinental rail lines in 1884, travel choices to Mexico were limited.[3] A very few travelers sailed south from California to Acapulco or Manzanillo before crossing into the interior. Most travelers endured enervating heat and violent storms on the Caribbean crossing to Veracruz. There were no direct steam lines between the two nations and visitors were subjected to interim visits to Havana, Tampico or other ports renowned for disease and disorder. Few travelers had kind words for their leisurely Caribbean cruises. Albert Gray was incensed at the indirect route that added "two extra, nauseating days" to his trip. "There is nothing to see or to do at these ports," he proclaimed, but "roll most unhappily at the slightest suggestion of a breeze." Others echoed his sentiments. "There was not much done that day except to lurch with the lurching ship. Now we go down, down, downy, and now we go up, up, uppy..." wrote Gilbert Haven, a Methodist minister moored off Tampico in 1875.[4]

Landfall in Veracruz was welcome, but not reassuring. travelers were struck by the beauty of the location and many even admitted that Veracruz appeared cleaner than most U.S. cities, but all knew the appearance was deceptive. The *Ferguson Anecdotal Guide to Mexico* aptly summed up the four plagues of Veracruz: heat, disease, mosquitoes and *el norte*, a powerful storm that sunk ships at anchor and sent clouds of sand rushing under door sills. Most Americans, with little understanding of the origins or transmission of tropical diseases, feared the very air of the city. As A.V. Kautz recalled of his journey in 1868, "Vera Cruz is admirably constructed for the cultivation and perpetuation of pestilential diseases." Both guidebooks and more seasoned travelers urged visitors to pass rapidly through Veracruz to the healthier air of the upland interior. In 1881 the newly arrived U.S. consul never made it out of the port city at all; he succumbed to the "black vomit" (cholera) upon arrival—a sobering lesson to incautious travelers.[5]

Most visitors were additionally overwhelmed by the physical collision with the alien culture, people and language that made itself felt the moment their ship dropped anchor. Steamers were besieged by boatmen bidding for the right to transport the passengers and baggage to the dock. One of the 1879 AID delegates described the scene as an "opera bouffé." "They were all looking up at us," he explained, "and we were all looking down at them, each boatman gesticulating and shouting "*un peso!*" in a shrill and squeaky voice." Ladies, animals, and boxes were lowered over the side of the boat in nets; men braved the rope ladders. The confusion of figures and language gave one a "perfect conception of the Tower of Babel," wrote Helen Sanborn after negotiating passage. She was unsure whether she had booked "passage for one, a dozen, or in fact anybody at all," until she and her trunks were on their way to shore.[6]

Before the completion of the Veracruz-Mexico City railway in 1873, a visitor's next task was to book passage on a diligence, or stagecoach, for the bone-rattling four-to-five day journey up through the mountains to Mexico City. Gilbert Haven found it difficult to appreciate the famous scenery, as "the stage reels to and fro among the stones and pits like a very drunken man and the passengers follow his example." Mary Hallock Foote found her scenery on the diligence itself, as she noted that her driver's goat skin breeches, "worn with the long yellow hair outside," comically suggested the legs of a satyr. He plied a whip and wore a small bag filled with small stones for pelting whichever of the eight horses appeared to be slacking, and she admired the "extraordinary neatness and precision in his aim." When roads were impassable due to rain or landslides, passengers traveled by mule or *litera,* coffin-shaped boxes that hung suspended from poles braced on the shoulders of Indian guides. If the entire journey had to be made in *litera*, the trip from Veracruz to Mexico City could take more than a week. Travelers seldom knew which was worse, the swinging, claustrophobic and extremely unstable *litera*, or the mule-drawn coaches, constructed without a single spring.[7]

Guides and drivers often entertained passengers with vivid accounts of recent bandit attacks, which lent additional color to the trip. A.V. Kautz's more experienced companions urged him to postpone his departure from the port as highwaymen usually targeted the stages that left Veracruz the day following the arrival of a steamer. Kautz watched curiously as his companions loaded their rifles and revolvers, all the while assuring him that the danger of robbery was greatly exaggerated. Brantz Mayer was one of very few Americans who felt that the apprehension and preparations for defense "gave a spice of adventure to our journey and repaid us for the slowness with which we crawled over the wretched road."[8]

Travel was transformed in 1873 when the completion of the Veracruz-Mexico City railway allowed travelers to climb the mountains in a mere twelve hours. Thereafter, travelers could sit comfortably in plush seats to enjoy the views, secure in the knowledge that an attached carload of Mexican soldiers assured the safety of the passengers. American accounts began to dwell on the staggering scenery of the trip and limited complaints to the inconvenient hour of departure. Although the railroad eliminated many of the hardships of earlier journeys, continued fears of political turmoil in Mexico kept the number of American visitors to Mexico during the 1870s to a minimum.

Travelers who wished to stray off the Veracruz-Mexico City corridor found the going even more challenging. Diligences, or closed carriages, crossed the northern deserts frequently but were seldom comfortable. John Finerty covered from eighty to one hundred miles a day in his grueling journey through the north. Although he grew to enjoy the largely male society of the diligences, sharing cognac, cigars and song to pass the time, he had a healthy respect for the rigors of the trip. "We changed mules very often and tore along the causeway as if Satan were behind us," he recalled. James Bates took a two day coach from Leon to Guadalajara, but could not recommend the excursion. "A long ride in one of these big coaches" Bates recalled, "under a blazing sun, choked with a cloud of ever present dust, and tossed back and forth from seat to roof as the mules gallop madly along to the loud shouts and perpetual flogging of the muleteers, is said to be a torture so excruciating that only the direst necessity will compel anyone to adventure it the second time." Adolph Bandelier, the Swiss-American archaeologist, wanted to avoid the tippy *literas* in the mountains south of Mexico City, but found few horses available for hire. He regarded his choice with apprehension:

I had to figure out ways and means of mounting my horse. This was no easy task. On whichever side I would place my foot in the stirrup the weight of my body threatened to demolish the horse. To leap into the saddle from behind would have resulted in breaking its spinal column, for the individual vertebrae seemed to hang loosely from the backbone like the beads of a rosary. Finally, I leaned the animal against the wall and so succeeded in due time and with great care to climb into the saddle.[9]

Nor was it easy to find accommodations after a day of strenuous travel. There was not enough demand to create a hospitality industry in Mexico and American travelers found food and lodging notoriously difficult to arrange. Priests and soldiers, the most frequent travelers in the Mexican countryside, boarded with colleagues in towns along the way. Well-to-do private Mexican citizens stayed with acquaintances or camped when traveling. Occasionally, stages promised overnight stops at inns, but the lodging was often in miserable, rodent-infested sheds designed to accommodate Mexican muleteers and their mules, not passengers. John Finerty found that accommodations were generally so "unspeakably vile that it was a blessed alternative to bivouac in the open air under the dews and damps of night." Albion Gray recalled the "execrable and deadly" drainage conditions at inns along the route to Puebla, which "decency forbad discussing in detail." Felix Oswald, who had traveled down the Pacific coast before joining a mule train through northern Mexico, heartily recommended his own practice of sleeping out under the stars and accepting the hospitality of the local Indians.[10]

The one exception in the hospitality field was the Hotel Iturbide in the capital, located in the former palace of Emperor Iturbide off the main square and across from the National Palace and the Cathedral. Its grand proportions and lavish decor offered American visitors a glimpse of the traditional style of the Mexican elite. Visitors entered through an archway (originally designed to accommodate carriages) into a spacious central courtyard ringed with balconies for several floors. Large rooms with French windows overlooked the marble-floored central patio on one side and the street on the other. Early visitors found the hotel a haven of luxury after the mule sheds of the countryside, although they still faulted the hotel for its lack of a heating system, separate ladies' parlor or adequate public reception rooms. The Iturbide adapted quickly to the growing numbers of American visitors, however, and by the early 1880s it offered English-language menus, an English-language travel information center, and an American-style dining plan. Other hotels followed the lead of the Iturbide and, by the late 1880's, Thomas Janvier was able to suggest a variety of hotels appropriate for American visitors to the capital, including one he highly recommended for "ladies traveling alone," and all of them speaking a "curious, but merchantable, variety of English."[11]

The completion of the international rail line from Mexico City to El Paso in the spring of 1884 marked the turning point in the experience of American travel to Mexico. The following winter the Raymond Excursion Company, an organizer of rail excursions to California, became the first company to organize a package tour to Mexico and in February 1885 seventy-three American tourists slept in American Pullman cars, ate food prepared by American cooks in the dining car, and listened to American guides during a four-week excursion to Mexico within their "portable" Pullman hotel. The first excursion was inscribed so rapidly that a second excursion train for forty additional tourists was organized for March. Enthused with success the company planned on five trips of sixty excursionists each for the 1885–86 season. Although other companies and private trains imitated the Raymond model, the company (later known as the Raymond and Whitcomb Company) set the standard for package rail tours to Mexico throughout the Porfiriato.[12]

The advent of rail travel and package tours removed much of the anxiety from the American travel experience in Mexico. Tourists had little need to worry about their possessions, safely stowed within the train itself, and no need to worry about their fellow travelers, who, like themselves, were bankers, manufacturers, authors, and other professionals with their families. Mary Blake and Margaret Sullivan, travel companions on the first excursion, did not have to down cognac and smoke cigars, as did Finerty in the male world of the stage coach, but were happy to spend their evenings with "the judge's pretty wards at their knitting and crochet; [and] the blonde haired Vassar girl sharpening her clever pencil." Traveling with one's own dining car and an American cook even eliminated anxiety over unfamiliar food. The excursionists on the first Raymond trips did not sit down to a Mexican meal until Zacatecas. Their second Mexican meal was organized in Puebla. Otherwise, on the train and in Mexico City (the only city in which the visitors left the train for a hotel) the Americans were served American food on an American time schedule.[13]

Train travel also eliminated the physical hardships of earlier journeys. "It is a little nest of comfort and luxury," noted Blake, "as these Mexican cities, enchanting as they are as case studies and full of brilliant novelty, have not as yet the slightest conception." "We live better on the train than anywhere we stop," agreed James Bates. The train became a refuge for travelers, meeting them after their excursions with a "welcome homelike face," not to mention homelike food, language and company. Travelers need no longer be heroic loners, braving disease, travel barriers, and inadequate accommodations. Maturin Ballou luxuriated "in the pleasure of seeing a strange and beautiful land, without a thought as to the modus operandi." Most travelers, like Arthur Spring, applauded the new travel technology. "The plan of spending our days visiting or sightseeing, passing to the next important point in the cool of the evening, and resting luxuriously for the night drawn up on some quiet side street, works wonderfully well," he concluded. "There is something gorgeous in the idea of a special train, that moves when one pleases and rests when one desires; that goes on like an obedient carriage horse, stopping here to let you pick flowers, and there for fear of disturbing your after-dinner coffee."[14]

Trains not only changed the mechanics but also the itinerary of American travel in Mexico. Before the northern route was opened, most travelers confined their explorations to the Veracruz-Puebla-Mexico City triangle.[15] The gravity-defying engineering of the Veracruz railway was a principal attraction; as was the surrounding scenery. Although few Americans actually visited the ruins of the Carlota Colony (founded by exiled Confederates near Córdoba) or retraced the routes of Hernán Cortés or Winfield Scott, most noted the history of the terrain along the rail route. A few hardy travelers reached Jalapa, the city of flowers, by the English mule-train; more often travelers undertook shorter excursions to nearby sugar, tobacco or maguey plantations. The popularity of these tropical attractions almost disappeared once Americans began to arrive from the arid north.

The experience of travel in the capital region changed as well. Americans had been accustomed to make their base in Mexico City and travel out to Teotihuacan to see the pyramids, to Puebla for a visit to the Cathedral and the Cholula ruins, and to the Shrine of Guadeloupe and the floating gardens of Xochimilco on the city's outskirts. In the city itself they had toured the

Art School of San Carlos, attended American community benefits at the Orrin Circus, paraded with the afternoon crowd along the Paseo de la Reforma, and climbed the hill of Chapultepec Castle. In between these outings they strolled down the streets of the capital, pored over the merchandise in the markets and watched the parade of Mexican humanity pass through the plaza in front of the Iturbide Hotel. Rail passengers, however, spent the bulk of their vacation in transit through the northern states, reducing their sojourn in the capital to one of many brief stops along the way. Accustomed to carefully mediated interaction with Mexicans at their preplanned excursion stops, they were more hesitant to branch out and explore on their own. Tours brought new visitors to Mexico, but these new travelers were less likely to have local acquaintances who could welcome them to join in local social activities, and, having a readymade community on the train, were less likely to seek out social interaction on Mexican terms.

What replaced the older images and itineraries was a northern rail route through new terrain and novel situations. Americans entered through El Paso in the evening and woke to find themselves in Chihuahua, two hundred and twenty miles to the south. During the first years of the Raymond Excursions the visitors were welcomed by the Governor of Chihuahua himself; they then visited the cathedral, convent and plaza, before hopping back on the train for another overnight journey to Zacatecas. In Aguas Calientes they gazed upon the famous hot springs, but most thought the bathing arrangements too promiscuous in gender and class to join in. From Leon a short excursion could be made to the ancient mining center of Guanajuato, with its sunken streets and famous "mummy" museum. In Queretaro they gazed upon the still functioning aqueduct and the Cerro de las Campañas, where the Emperor Maximilian was executed in 1867. Travelers occasionally took advantage of the proximity of mining towns in the north to glimpse the hardships of the mining life, but most were content to use their free moments to wander in nearby markets.

Finally, after sixty-two hours of rail time spread out over four to five days, the visitors awoke in the central rail station in the City of Mexico. Once in the city excursionists repeated some of the itinerary of earlier travelers, but with an abbreviated schedule and under the supervision of their hired guides, not local hosts. They attended the theatre and the circus, boated in the Xochimilco canals, toured art galleries and cathedrals, and enjoyed the music of the Alameda and the sight of the Mexican gentry along the Paseo. Depending upon the season and the health bulletins, a very few ventured a brief visit to Veracruz before reembarking on the train north. During the following years the construction of rail spurs to Guadalajara and Morelia incorporated new territories into the itinerary, but the general pattern remained the same. The program for the "Pennsylvania Tour to Mexico" was typical; the train stopped five days in the capital, two in Puebla, one each in Chihuahua, Zacatecas, Aguas Calientes, Guanajuato, Queretaro, Veracruz and Cholula, half days in Leon and Silao, and mere hours in Torreón and Tlaxcala.[16]

The new rail route dramatically altered not only the geographic but the psychological encounter with Mexico. Border crossings and other symbolic entrances have always offered travelers a convenient moment to reflect on the impending journey and are often invested with disproportionate significance. After 1885 most travelers no longer entered Mexico through the chaos of Veracruz, but remained in their familiar coaches as they crossed into Mexico through the border town of El Paso. Some travelers were relieved at the ease. "Just think," wrote Sylvester Baxter, "we are really abroad, in a foreign country without crossing the ocean!" Others, like Mary Blake, lamented the construction of the railroad bridge, which spirited passengers across "with no more consciousness of change than in passing from one portion of a frontier town to another." Blake missed the "delicious slowness and uncertainty" of the older rope ferries, "which were partial preparation for the strangeness beyond." Travelers looked quickly for signs of Mexican life. McCollester, from behind the windows of his train car, was convinced that "we had alighted upon a new world. The people, look, appear, and talk so strangely." Captain C.H. Wilson agreed that "in the twinkling of an eye" everything changed—the streets, houses, people and goods. Others were less romantic. Nevin Winter urged travelers to choose an evening departure if possible and use the first two hundred miles to gain a little extra rest as nothing significant was to be seen until one reached the outskirts of Chihuahua.[17]

The geography of the new border crossing altered American stereotypes of the southern nation as well. Just as American travelers to London knew to look for Big Ben, American travelers to Mexico had once known to look for volcanoes, churches and tropical foliage. The description Adolph Bandelier left of the view from his window on the Veracruz-Mexico City railroad perfectly captured the older image of Mexico. "There would thus develop a picture," wrote the archaeologist, "the foreground of which consists of plantations of sugar cane and tobacco in light green, tropical shrubbery, reed huts thickly shaded by bananas and surrounded by tree like hibiscus on which the great red blossoms take the place of missing leaves. In place of the lantanas and red abutilons of the vicinity of Vera Cruz, the bells of morning glories and scarlet red marigolds shine forth." Bandelier completed his picture with a small village where a golden-domed church gleamed beneath the cliffs and peaks of mountains beyond.[18]

After 1884 the Mexican landscape was first glimpsed by most travelers at daybreak, when they awoke to find themselves anxiously searching for evidence of Mexico from the window of their train. "My first view of Mexico was at dawn when I rolled up the curtain," wrote T.B. Evans, "Such a country! Nothing but a wide stretch of sand as far as the eye could see....Scarcely a living shrub or bush; little patches of dried up sage brush and great clumps of giant cactus...one dead stretch of desert."[19] Bandelier's "picture" captured the older stereotype of a nation seductively dangerous in its tropical fecundity, populated with layers of alien cultures and ancient civilizations. In contrast, the new stereotype of the Mexican landscape was that of a vacant land, devoid of human history.

The isolation travelers felt in the north was both physical and cultural. Americans were seeing more of the Mexican landscape, but they were experiencing less of Mexican life. Earlier travelers may often have been displeased by the Mexican inns they encountered, but they shared the hardships with local travelers, and often recorded detailed descriptions of their Mexican companions, as did A.V. Kautz of his stagecoach party in 1868. For several days he listened and watched the interactions between a large Mexican family with several children, a local widow with an unhappy two-year old, a single gentleman from Spain, the drivers and cargo handlers, and, the only Americans on board, his companion and himself. Louise Palmer Heaven crossed northern Mexico in a wagon train with her husband and children in 1884 and enjoyed the gracious hospitality of northern ranchers who sent out messengers to welcome the travelers to their homes. John Finerty enjoyed his conversations with Mexicans of all classes, although he found it "rather awkward" to address the many with the unexpected name of Jesus.[20]

In contrast, the era of train travel ended the cooperative experience of travel and replaced it with the hierarchical framework of observer gazing upon the observed-—when they could find anyone to observe, of course. Physically limited to the narrow rail corridors, Americans traveled through areas in which not only the inhabitants but the regional lifestyle was hidden from view behind distant hacienda walls or in mountainous Indian villages. Undaunted, Americans replaced communication and interaction with Mexicans with unidirectional scrutiny of the limited material in their view. Charles Dudley Warner, watching villages flash by his window, asserted that "the favorite occupation of the men, clad in big hat, cotton trousers and ragged colored serape drawn about the shoulders, was to stand perfectly motionless, holding up some building." It would be interesting to know how village observers of the American tourists described the apparently favorite occupation of the seated passengers hurtling by, but there were few opportunities for interchange even when the trains did stop. On the train or at the inn Americans were increasingly likely to travel beneath the watchful eye of a professional guide and interaction or conversation with locals was unnecessary and often impossible. As Alden Case noted, if "one is on an American conducted train, with a few American passengers, what matters if he does not 'sabe' a dozen Spanish words?" Even travelers who did step out of the tourist track in later years adapted their itineraries to the location of resident American merchants and missionaries. Independent travelers like Flavel Tiffany, Charles Flandrau and Stanton Kirkham enjoyed greater exposure to the geography of Mexico, but the same isolation from Mexican life as they were passed from one American acquaintance to the next across the countryside. From the perspective of train-era travelers the rail carriages, hotels, and expatriate communities became not so much gateways to new horizons as islands of familiar culture in an alien wasteland.[21]

The new travel era was marked not only by a change in the travel experiences of Americans in Mexico, but in the objectives of travelers as well. Travelers to Mexico prior to 1884 were generally potential investors, missionaries or self-styled journalists. Although they were often surprised by the reality of Mexican conditions, their clearly defined roles provided a ready framework to guide their interaction with and responses to Mexico. In contrast, the ease of rail travel brought a new class of travelers to Mexico whose only explicit goal was a leisurely vacation. More Americans could contemplate a visit to Mexico, but with less motivation to learn from the encounter. Unfortunately the changing makeup of visitors was ill-suited to fulfill the objectives of the Porfirian promoters. The assiduous attention paid early travel groups, the suggested itineraries in government sponsored guides, and the clear continuation between government approaches to official visitors, like the AID delegation, Grant, and private travel excursions, revealed how Mexican leaders hoped to use tourism in their campaign to raise Mexico's international profile. It quickly became clear that however Mexican promoters might have hoped to frame the visit to Mexico; American travelers were driven by alternative aims. The pattern of travel that emerged in Mexico was neither an extrapolation of the AID model or a transposition of the European tradition; Americans in Mexico were creating a new model of travel, the escapist vacation.

Early rail travelers experimented with a variety of travel models before the new conventions of leisure travel emerged to guide American vacation behavior in Mexico. Initially, American pleasure travelers in Mexico did model their excursions after the European grand tour. The European comparison appealed in several ways to American tourists. For one, it was a familiar model (if not from experience, than from books or articles) and provided a ready conceptual framework to guide the travelers' activities and reactions. In Europe Americans visited cathedrals, art galleries and historic sites; in Mexico they could do the same. Visiting Governor of New Mexico L.A. Shelden's 1884 inventory of Mexican attractions neatly duplicated the building blocks of the classic Grand Tour: ruins of ancient civilizations, sites of momentous battles, legacies of Western civilization, beautiful mountain views, cosmopolitan people, artistic wares, and picturesque dress. Mexican-planned itineraries encouraged the grand tour model as well in the excursions arranged for the AID mission and promoted in later Mexican-written guides. The Mexican use of the grand tour model was not necessarily driven by the desire to place the nation within the European standard; the grand tour was simply the model of pleasure travel familiar to both nations.[22]

Certainly the grand tour model permeated travelers' written accounts of their journeys. First, the practice of maintaining a journal was a mannerism of grand tour behavior. Then, within the journal, European landscapes provided a standard, a vocabulary and a stance for evaluating Mexican scenery. On sighting Orizaba from the windows of the Veracruz train, Gray enthused, "It was a revelation of natural beauty. It was Switzerland beside Andalusia, Norway by the Delta, England and Italy side by side." Both Baker and Baxter described the pine-covered hills outside the capital as "alpine pastures" with their "alpine looking cottages." The travelers themselves completed the European metaphor. Traveling in what he thought was a remote Cuautla valley, Baxter was surprised to come across "a party of American tourists passing the time in placid ease, just as they might be encountered at a nice Swiss inn in some Alpine valley." Ford praised Veracruz as "a tropical Venice" and G.B. Cole endorsed a visit to Chapultepec castle by likening it to St. Peters in Rome. Ida Morris began her description of Mexico with a conventional allusion to "skies of Italian blue," but quickly abandoned the metaphor, although she clung to the overstated style of Victorian landscape descriptions. "The mountains unfold like a grand panorama," she began,

> groves of stately palmetto lift their plume like crests, swayed by the breeze the royal bloom of the wisteria hangs in great festoons from the trees to which cling brilliant orchids. Festoons of scarlet throated honeysuckles, and strange wild vines, conceal rugged brown rocks, or climb and climb, draping themselves in loops and festoons on tall trees.

Smith, who praised the snowcapped volcanoes atop the "silver lakes, [and] Tenochtitlán like a jewel in the midst of this vast stretch of green and gold," was obviously more comfortable in comparing Mexico to a treasure house, but his words are little different in spirit from less mercenary descriptions. Whether in comparing Mexican to European mountains or in subjecting Mexico to mercantile rhetoric, travelers inventoried the scenic wealth of Mexico for their readers at home.[23]

The European model and European allusions also had the advantage of elevating the American continent before the eyes of the world at a time when many were beginning to think of the hemisphere as a U.S. hinterland. Ballou chastised Americans for their ignorance of their neighbor, of which "the average American knows less than he does of France or Italy, but which rivals them in natural picturesqueness, and nearly equals them in historic interest." Blake agreed that thousands succumbed to sentimental "pilgrimages to the Old World," but, "when every allowance has been made, there still remains an unaccountable lack of curiosity and knowledge concerning that portion of the world which is essentially ours." The *Two Republics* had long maintained that Mexico was "not dissimilar to Europe" in its possession of intricate history and beautiful scenery, and deserving of more attention from the world beyond.[24]

European associations not only elevated the status of the continent, however, they elevated the status of the tourist. Through the proper style of travel, American tourists underlined their association with Anglophile, upper-class practices.[25] The European travel model had encouraged travelers to broaden their minds through study and refine their sensibilities through the contemplation of beauty, and early American travelers bound for Mexico pursued both enlightenment and prestige in their imitation of this Grand tour tradition. In the early years Americans prepared for their journey to Mexico with Prescott, Calderón de la Barca, or one of the recently published Mexican guides. During the evenings they gathered in their dining car for lantern slide shows and lectures. They studied the vegetation, the topography and the geology along with the artistic and architectural traditions of the Southern nation. They may have been traveling in Mexico, but they were playing out a European fantasy as well.

Educational travel not only allied Americans with the European vision of travel as self-improvement, but it allowed travelers to share in the European enthusiasm for exploration as they too pushed back the frontier of the unknown. Americans were quick to record the height of mountains, depth of mines, population of towns and pounds of produce as if the measurements themselves sufficed to tell the story. And, indeed, the measurements did offer a convenient frame of reference for readers and travelers alike. If the population of Toluca could be equated with that of a small American town, it relegated Toluca to a familiar category, leaving little impulse to investigate the history or economics of the Mexican town. The Paseo was one of many symbolic centers of the capital that was converted to numbers (an avenue three miles in length and two hundred feet in width, with seven great circles, each three hundred feet in diameter), leaving a portrait that communicated little of the vital social and cultural role the Paseo played in Mexican life. Marked rail distances further simplified the process. Travel writers seldom described Zacatecas in terms of its regional or national role in Mexico, but were content to note that it was 267 miles from Torreon, 439 from the City of Mexico, and, most importantly, 3,191 from New York. Baxter lightly (and incorrectly) dismissed the ruins of Teotihuacan as "the Aztec city at kilometer twenty-four."[26]

Not surprisingly, explicit echoes of the literary conventions permeating travelogues of European exploration in Africa and the Orient reappeared amid Americans accounts in Mexico. After all, Mexico was, in Crawford's words, "more foreign, indeed, to our Anglo-Saxon ideas and customs than any of the cultured countries of civilized Europe." Grand tour analogies may have been useful for guiding travelers' responses to cathedrals, art academies and landscape panoramas, but they offered little help in interpreting the ubiquitous discomforts of the road or the everyday encounters with the curious natives of Mexico. By framing their journeys in the tradition of Oriental and African explorations, however, Americans tamed the unsettling experience of traveling through an alien landscape by translating it into the conventions of another, more culturally familiar literary genre.[27]

Mexico, for example, was often depicted as America's own "orient" in American accounts. Bates wondered why "our painters go to Tangiers and the distant Orient for subjects," when all around her she found subjects fit for the artist. Maturin Ballou also summed up the attractions of Mexico in orientalist terms. "It has not the halo of Biblical legends to recommend it to us," he conceded, "yet Mexico is not lacking in numberless legends, poetic associations, and the charm of a tragic history quite as picturesque and absorbing as that of any portion of the East. Evans agreed that "everything recalls the scenes we have read of through Egypt and the East." Bates, waking up in Chihuahua, found it so strange "were I told we were in Palestine or Egypt, all about me would confirm it." McCollester likened his journey through Mexico to a cruise up the Nile to Thebes, while Albion Gray explained Mexico's appeal as "semi-oriental," a charm "only to be experienced in those fair and fatal Southern lands."[28]

Oriental allusions were hardly neutral, but rather were infused with racist condescension as they clearly revealed how closely Americans allied themselves not with their newly discovered neighbors, but with the European perspective on the non-European world. Idealized European behaviors set the standard not only in the esthetics of landscapes, architecture, and beauty, but in assumptions of behavior in public and private life. Creelman, for example, found Mexican descent from "Oriental blood" a ready explanation for the failure of democratic institutions. Crawford's equation of Mexican "orientalism" was less specific, but equally dismissive. "There is an oriental effect in much of the landscape," she wrote in a revealingly selective list, "in the primitive methods of husbandry, in the flowing garb of the people, and in the dashing ease in horsemanship; while the swarthy faces and piercing black eyes vividly recall the descriptions of the Egyptians and Bedouins of the Arabian deserts." Crawford even found the orientalist perspective a convenient way to distance herself from nearby misery as she noted that "The crowds of beggars that gathered around the train wherever we stopped, some of them horribly deformed or covered with leprous sores, also brought to mind the interesting book trip up the Nile that Warner has given us." On a lighter note, Sylvester Baxter suggested that travelers discomfited by the scanty clothing of the male Indians might imitate the example of his female friends in Egypt who "agreed among themselves to regard [the natives] as bronze statues, and after that they got along very comfortably."[29]

Organizational motifs of the African travel tradition, particularly the image of the Western explorer in the heart of the untamed wilderness, also reappeared in American accounts of Mexico. The conflict between physical and mental, instinct and reason, and savage and civilized carried over from the African accounts into discussions of Mexican-American encounters. Lone travelers in Mexico were the most likely to portray their journeys in terms of a heroic sojourn among the uncivilized, but even members of group tours found occasional moments in which to enjoy their encounter with the primitive.[30]

Many Americans found this opportunity to confront "savagery" in a visit to the bullfights in Mexico City. They fully expected to be disgusted and were seldom disappointed. Shelden found the whole scene "brutal" and left early. Evans admitted that the initial band music and processions were enthralling, but found the actual sport "mere torture and butchery." American tourists excused their attendance as necessary to their examination of the nation. "I went to the amphitheater not in any hopes of enjoying the spectacle," wrote Harrison, "but rather to study the conduct and bearing of an emotional race under pressure." Ballou, like many others, found proof of Spanish degeneracy in the show, commenting that "only among a semi-barbarous people and in a Roman Catholic country would such horrible cruelty be tolerated." Bates, who left in disgust after the first fight, was equally convinced that "No countries except Spanish countries could have this amusement."[31]

As early as 1881 the *Two Republics* commented on the American visitors' fascination with bullfighting, which, it perceptively noted, had come to stand for the "alpha and omega of all that is atrocious and wicked" in Mexico. In 1886 the same paper jokingly consoled the Raymond excursionists for their presumed disappointment when they did not witness "what they had been led to believe was the height of Mexican sport, namely, horses galloping about with their entrails hanging out and trailing on the ground." At the time the newspapers of Mexico City were hotly debating the recent government decision to legalize bullfighting in the capital, a sport which had been banned from the city for several years. While some papers defended bullfighting as a national sport, others agreed with the foreign visitors that it reflected badly on the Mexican population. Even more controversial was the proposal of an American entrepreneur to bring prize fighting to the city. The editor of the *Two Republics* agreed that bullfighting was objectionable, but pointed out that most Mexicans found American prize fights far more barbaric. Twenty years later traveler F.W. Grey encountered the same opinions, as he noted that Mexicans "think a boxing match a most brutalizing sport, yet they think bullfighting is elevating and can see absolutely no harm in it." Despite their protestations, American visitors were drawn to the bullfights and considered a description of the savage display and their predictable revulsion an indispensable part of their Mexican diary.[32]

Not every traveler attended a bullfight, but most visitors considered an experiment with pulque as intrinsic to the itinerary as the obligatory visit to the National Cathedral. Pulque, the fermented sap of the maguey cactus, was the humble beverage of Indian Mexico and all aspects of its production and consumption fascinated Americans. The distinctive maguey plant had come to symbolize Mexico to Americans entering the country from the north, just as the humble cantinas came to represent (to Americans) the failings of the Mexican working class. American travelers admitted that public drunkenness was far rarer in Mexico than at home, but they still blamed cantinas for corrupting morals and lamented the waste of land and labor devoted to the cultivation of an article of luxury and enslavement. Even though Americans invariably disliked the drink (Harding called pulque "the most atrocious beverage that ever man put into his stomach"), travelers recounted the visit to cantina or storefront, invariably undertaken under the watchful eye of a guide, as a thrilling brush with native Mexico. Blake was entranced by the names of cantinas (the "Flight of time," the "Tempest of love," the "Triumph of dynamite") but, like other travelers, disappointed by the beverage itself. It was, she concluded, the "sourest, thinnest, saddest means of reaching exhilaration that the mind of man has ever conceived."[33]

Americans also found the opportunity for an encounter with "savagery" in a gratuitous flirtation with the threat of banditry. Adolph Bandelier seemed to take perverse glee in writing home to his family of his dangerous travels over the "highly unsafe" roads of the sierra. Bandelier assured them that he carried no money, wielded a ready gun and "under no circumstances" accepted escort from an Indian or mestizo. Louise Palmer Heaven described her carriage where "rifles and shotguns guarded the doors, pistols were slung in all available corners, and cartouche boxes served for footstools." One of Ida Morris's companions flaunted her possession of a concealed stiletto, while

Evans travelled in a party where "even the ladies were well strapped with belts and colts under cover."[34]

In reality there was little danger to most Americans from bandits by the 1880s. The only time Bandelier was driven to defend himself was in an unexpected encounter with a wild steer, which "soon disappeared when I approached him with my gun." Alden Case had been so thoroughly frightened by rumors of bandits that he almost shot his hotel roommate one evening. Bishop, who explored "remote parts of Mexico," concluded that the "ordinary travelers run little if any more danger of robbery than at home." McCollester was relieved to find conditions in Mexico City no worse than those in Chicago, "or in Washington, where people are compelled to chain the door rugs to the steps and attach burglar alarms to the windows of their houses and stables."[35]

Yet banditry became a stereotype that American visitors prolonged in their contact with Mexico. The threat of danger added both romance and distinction to their odyssey. Members of Thomas Price's party had been warned of the danger of bandits before their diligence ride to Pachuca, and were amused when they recognized the voice of a galloping horseman, who shouted "your money or your lives," as that of a joking friend. Ida Morris described her first glimpse of robed Mexicans as "brigands, everyone, to our imagination." Helen Sanborn could not repress a shudder when confronted with "the villainous faces of those we met...in which the word *desperado* was plainly written." The Pennsylvania Railroad Company even promised prospective tourists a visit to Silao, once the home of "banditti" and still famous for the "daring deeds of the famed robbers." Aboard the Veracruz train Henry Bishop's attention was arrested by a "lawless and bizarre" figure in his coach. This turned out to be his "first view at close quarters of a dashing type of Mexican costume and aspect....Our new friend was dressed in a short black jacket under which showed a navy revolver, in a sash; tight pantaloons, adorned up and down with rows of silver coins; a great felt sombrero, bordered and encircled with silver braid; a red handkerchief knotted around his neck. A person in such a hat seemed capable of anything." In the end, the amiable young man (who was actually a local planter) let them all try on his hat and his "lawless" aspect.[36]

The craze for mountaineering best illustrates the eclectic mix of allusions Americans applied to their travel experience in Mexico. A European sport transplanted to the "Alps" of the new world, it glorified the American landscape while providing an encounter between the savage and the civilized. Physically, mountain climbing enjoyed a reputation as the consummate test of manhood, offering proof of one's personal fortitude in an age of increasing social interdependence. The visual experience was also vested with symbolism.

Climbers aspired to luxuriate in views enjoyed by no other, chasing enlightenment in the landscape. From their god-like vantage point climbers could trace
the geologic evolution of the region and the altitudinal effect on plant and
animal life. They could even evaluate the achievements of human civilization
upon the face of the earth, and place themselves literally above the horde.

Adolphe Bandelier was one of many travelers who climbed the volcano
Popocatépetl during this era, and he was explicit in justifying his ascent as an
educational and psychological quest. He was sure that this "test of strength"
would win him respect from the local Indian population whose assistance he
needed for his fieldwork. Unfortunately, the climb did not prove to be the em-
powering experience Bandelier sought. Bandelier was particularly incensed
by the guide, who climbed effortlessly ahead with no apparent concern for
his charge. Finally, Bandelier arrived at the snow line, where "sat our guide,
smiling like an idiot and drinking mescal. I could have choked the dog." During a later climb he made a similar complaint when he stated, "My Indians
left me wholly in the lurch as each one followed his own path without being
concerned in the least about me." Annoyed by their tendency to chase rabbits
or race ahead, Bandelier finally discharged his pistol to remind 'his' Indians
of their proper employment in attending his ascent.[37]

Despite Bandelier's vexing guides, he managed to enjoy the "wonderful
power which those masses exercise upon human beings. The great weirdness,
the mysteriousness in its majestic aspects, I have felt in my deepest soul."
The contrast between Bandelier's romantic encounter with the mountain and
his disdain for the mountain's inhabitants reappears in his description of the
sulphur mine operating inside the core of the volcano. "A regular business is
carried on," he noted without mentioning the human workers, "the sulphur
is broken, packed into sacks, and pulled up with a great windlass."[38] Bandelier apparently did not find the native Mexicans, who ascended the volcano
regularly without horses or assistants, carried their own provisions, and lived
for weeks at a time amidst the majestic mountain peaks, ennobled by the
experience.

Bandelier's account was perhaps one of the most explicitly self-centered,
but not particularly distinct from the many left by other American moun-
taineers in Mexico. In 1887 the *Two Republics* complained that "although
the peak of Popo has been ascended by hundreds of people, including quite
a number of ladies, nearly every person who makes the ascent writes out a
long account of it for the newspapers." The marketability of such accounts at-
tested to their popularity, but it was not the scenery of Mexico which seemed
to drive their appeal. Climbers like D.S. Richardson paid as much attention
to describing their own appearance on the ascent of the Volcano Popocate-
petl as the terrain through which they passed. Through Richardson's account

the reader shared in the exciting career of the explorer. "The sight of three white men on foot was a novelty sufficient to excite the curiosity, if not the suspicions of the natives whom we met," wrote Richardson, "even donkeys pricked up their ears in astonishment at the unusual apparition." At the centerpiece of the mountaineering accounts was the Western mountaineer, rarely the Mexican mountain.[39]

Americans also spent their travel time in the pursuit of more accessible scenery. Few traveled with camera or brush like the grand explorers they modeled themselves on, yet nearly all joined in the quest for visual souvenirs. Ida Morris described her travels as the process of "making pictures" for future remembrance. McCollester, on watching a cow kick its milkmaid, regretted that "our artist was not present to take a snapshot of them; it would have made a ludicrous picture." Baxter and Moran found "a picture at every step." The search for 'pictures' allied Americans once again with the British travel tradition as tourists searched the physical and human landscape for the picturesque and the sublime—Victorian catchwords for amusing regionalisms and the soul-transforming universal. 'Picture-making' revealed not only the landscape, but the values of the observer as it provided a testimony to their esthetic standards. Tourists recorded swarthy muleteers whose "costumes seemed borrowed from Carmen," wrinkled old crones washing clothes in streams, sleepy tiendas, and caballeros in broad sombreros. One writer scoffed at a companion who "searched out hundreds of subjects in several cities" in his quest to find the most photogenic string of pack mules. Americans even disrupted religious services in their quest to photograph the curiosities of Catholicism.[40]

Translating Mexico into pictures also helped Americans inure themselves against scenes of misfortune by dehumanizing the poor and reducing misery to merely another aspect of the landscape. In 1885 Arthur Spring noted that "There are many miles where nothing human is seen but wretched natives in small clusters of rude huts...But the scenery always has the merit of novelty; and the 'natives,' however squalid, are ever picturesque." Blake found the men, women and children "picturesque in rags and brilliant scarfs," while "the bronze skinned beggar dozing against some crumbling corner of a white adobe wall" lent additional appeal to the scene. On visiting the mines Crawford described the "dreadful feeling of oppression and fear of being buried alive" in the "windings of these subterranean labyrinths and corridors." Even so, she found it a "picturesque sight to see the long line of white garmented workers entering a cleft in the mountainside and disappearing from the light of day." Bates sighted beggars "in the most picturesque of parti-colored rags;" while Isaac Ford applauded beggars in Orizaba who were "in accord with their surroundings. The lowly beggar lying in a heap and mumbling for alms is in the right place under the crumbling church tower. The meek burro is at home in the crooked lanes and deep defiles." The beggar, the crumbling wall, the donkey, and the crooked lanes enjoyed equal status in the pictography of the American travel account.[41]

Those who eschewed photography found other diversions. Freed from lengthy struggles to negotiate passage and accommodation, many travelers devoted their new leisure hours to shopping. Blake was surprised at her accumulating treasure horde, which provided a virtual map of her travels. "You gather a pretty bit of pottery here," she explained, "a shilling vase there. You negotiate for a zarape at Leon, and a pair of coarse leather sandals at Zacatecas. You buy a broken idol at Cholula, a reboso at Silao, a basket at Guanajuato, an onyx paper weight at Puebla, a handful of opals at Queretaro. And of course, you get a Guadalajara water jar, some Aguas Calientes feather work, a cotton image at Chihuahua, a Guadelupe duck, and a living, breathing Mexican mocking-bird." While strolling through a cemetery, Frank Green's traveling companion was overwhelmed with the urge to carry off the skull of some "defunct Mexican....doubtless to show it to his admiring friends in Jersey City." Francis Smith, a self-proclaimed "tramp" traveler, belied his anti-materialist stance in a ruthless pursuit of objects. Entranced with the sight of an embroidered altar cloth and an antique priest's chair, he deceived the sellers into thinking that the purchases were meant as gifts for clergy back home, not decorations for his own apartments. Like Bandelier, he assumed that his esthetic refinement excused his highhanded behavior.[42]

The impulse to convert the experience in Mexico into a series of visual or physical tokens was not unexpected. Even today snapshots and souvenirs serve an emotional role in helping tourists to psychologically place themselves in the scene and garner trophy-like proofs of the journey. Yet the kinds of sights and souvenirs Americans sought out revealed that they had begun to deviate from the educational travel model that shaped earliest interactions with Mexico. In the 1890s travelers continued to gather in their Pullman cars for lectures on Mexico, but their attention and enthusiasm had shifted from the cathedrals to the flower vendors, urchins and mules in the foreground. Tourists wandered away from the uplifting itineraries planned by their guides as they sought out encounters with the Mexico of pulquerias and streetsweepers. "What a busy, bohemian like day that was!" recalled Mary Ashley Townsend, who presaged the new travel model as she roamed with her daughter through Mexico City in 1881. They visited the pawn shops, the match factories and the cigar makers, "with no guide save our own inclination."[43]

The new icons of the Mexican journey, the market places, the burros and the maguey, appeared in countless travelogues, replacing the older symbolic markers of the battlegrounds, cathedrals and ruins of past guides. This was the 'real' Mexico American tourists increasingly preferred to the orderly itinerary of convention. Tourists like Charles Dudley Warner were content to soak up the "animated spectacle" of the markets, where Indians, flowers, baskets, and pottery were listed in categorical style, with equal value to the dispassionate observer from the north. Finding beauty in the subject of the Mexican poor signaled no shift in cultural hierarchies however. "The sad pity of it," concluded Warner even as he basked in the charm of the local children was that they "will all grow up and become Mexicans."[44]

The fading interest in studying Mexico almost eliminated interest in historic Mexico. Tourists throughout the Porfiriato continued to carry copies of William Prescott's *Conquest of Mexico* tucked in their baggage, but over the years they ceased to regard the work as history and grew to regard it as romantic fiction, lending color to their vacation. The traveler attitude echoed in the scholarly world. In the 1880s the Morgan-Bandelier thesis reclassified the Aztec world from an empire to a "loose military confederation" and likened the palace of Montezuma to a "large joint-tenement house." Archaeological sites and treasures fared even worse. Isaac Ford suggested that two or three "protracted morning hours" in the National Museum would cure any zealous tourists of their fascination with the Aztec past. Bates studiously gazed upon the "hieroglyphs" of the Calendar Stone and gathered relics at the ruins in Tula, but found it hard to reconcile thoughts of the ancient past with the "sun-filled present."[45]

Bates did not even bother to visit Teotihuacan as he could glimpse the site from the windows of his train car. Train travel may have improved American access to remote Mexico, but it reduced the pre-Columbian heritage of Mexico to yet one more vignette in the rapidly passing landscape. As Flavel Tiffany recorded in his lecture on the rail route to Veracruz, "On the way are immense fields of cactus planted in regular rows across the country. On the left are some pyramids, or *teocalli*, of immense interest to archaeologists. The aloe plant is the staple product...." Harding paid a visit to Teotihuacan but did not bother to comment on the ancient site other than to note that he bought there a half-gallon of clay idols. Smith summed up the stance of those who opted to forego inquiry for intuition. After all, he reasoned, the sight of a pretty Indian girl in the sunlight near a lizard "told the whole story of Mexico."[46]

Travel accounts mirrored the diminishing interest in the facts of Mexico. The long chapters on the history and government that characterized earlier accounts were replaced by quaint descriptions of regional life and curious customs. Smith was explicit in describing his portrait of Mexico as an attempt to "present what would appeal to the painter and idler....I have watched the naked children at play and the patient peon at work, and the haughty hidalgo, armed and guarded, inspecting his plantation, and the dark skinned señorita with her lips pressed close to the confessional, and even the stealthy fugitive glance of the outlaw, without caring to analyze any of the many social and religious problems which make these conditions possible." Flandrau agreed completely. "Mexico," he wrote, "is one long, carelessly written but absorbing romance."[47]

The shift from educational to escape travel reflected the growing acceptability of leisure and vacation activities as respites rather than occasions for self improvement, but it was only made possible by the liminal situation of the traveler. Both the physical and psychological circumstances of vacation travelers placed them outside their normal roles and responsibilities. They were not burdened with the obligation of defending rational religious practices or American-style progress, but were free, temporarily, to indulge in the attractions of the primitive life. Ford, who traveled through Mexico investigating the potential for a U.S.-Mexican commercial union in 1893, epitomized the two distinct attitudes. In his professional capacity he insisted that "Civilization is doing a great work in that benighted land." Yet in his moments of leisure he sought out vistas "not despoiled of picturesque quaintness by modern innovation." Helen Sanborn worried that any modernization might cause Mexico to lose some of its attraction, "for the really appreciative traveler will prefer the grandeur of nature to the comforts of modern life, and the primitive characteristics of Mexico to the elegance of civilized society." Ballou also worried that "The next score of years, while they will probably do much for the country as regards commercial and intellectual improvement, will prove fatal in a degree to the picturesqueness which now renders Mexico so attractive." Gray condemned the poverty and indolence of the South, but admitted that Indian villages were refreshing to eyes fresh from the north precisely because they were "suggestive of everything but progress."[48]

Time in Mexico was a time out of both the march of history and the responsibilities of civilization. In 1909 Davis Stanton urged Americans to visit Mexico in order to "elude the commercial spirit altogether," for "surely there is need to-day of escaping now and again from the atmosphere of affairs, of hurry and worry, into one more genial and indolent where money is not everything." Wallace Gillpatrick traveled through northern Mexico with an aspiring American mining engineer, and battled his dueling emotions of pride in and pity for the boy's situation: "For him the purple distant mountains had no meaning, save that perhaps they concealed rich veins of ore. The clear, leaping streams were good for one thing alone – to turn a turbine wheel in an ore mill."[49] In Mexico the American tourist found a respite from the tensions of the "go-getter" identity they assumed at home, but only by preserving a firm division between their worlds of work and play.

Escape travelers even moderated their condemnation of Catholicism and poverty. While most visitors were willing to repeat old assumptions that Catholicism lay at the root of Mexico's problems (inhibiting political development, thwarting ambition and diverting wealth) and contributed little to spiritual growth, they were also delighted by the beauty of the rituals. Many, like McCollester, were attracted by the "ingrained religion" of the people and the air of devotion evident during Mass. Crawford was struck by the beauty of the angelus in Tula, where listeners in the streets and stores momentarily ceased their actions and bowed their heads. Gray's description of the church in Orizaba captured the American vacationers' ambivalence towards Catholicism. The church was "crumbling without, tawdry within, a brace of not-unhappy looking cripples at the door, and inside the usual assortment of mantillaed dames and mumbling beggars, a drowsiness and dreariness of both faith and climate investing the whole with a charm which no soul with any music can resist."[50]

One of the few travelers who professed outrage over the situation of the poor was a very young Nellie Bly, the pseudo-name of Elizabeth Cochrane, then of the Pittsburgh *Dispatch*. Having already acquired a local reputation as a champion of the working class, Bly persuaded her editor to let her, with mother along as chaperone, join the flow of tourists to Mexico in the spring of 1885. Twenty-one year old Bly found beauty, romance and antiquity in Mexico, but was horrified by the life of the peon. "As a people they do not seem malicious, quarrelsome, unkind, or evilly disposed," she noted, "Yet most of them live and die homeless, poor, uncared for, untaught." Bly faulted not only the Mexican elite, but the American travelers and residents who she considered notably stingy in sharing their good fortune with the servants and workers who surrounded them.[51]

Bly's pathos had been her trademark in the *Dispatch*, but her critiques of Mexico found no similar reception. At the outset of her journey Bly had received complimentary passes from the Mexican railroads, and assiduous attention from the Mexican and American officials she sought out, but as her writing cooled so did her Mexican welcome. Her articles from the *Dispatch* were recirculated and reprinted in Mexico, and after her explicit condemnation of the second Díaz regime as a virtual monarchy and a "republic in name only." Bly found her writing condemned in the capital's newspapers. When a threatening note appeared beneath her hotel door she decided it was a good time to return home.

Bly had a tendency to exaggerate when it came to depictions of the dangers she faced in her career and enjoyed portraying herself as the ingénue among rogues, so it is certainly reasonable to question how threatening her situation had truly become. True or not, the threats against Bly became a more important element of her storylines as the weeks passed, and revealed, once again, the romantic preferences of the American reader. Bly had set out for Mexico as if it were another neighborhood of Pittsburgh in need of exposure. She had ridiculed the "widows of the crankest type writing up Mexico, each expecting to become a second Humboldt and have their statues erected in the public square" and prided herself for endeavoring to compile a serious study of the nation. Yet when it became clear that neither Mexicans nor Americans were interested in descriptions of the miseries of the Mexican underclass Bly began to bolster her accounts with the staple portraits of bullfights, festivals and promenades along the Paseo. Americans did not want to read about Nellie Bly, the muckraker, abroad, but rather Nellie Bly, the adventurer. In the end it was not the pathos of the wretched poor that dominated her stories, but the daring of the American girl who hid her notes in her lingerie to thwart her Mexican censors. Mexico had been converted from an object of study to a stage set for American pluck.

Unlike Bly, most Americans in Mexico still blamed the poverty they saw on the characteristics of the peons themselves, not their situation, but within the new genre of travel literature these condemnations were increasingly tinged with envy. "Pleasure-loving" peasants were still critiqued for their lack of ambition, but they were also admired for their contentment. Addie McGrath comforted herself with the thought that because the poor "possessed nothing, they had nothing to fear." Baxter was convinced that the Mexican natives were better off than American workers, because "they are so ignorant that they have no idea of any other conditions," and because they were not plagued by jealousy like Americans. Morris agreed that the peon "easily earns all he needs, and he cares for no more." Bates found Mexico a "loafer's paradise," where even the beggars seemed to have "good muscles, healthy flesh, and a mildly happy look." And, of course, poverty was no hardship in "a country of perpetual Spring and Summer" where nature's abundance conspired to rob man of initiative. Baker was sure that the natives' "wonderful physical health" was, in fact, due to their simple life. If the women of the Mexican lower classes led a strenuous life, at least they did not suffer "from the special diseases which embitter the lives of their more civilized sisters." Nor did they "break down before thirty-five with nervous prostration." Sadly, while the tourist stereotype of the cheerful, healthy, and contented peasant may have made it easier to vacation amidst the poverty of the Mexican native, it was hardly accurate.[52]

By the end of the Porfiriato American vacation tourism was firmly established in Mexico. Americans wandered away from the galleries and cathedrals they had contemplated in the early 1880s to the pulquerias, the flower markets, and mule trains of Mexican villages. Within a few years the package tours of the twentieth century would follow the same route, abandoning the museums for the alleys, and eventually the beaches, of the 'real' Mexico. While Porfirian promoters could be content that travel in Mexico was no longer regarded as a perilous adventure (William Carson was only mildly surprised to encounter fifty widows from the American West enjoying a group tour of Mexico City in 1909, just down the street from hundreds of American shriners on convention in the southern capital) the increasing tourism had done little to improve American respect for the southern nation. Flandreau was horrified to find tourists requesting governors to pose for pictures, appropriating boy guides as if they were pets, and leaving orange peels on Cathedral pews.[53]

The new tourism had also changed the conventions of travel writing, dragging the armchair travelers back home away from the contemplation of history and along on the new escapist itineraries as well. The detailed descriptions of Mexican politics, economics and society that characterized early Porfirian-era accounts of Mexico gave way to cliché-ridden portraits of carefree, timeless Mexico, an appropriate backdrop for a pleasure vacation or a literary interlude. Travel writer Maturin Ballou described his 1889 excursion as a "holiday journey...an excursion into Aztec land, full of novel and uninterrupted enjoyment." Ida Morris termed Mexico the land of the "Lotus Eaters," while Captain C.H. Wilson fondly recalled his journey to the land of the "bygone Aztecs," "a free and easy, pleasure-loving race."[54] For their expert witnesses American travelers turned to the flower vendors and shopkeepers they could barely converse with, and away from the interpretations the Mexican promoters had been so eager to provide. The wonderland image of Mexico was hardly the progressive Mexico Porfirian Liberals had hoped to promote, but it was the Mexico that American tourists and readers wanted to find.

The history of American travel in Mexico revealed two struggles, one between nations to determine the itinerary and attitude of travelers within Mexico, the second within the minds of the Americans themselves. During the AID and the Grant visits Mexican promoters had proudly showcased the history, art, cultural heritage and progressive orientation of Mexico City as the centerpiece of the nation. The Mexican promotional objectives, however, clashed with the interests of vacationing visitors who staged their own encounters with Mexico, choosing entertainment and relaxation through superficial contacts over studious inquiry. For Americans like Isaac Ford, Mexico City lacked the "strong coloring of characteristic costumes and the quaintness of old time simplicity." Arthur Spring admired the cathedral and plaza of Chihuahua, but urged his readers to imitate his example and turn their attention to the costumes, markets, and children of Mexico. "After all," he reasoned, "the people are the chief object of interest."[55] Americans emphasized Mexican timelessness rather than Mexican history, Mexican primitive exoticism rather than Mexican civilization and the ubiquitous happy peasant rather than the hardworking citizen. The authentic Mexico sought by American visitors was increasingly found in the forgotten byways of sunny villages, not amidst the bustling streets or architectural jewels of the capital.

The failure of the Porfirian campaign is even more pronounced when contrasted with the pattern of American travel in Europe in the same era, where travelers modified the grand tour tradition only slightly as entire families embarked upon genteel tours of monuments and museums. While visitors would continue to approach European travel as an uplifting opportunity for study and personal improvement, the escape travel model that emerged in Mexico underlined and perpetuated the American belief that Mexico had little history or culture worth studying; her character could apparently be imbibed with the pulque and the sunshine. Europe was examined methodically, Mexico, in contrast, was to be experienced. The geographic divide in styles clearly illustrated the limits of American regard for Mexico.

Although American travelers to Mexico began as proud emissaries from the future, during the course of the Porfiriato they were increasingly likely to pose as temporary fugitives from modernity as well. This ambivalence toward the culture of progress reflected the second arena of struggle over the interpretation and ultimately played the greatest role in shaping American cultural relations with Mexico and other nations that became part of the new leisure horizon of the U.S. The liminal situation of the pleasure traveler, from both their own roles at home and the demands of their host's culture, granted travelers the freedom to indulge in a temporary revolt against their own professed values. The tourist guise permitted Americans an outlet for the nostalgia they felt toward a romanticized past and allowed them to claim a continuing connection with the primitive, but it never required them to abandon the advantages they enjoyed from their complicity in modern life.

The bifurcation of work and leisure realms that was then evolving in domestic American life echoed in the physical division of the world envisioned by the tourist: Americans studied Europe, they played in Mexico. Mexico, through the eyes of the traveler, could never be a sister nation of enterprise and republicanism, but merely a refuge for the endangered peoples of an industrializing world. In slipping off the beaten track, contemplating the sun-drenched gardens and exchanging smiles with passing Indians, Americans convinced themselves that there was no real choice for development but the frenzied life they led at home. While the Mexican wonderland had its own charms, it was incompatible with progress and the progressive identity Americans had chosen for their future. Yet, by escaping as individuals on sabbatical from their responsibilities at home, they could indulge in a fantasy of personal communion with "authentic" Mexico and convince themselves that they had not lost touch with their own primitive innocence in the rush for progress. In compartmentalizing their misgivings, however, Americans compartmentalized Mexico as well. The Mexico that American tourists sought was a land divorced from evolution, not a viable alternative model of social development.

In the end the emergence of American tourism in Mexico did little to improve American images of Mexico. It did not validate Mexico's existence as an autonomous, viable nation, but sentenced Mexico to play a static role in a primitivist American fantasy that stripped the nation both of its rich past and its potential for future change. American visitors and travel accounts rejected both the historic cathedrals promoted by the nation's leaders and the mines marketed by the financiers in their quest for the sleepy burros, picturesque beggars and colorful *pulquerias* that populated their fantasies. The condescension was more than insulting; it could be fatal for the survival of an independent Mexican nation. The Porfirian Liberals had pursued both contact with the American public and a reputation for progressivism as a means of increasing Mexico's international stature and providing increased security for the Mexican nation-state, but from the American tourist perspective any Mexican development only undermined her claim to sovereignty. Because American tourists saw only primitive Mexico as authentic, progress equaled Americanization in the American mind and only de-legitimized the nation. The "wonderland" image left Mexico only a narrow ledge of legitimacy in the American mind—once the 'authentic' Mexico of the burro in the village plaza disappeared, what would justify the continued existence of an autonomous state?

NOTES

1. The labels of "traveler" and "tourist" are used interchangeably in this chapter as it explores similar experiences of role playing and identity formation in both educational and vacation travel. Favorite studies of travel and identity include Dean MacCannell, *The Tourist: A New Theory of the Leisure Class* (New York: Schocken Books, 1976).Mary Louis Pratt, *Imperial Eyes: Travel Writing and Transculturation* (London: Routledge, 1992); David Spurr, *The Rhetoric of Empire: Colonial Discourse in Journalism, Travel Writing and Imperial Administration* (Durham: Duke University Press, 1993); John Urry, *The Tourist Gaze: Leisure and Travel in Contemporary Societies* (London: Sage, 1990); and Pierre Van den Berghe, *The Quest for the Other: Ethnic Tourism in San Cristobal, Mexico* (Seattle: University of Washington Press, 1994).

On the conventions of Victorian travel writing, see Ahmed Metwalli, "Americans Abroad: The Popular Art of Travel Writing in the Nineteenth Century," in *America: Exploration and Travel*, ed. Steven Kagle (Bowling Green: Popular Press, 1979), 68–82; and Alan Sillitoe, *Leading the Blind: A Century of Guidebook Travel, 1815–1914* (New York: MacMillan, 1998).

On American writing on Mexico, see Drewey Wayne Gunn, *American and British Writers in Mexico: 1556–1973* (Austin: University of Texas Press, 1973) as well as his bibliography, *Mexico in American and British Letters: A Bibliography of Fiction and Travel Books Citing Original Editions* (Metuchen, N.J.: Scarecrow Press, 1974); Garold Cole, "The Birth of Modern Mexico, 1867–1911: American Traveler's Perceptions," *North Dakota Quarterly* 45 (1977): 54–72; and Clinton H. Gardiner, "Foreign travelers Accounts of Mexico, 1810–1910," Americas, VIII (January 1952) 321–351.

2. Helpful discussions of this shift in travel models can be found in John Jakle, *The Tourist: Travel in Twentieth Century America* (Lincoln: University of Nebraska Press, 1985); John F. Sears, *Sacred Places: American Tourist Attractions in the Nineteenth Century* (New York: Oxford, 1989); and William Stowe, *Going Abroad: European Travel in Nineteenth Century American Culture* (Princeton: Princeton University Press, 1994).

3. The final spike of the intercontinental line was driven March 8, 1884 and the line opened to passenger traffic in April. *Two Republics*, 4 May 1884.

4. Gray, 19; Haven, 42; also Bishop, 24–25; and Henry C.R. Becher, *A Trip to Mexico: Being Notes of a Journey from Lake Erie to Lake Tezcuco and Back* (Toronto: Willing and Williamson, 1880), 8–17.

5. *Ferguson's Anecdotal Guide to Mexico, with a Map of the Railways: Historical, Geological, Archaeological and Critical* (Philadelphia: Claxton, Remsen, and Haffelfinger, 1876); also George Canady Harding, "Pencil Notes of a Brief Trip to Mexico," in *The Miscellaneous Writings of George Canady Harding* (Indianapolis: Carlton and Hollenbeck, 1882), 26–29; A.V. Kautz, "Notes of Travel in Mexico," *California and Overland Monthly* (April 1883) 397; *Two Republics*, 20 March 1881.

6. "The Commercial Expedition to Mexico," *Frank Leslie's Illustrated Weekly*, 15 February 1879, 430–1; Helen Josephine Sanborn, *A Winter in Central American and Mexico* (Boston: Lee & Shepard, 1886), 224–5.

7. Gilbert S. Haven, *Our Next Door Neighbor: A Winter in Mexico* (New York: Harper, 1875), 69; Mary Hallock Foote, "A Diligence Journey in Mexico," *Century Magazine*, November 1881, 1–15; Gustavo Adolfo Baz, *Historia del Ferrocarril Mexicano* (1874; reprint, Mexico: Cosmos, 1977), 8–10.

8. A.V. Kautz, "Notes of Travel in Mexico," *California and Overland Monthly* (April 1883) 398; Col. Brantz Mayer, "The City of Mexico," *Frank Leslie's Popular Monthly* (February 1878), 146.

9. Finerty, 225–6, 250; Bates, 29; Adolph Bandelier, *A Scientist on the Trail: Travel Letters, 1880–81*, George Hammond, ed. (Berkeley: Quivira Society, 1949), 118.

10. Finerty, 316; Gray, 26; Felix Oswald, *Summerland Sketches: Rambles in the Backwoods of Mexico and Central America* (Philadelphia: J.B.Lippincott, 1880), passim. For other pre-railway accounts of travel in the north, see Rev. J. Hendrickson McCarthy, *Two Thousand Miles through the Heart of Mexico* (New York: Phillips & Hunt, 1886); and H.H. Jackson, "By Horsecars into Mexico," *Atlantic Monthly*, March 1883, 351–366.

11. In the 1970s the Iturbide Palace was converted into a museum and cultural center by Banamex, the National Bank of Mexico. For contemporary accounts see Maturin Ballou, *Aztec Land* (Boston: Houghton Mifflin, 1890), 176–8; Mary Elizabeth Blake and Margaret Francis Buchanan Sullivan, *Mexico: Picturesque, Political and Progressive* (Boston: Lee and Shepard, 1886) 64–7, Finerty, 253; "The Prospective American Influx," *Two Republics*, 19 June 1881; and Thomas A. Janvier, *The Mexican Guide* (New York: Charles Scribners, 1890), 103.

12. *Two Republics*, 10 February, 12 March, 5 and 17 April 1885.

13. Blake and Sullivan, 26; other accounts of early Raymond Excursion trips include Arthur L. Spring, *Beyond the Rio Grande* (Boston: J.S. Adams, 1886); Frederick Ober, *Travels in Mexico and Life Among the Mexicans* (Boston: Estes and Lauriat, 1884); and the *Two Republics*, 18 March 1885. On rail tourism social dynamics, see Sarah Herbert Gordon, "A Society of Passengers: Rail Travel, 1865–1910," (Ph.D. dissertation, University of Chicago, 1950).

14. Blake and Sullivan, 25–26; Bates, 102; Spring, *Beyond*, 25. Later travelers expressed similar sentiments, see Sullivan Holman McCollester, *Mexico Old and New: A Wonderland* (Boston: Gardiner, 1899); and Ballou, iv.

15. Early guides illustrate the Veracruz-Mexico City focus, see Ireneo Paz and Manuel Tornel, *Nueva Guia de México: en Ingles, Frances, y Castellano* (Mexico: Imp. de. I. Paz, 1882); Frederick Ober, *Mexican Resources: A Guide to and through Mexico* (Boston: Estes and Lauriat, 1884); Benito Nichols, *Nichol's Guide to Mexico: Commercial and Official Guide of the Republic of Mexico* (Mexico: B. Nichols, 1884); Alfred R. Conkling, *Appleton's Guide to Mexico: Including a Chapter on Guatemala, and a Complete English Spanish Vocabulary* (New York: D. Appleton and Co., 1883); Leonidas Hamilton, *Hamilton's Mexican Handbook: A Complete Description of the Republic of Mexico* (Boston: Lothrop & Co., 1883); Thomas A. Janvier, *The Mexican Guide* (New York: Charles Scribners and Sons, 1886); *Ferguson's Anecdotal Guide to Mexico, with a map of the Railways: Historical Geological, Archaeological and Critical* (Philadelphia: Claxton, Remsen, and Haffelfinger, 1876); "A Few Attractions of Mexico," *Two Republics*, 20 March 1881; and Vincent G. Manero, *Guide for Mexico* (Mexico City: Tip. Gonzalo Estevez, 1878).

16. Pennsylvania Railroad Company, *Pennsylvania Tour to Mexico: Affording Four Weeks in the Land of the Aztecs* (Philadelphia: Allen, Carr and Scott, 1891), 17–30; also see [Ferrocarriles Nacional] *Mexico from Border to Capital: A Brief Description of the many interesting places to be seen en route to Mexico City via the Laredo, The Eagle Pass, and the El Paso Gateways*, (Mexico City: Ferrocarriles Nacional, n.d., [c1914]).

17. Sylvester Baxter, *The Cruise of a Land Yacht* (Boston: Author's Mutual, 1891), 83; Blake and Sullivan, 9; Sullivan Holman McCollester, *Mexico Old and New: A Wonderland* (Boston: Gardiner, 1899) 8; Captain C.H. Wilson, "Through Mexico in a Private Car," *Frank Leslie's Popular Monthly*, April 1899, 639; Nevin O. Winter, *Mexico and her People of Today* (Boston: L.C. Page, 1907). 267.

18. Adolph Francis Bandelier, *A Scientist on the Trail: Travel Letters of A.F. Bandelier, 1880–81*, eds. George P. Hammond and Edgar F. Goad (Berkeley: The Quivira Society, 1949; reprint New York: Arno Press, 1967), 66–67.

19. T.B. Evans, *From Geneva to Mexico: A Record of a Tour through the Western Part of the U.S. and the Greater Part of Old Mexico*, (Geneva, Ill.: Geneva Republican, 1893), 40–41.

20. A.V. Kautz, Notes of Travel to Mexico," *California and Overland Monthly* (April 1883) 398; Louise Palmer Heaven, "Nine Days Travel in Mexico," *Overland Monthly* (September 1884) 224–235; Finerty, 253.

21. Charles Dudley Warner, "Mexican Notes," *Harpers Magazine* (April 1887) 803; Case, 24.

22. Shelden, 21–2; Janvier, *The Mexican Guide*, 1886, Antonio Garcia Cubas, *Album del Ferrocaril Mexicana*, 1877; Nichols, *Nichols Guide to Mexico*, 1884; Manero, *Guide for Mexico*, 1878; James Joseph Fitzgerrell, *Fitzgerrell's Guide to Mexico* 3rd. ed., (México: Imp. de la Secretaría de Fomento, 1906).

23. Gray, 30; Baker, 111; Baxter, *Cruise*, 183; Baxter, "A Plunge," 314; Isaac Ford, *Tropical America* (New York: Scribners, 1893), 3; and G.B. Cole, "An Old Imperial Residence, Castle Chapultepec, in Mexico," *Overland Monthly and Out West Magazine*, (April 1885) 379; Ida Dorman Morris, *A Tour in Mexico* (New York: Abbey, 1902), 10, 72; Francis H. Smith, *A White Umbrella in Mexico* (Boston: Houghton Mifflin, 1889), 119.

24. Ballou, 1; Blake and Sullivan, 7–8; *Two Republics*, 16 February 1884.

25. On Victorian visions of travel and historical study, see Daniel Walker Howe, "American Victorianism as a Culture," *American Quarterly* 27 (December 1975): 507–32; and Peter Bowler, *The Invention of Progress: The Victorians and the Past* (Oxford: Basil Blackwell, 1989).

26. Blake and Sullivan, 71; Robert Barrett, *Modern Mexico's Standard Guide to the City of Mexico and Vicinity* 3rd. ed., (New York: Modern Mexico, 1903); *Pennsylvania Tour*, 30; Baxter, *Cruise*, 242; Bates, 88; Harding, 61.

27. On the Africanist and Orientalist travel models, see Edward Said, *Orientalism* (New York: Pantheon, 1978); Catherine Barnes Stevenson, *Victorian Women Travel Writers in Africa* (Boston: G.K. Hall, 1982); and Shirley Foster, *Across New Worlds: Nineteenth Century Women travelers and Their Writings* (London: Harvesters Wheatsheaf, 1990); Crawford, 1.

28. Bates, 21–2; Ballou, 7. Some writers even argued that the Mexican ruins were clear evidence of Eastern activity in the Americas. See McCollester, 208; and Channing Arnold and Frederick J. Tabor Frost, *The American Egypt: A Record of Travel in Yucatan* (London: Hutchinson, 1909); [5] T.B. Evans, 44; Bates, 15; McCollester, 32; Gray, 21.

29. Crawford, 25, 41; Sylvester Baxter, "A Mexican Vacation Week*,"* *Atlantic Monthly*, (July 1885) 47.

30. The theme of the "heroic encounter with the wilderness" was popular in contemporary domestic literature as well. See Richard Slotkin, *The Fatal Environment: The Myth of the Frontier in the Age of Industrialization, 1800–1890* (New York: Athenaeum, 1985).

31. Shelden, 17; T.B.Evans, 67; William Richard Harris, *Days and Nights in the Tropics* (Toronto: Morang and Co., 1905) 122; Ballou, 182; Bates, 84.

32. *Two Republics*, 8 May 1881; *Two Republics*, 9 March 1886; *Two Republics*, 23 April 1886. On the plan to bring prizefighting to Mexico, see Schell, *Integral Outsiders*, 40–41; F.W. Grey, *Seeking Fortune in America* (London: Smith, Elder, 1912), 220.

33. Ballou, 192, Becher, 42; Harding, 58–59, 112; Blake and Sullivan, 56, 94.

34. Bandelier, 97–98; Louise Palmer Heaven, "Nine Days Travel in Mexico," *Overland Monthly* (Sept. 1884) 224; Morris, 42; T.B. Evans, 40.

35. Bandelier, 103; Case, 75; Bishop, 90–92; McCollester, 81.

36. Thomas W. Price, *Notes of a Plain Businessman: Originally Published as Letters in the Hartford Churchmen* (Hartford, Conn.: n.p. 1878), 42–3; Morris, 41; Sanborn, 226, 228; Pennsylvania Railroad Company, 33; Bishop, 26–7.

37. Bandelier, 82–3, 87, 105.

38. Ibid., 88–90.

39. *Two Republics*, 19 May 1887; D.S. Richardson, "Two Nights in a Crater," *Overland Monthly and Out West Magazine*, (March, 1888) 308–309.

40. Morris, 93; McCollester, 42; Baxter, *Cruise*, 212; Blake and Sullivan, 11; Price, 84; Grey, 222. On Victorian landscape esthetics, see Beth L. Lueck, *American Writers and the Picturesque Tour: The Search for National Identity, 1790–1860* (New York: Garland, 1997).

41. Spring, *Beyond the Rio Grande*, 16; Blake and Sullivan, 20, 38; Crawford, 83, 91; Bates, 222–3; Ford, 248.

42. Blake and Sullivan, 128; Frank W. Green, *Notes on New York, San Francisco and Old Mexico* (Wakefield, England: E. Carr, 1886); Smith, 25, 81, 98–9.

43. Mary Ashley Townsend. *Here and There in Mexico: The Travel Writing of Mary Ashley Townsend.* Ed. Ralph Lee Woodward, Jr. (Tuscaloosa: University of Alabama Press, 2001), 241.

44. Charles Dudley Warner, "Mexican Notes," *Harper's Magazine*, (June 1887) 27.

45. Ford, 322, 307, 293; Bates, 54–55. Popular American loss of interest in Prescott echoed the scholarly world's demotion of the Aztecs. See Benjamin Keen, "Montezuma's Dinner," in *The Aztec Image in Western Thought* (New Brunswick: Rutgers University Press, 1971), 380–410; and Johannson, *To the Halls of Montezuma*, 154–160.

46. Flavel B. Tiffany, *Land of the Aztecs* (Kansas City: Franklin Hudson, 1909) 36, 88; Harding, 61; Smith, 109–110.

47. Smith, 1–2; Flandrau, 22.

48. Ford, 298, 322; Sanborn, 250; Ballou, 36; Gray, 63.

49. Stanton Davis Kirkham, *Mexican Trails: A Record of Travel in Mexico, 1904–07, and a Glimpse of the life of the Mexican Indian* (New York: G.P. Putnam, 1909), v-vi; Wallace Gillpatrick. *Wandering in Mexico* (London: Evelyn Nash, 1912) 21.

50. Shelden, 14; McCollester, 57, 77; Ballou, 187; Crawford, 146–7; Gray, 32.

51. The *Dispatch* articles were compiled as *Six Months in Mexico, by Nellie Bly*, [Elizabeth Cochrane], (New York: Munro, 1888). Also see Mignon Rittenhouse, *The Amazing Nellie Bly* (New York: E.P. Dutton, 1971) 39–49; and Brooke Kroeger, *Nellie Bly: Daredevil, Reporter, Feminist* (New York: Times Books, 1994).

52. Addie McGrath, in Thomas, *Journalists Letters.* 89; Baxter, *Cruise,* 118; Morris, 79–80; also Ford, 330; Bates, 23; also "Plenty Without Wealth," *New York Times*, 18 May 1884; Anonymous, in Thomas, 95; Baker, 67; Harding, 113–4; Blake and Sullivan, 89.

53. Carson, 336; Flandreau, 227–229.

54. Ballou, iv; Morris, 1–2; C.H. Wilson, "Through Mexico in a Private Car," *Frank Leslie's Popular Monthly*, April 1899, 640.

55. Ford, 304; Spring, 10.

Chapter Seven

Minerals and Aztec Villages: Mexico on the American Fairground

In 1885 the Mexican government mounted a lavish display at the New Orleans Cotton Centennial as part of its public relations strategy to improve American knowledge of Mexico. International expositions were the most prominent arena for publicizing new products and producers and celebrating the advance of human civilization in the late nineteenth and early twentieth centuries, and the Mexican organizing committees were eager to array Mexico's wealth "before the eyes of the entire world." Despite mounting a lavish display, the fair failed to fulfill the Díaz administration's goal of gaining international respect for Mexico's history, culture and people. Although Mexico participated in later American fairs, hosting popular exhibits at the 1893 Columbian Exposition in Chicago, the 1901 Pan American Exposition in Buffalo, and the 1904 World's Fair in St. Louis, the Cotton Centennial proved an anomaly. Mexico's U.S. exhibits never again matched the scale or complexity of the display at New Orleans, reflecting Porfirian disillusion with the American venue after 1885.[1]

Ironically, despite the Mexican government's reduced interest in participation, in the years following 1885 Mexican and other "Latin" exhibits grew in popularity with American audiences.[2] Their popularity, however, signaled the failure, not the triumph of the original Porfirian objectives. For the fairground, like the tourist industry, was a consumer driven venue and not an easily controlled medium for transmitting information. Despite the best efforts of Mexican promoters to frame material in accord with their national objectives, they could not control which images of Mexico were preferred by viewers. The preference among American fairgoers for simplistic and romantic images of primitive Mexico inexorably altered the displays on Mexico at fairs, encouraging profit seeking exhibitors and marketers to shape their own "Latin" corners for visitors. Ultimately, the image of Mexico that

American audiences sought out on the fairground was not the progressive Mexico once promoted by the Porfirian leadership, but the romantic, carefree Mexico of their dreams. The history of Mexico's participation in international exhibitions in the U.S., the disappointing American response to the Porfirian overtures and the emergence of an alternative image of Mexico within the fair illustrates yet another aspect of the competing cultural visions of Mexico within the two nations in the new international era.

Mexico contributed to fairs in Europe in 1851, 1855, and 1867, but the 1876 Centennial Fair in Philadelphia marked the first time the President's cabinet devoted sustained attention to planning Mexico's displays abroad. The Mexican display was planned prior to the coup that brought Díaz to power, but the experience at this fair foreshadowed later Porfirian policy, showing continuity in both objectives and personnel. Mexico, according to U.S. Foreign Minister John Foster, had been "greatly pleased" at the invitation to participate in the Philadelphia Centennial and instantly accepted. Gabriel Mancera, one of the principal Mexican exhibit organizers, saw the Centennial as a chance to help demolish the "countless mistakes and the incomprehensible preoccupations that the American people...hold toward Mexico." The Mexican government selected representative archaeological treasures, commissioned artisans to produce examples of Mexican furniture, textiles, metalwork and other manufactures, gathered samples of Mexican minerals and gems and shipped 123 paintings, 145 photos and 124 sculptures from both public and private collections to Philadelphia. Although Mexico was not one of the largest foreign exhibitors, it was respectably represented.[3]

Between May and November of 1876 over ten million people, an estimated twenty percent of the American population, visited the fairgrounds in Philadelphia. The opportunity for publicizing Mexico among the American people was great, but guides and reviews of the Centennial exhibits suggest that few Americans were impressed with the Mexican displays. Frank Norton's *Illustrated Historical Register of the Centennial Exposition* dismissed the Mexican collection as "bits of pottery, shoes, hats, wines, wood and tobacco." J.S. Ingram examined the archaeological material and concluded that the items were "perhaps interesting to ethnologists, but to us we confess they were not particularly attractive." The "Special Catalogue" for the Mexican section (privately written by Philadelphia entrepreneurs for sale at the fair) included little discussion of the actual items, but numerous critiques of Mexican history. It lamented the evidence of Spanish influence on Mexico and faulted the exhibit for lacking the organization necessary to educate Americans on Mexico's struggle for "civilization and progress." Frank Norton agreed. The exhibit, he noted, "is not of a collective system, or official character, neither has it a historical aspect, by means of which might have been presented in progressive series the relics of the Aztec civilization, the state of the national industry, when the country accomplished its independence, and its present products and manufacturers."[4]

The comments suggest that reviewers preferred displays that followed familiar evolutionary trajectories depicting a nation triumphing over the Indian and Spanish influences of the past. As it was, the only Mexican display at Philadelphia that garnered consistent praise was the collection of national minerals and gems. Commentators who struggled to describe their reaction to the work of Mexican artisans and artists raved effortlessly over the samples of lead, iron, tin, copper and coal, and were particularly captivated by a four thousand pound silver nugget. Unfortunately, the enthusiasm missed the point of the exhibit from the Mexican perspective. The mineral display was one of several exhibits designed to raise the profile of Mexican commerce in the U.S., but the tone of American discussion emphasized instead the opportunities for Americans in Mexico. *The Centennial Exposition* offered little comment on the displays of Mexican manufactured goods other than to report on wages and note that Mexican production was insufficient to meet local demand. Reviewers mistakenly asserted that Mexican manufacturers had been uninterested in participating in the fair, compounding the impression that Mexico was bereft of forward-looking producers. Detailed discussions of Mexico's natural resource potential, wage costs, land prices, laws and available production technology suggested that Americans' fascination with the possibilities of exploiting Mexican labor and resources blinded them to the Liberals attempt to showcase Mexican abilities.[5]

Mexico's reception at the Centennial was disappointing but valuable nonetheless. It exposed Mexican representatives to some of the problematic patterns that would recur in U.S.-Mexican cultural relations, particularly the tendency of Americans to focus on markets for American investments and exports rather than the marketability of Mexican production, and may have suggested the tack Zamacona would later take in his strategy to win recognition of the Díaz regime. The 1876 Centennial also provided Mexican organizers with the opportunity to observe the difficulties Americans encountered in confronting the complexities of Mexican culture and history. The guide to Mexico prepared for Philadelphia by geographer Antonio Garcia Cubas presaged many of the themes developed in the later "sister republics" campaign in its treatment of the geography, habits and character of Mexico and the Mexicans. The Philadelphia experience was particularly important for at least three members of the original 1876 commission—Manuel Zamacona, Gabriel Mancera and Manuel Romero Rubio—who enjoyed long careers in the Díaz administration and were influential in organizing future promotional campaigns. Finally, the Philadelphia fair also inspired Mexican visitors. One of these, Carlos Zaremba, recalled his experience in Philadelphia as he later attempted to convince New York investors and Washington diplomats to support an international fair in Mexico City in 1892.[6]

In 1884, eight years after the Philadelphia Centennial, the Mexican government committed itself to sponsoring a lavish display at the New Orleans Industrial and Cotton Centennial Exposition. Díaz took a personal interest in the representation of Mexico at the fair, initiating a pattern that would be repeated throughout his regime. He issued a national appeal encouraging regional artisans to dedicate themselves to creating fine samples of Mexican workmanship. He invited manufacturers to collect their best products and personally solicited special contributions from prominent citizens. Díaz became involved in even the smallest details of the exhibit. He personally wrote Jaime Torres to request him to allow ten magueys on his ranch to flower (ruining their production of pulque) before donating them for the "glory of Mexico" in New Orleans. Díaz charged the Secretaría de Fomento with the task of surveying the different Mexican states to compile geographic data and make recommendations for the content of exhibits. Finally, he urged the Mexican rail and steam lines to offer special fares for passengers travelling to the exhibit and free shipment of materials to the fair.[7]

Preparations for the fair received wide coverage in Mexico. National newspapers published letters from commissioners and representatives describing the 250,000 square foot space allotted to Mexico at the fair (the Mexican display in Philadelphia had occupied only 5,000 square feet) and the additional areas reserved in four of the five main exhibition halls. Drawings of the proposed mineral pavilion, manufacturers building and bandstand accompanied descriptions of the five-acre tropical garden. Mexican papers reported on the state contests to select the finest examples of metallurgy, industry and art for display as well as the horticultural collection that would landscape the fairgrounds.[8]

The New Orleans Centennial provided Mexicans with an opportunity for taking stock of their nation at a moment when Mexico, replete with new railroad links to the north, appeared poised at the brink of engagement with the world beyond. The official organizing committee noted the heavy responsibility of studying "the diverse fields of human knowledge, the enterprises of transport by sea or by land, the press, the producers, the merchants, and the artist, and all those hardworking, useful and wise men of many nationalities who populate our land...." It praised the government for "raising, before the eyes of the entire world, the image of Mexico to the height that its virtues, its riches, and its glories deserve in the grand hierarchy of civilized nations." The Secretaría de Fomento commissioned a four hundred page survey of Mexican resources and geography for distribution to American fairgoers, noting that "None of the civilized nations that populate the globe is less known, nor with less accuracy judged by others than our own." The Secretaría de Fomento also seized the occasion of the fair to publish a seven hundred page survey of

Mexican mining practices and laws, and an equally detailed survey of commercial agriculture in Mexico. The Agricultural Committee noted that, despite the natural abundance and variety of Mexican production, "our agricultural wealth is little understood by foreign nations." The committee expected the abundant samples of "fibrous plants, aromatic herbs, juicy fruits, [and] elastic canes" to convince Americans of "the fertility, fecundity, and richness of Mexican soil." The editor of the *Two Republics* angrily denounced a North American journalist who had assumed that the Mexicans would have little of their own work to display. "The useful products," the northerner had written, "will probably be chiefly confined to those which have been evolved on Mexican soil by Yankee and German enterprise." The New Orleans exhibit, editor Clarke retorted, would prove once and for all to the American people that Mexico did "amount to something."[9]

As the excitement mounted in the final months of 1884, the *Two Republics* reported on the special trains carrying the displays to New Orleans. Throughout twenty states, the correspondent noted, "all along the route of the Mexican Central are loaded cars awaiting to be attached to this special." On the cow-catcher of the lead car the engineers had mounted a pedestal, adorned with "scientific, artistic and industrial objects, [and] crowned with a handsome statuette representing 'progress.'" The engine itself was buried under the entwined banners of the U.S. and Mexico. In the following cars the journey was made festive by the music of the orchestra, whose members clad themselves in the indisputably Mexican "charro" costume. Next passed cars crowded with the waving fronds of tropical and temperate plants gathered from all regions of Mexico and accompanied by "capable and competent gardeners," cages of exotic animals and birds, and, finally, a flat car with mounted cannon and an artillery guard. A steamer gathered additional exhibits from Veracruz, Tuxpan and Tampico. Over the following weeks the exhibit was supplemented with two hundred members of the Rurales cavalry force, bulls, bullfighters and a variety of Mexican dance companies.[10]

The imposing exhibit proved the commitment of the Díaz administration to promoting Mexico abroad, just as it revealed a proud vision of the Mexican national identity. The Díaz administration did not choose a European-style orchestra to represent Mexico, but rather an "orquesta típica," which played Mexican airs on Mexican instruments accompanied by regional dance demonstrations. The architectural design of the Mexican exhibition halls also revealed confidence in the national heritage. Although the iron frame of the metallurgy pavilion was assembled in Pittsburgh, Díaz dispatched Mexican artisans to Pittsburgh to execute the "Moorish palace" designs. The residence for the cavalry and band members had been designed to resemble a colonial hacienda.

The Mexican exhibits also reflected diverse segments of the society as fine European-style lace work was displayed alongside Indian weaving, chemicals alongside medicinal plants and railroad and telegraph atlases alongside pre-Columbian antiquities. More than one hundred wax figurines illustrated the many races, Indian nations, classes and professions of the Mexican republic. "Coppery" tinted vaqueros and peons appeared beside olive-skinned señoritas. Water carriers, tortilla makers, soldiers, burro drivers, woodcutters and bull fighters appeared in miniature, carved in wax and dressed with exquisite attention to detail. As the Mexican Organizing Committee proudly noted, Mexico was a product of "all those hardworking, useful and wise men of many nationalities" who populated its soil.[11]

Unfortunately, the underfunded and poorly planned Cotton Centennial was a financial and organizational disaster. Months behind schedule, it finally opened on the eve of the hot and humid yellow fever season of 1885 rather than the cool autumn months of 1884. The polished Mexican exhibit, however, provided a welcome contrast to the general confusion. Mexico was "at the head of all the foreign countries," wrote Eugene Smalley for *Century* magazine. In sheer size the Mexican display dwarfed other presentations, even those of the American states. The Mexican exhibits alone occupied seventy-six of the two hundred forty-nine acres of the fairgrounds. Americans crowded the counters where "rare and curious things" from the neighboring republic were displayed. The archaeological exhibits were sure to "engross the attention of scholarly visitors," wrote Lafcadio Hearn for *Harpers Weekly*, especially those "interested in the question of Egypt in America." Other visitors gathered to see the finely worked metals and woods, embroidered cloths, leatherwork and pottery, which shared space with busts of prominent historical figures and samples of Mexican religious art. The agricultural committee displayed samples of sugar cane, cotton, silk and chocolate, sixty specimens of dyewood, and three hundred eighty-nine varieties of coffee beans. Manufacturing displays included furniture, inlaid wood, marble, liqueurs, medicines and textiles. There were also exhibits on the science, armaments, stamps, maps, uniforms, lithographs, and history of Mexico.[12]

Many of the Mexican exhibits invited participation. The Mexican band, with its ornate national costume, provided "magnificent music" and was wildly applauded. The band members were even invited to join Jefferson Davis in greeting the arrival of the Liberty Bell at the New Orleans train station, where they pleased the crowd with a Mexican rendition of "Dixie." Fair visitors sampled Mexican hot chocolate (the "special treat of the ancient Aztecs" noted its vendor) while wandering the paths of the Mexican tropical garden. Throughout the course of the centennial the Mexican Commission organized special feast day celebrations when bullfights, regional dances, and cavalry movements amused the fairgoers.[13]

Although the Mexican exhibits proved popular with American fairgoers, New Orleans did not set a pattern for future Mexican participation in

American fairs. In the years following the Cotton Centennial, the Mexican government pursued trade and investment promotion through alternate channels, including the Secretaría de Fomento, professional diplomatic staff and Mexican trade clubs. Mexico continued to send popular gem and mineral displays to fairs along with art and archaeological treasures, but the Porfirian administration never again mounted an exhibit in the U.S. the size or scope of that dedicated to the Cotton Centennial.

The decision to pursue more specialized communication strategies reflected the Porfirian administration's frustration with the outcome of the fair as a vehicle for national publicity. Mexico had endeavored to convince Americans of its commitment to progress, but neither the Mexican-owned steamship anchored by the fairgrounds nor the model of the proposed Tehuantepec rail/sea line inspired the interest that the colorful Rurales provoked. The New Orleans *Times Picayune* admitted that contemporary Mexico was "in line with modern progress," yet according to the writer the authors of that progress were not the Mexican people, but the railways. "Railways," the *Picayune* noted, "penetrate her wonderful valleys, teeming with the populace of the tropics, blooming and fruited like the gardens of paradise, and the locomotive with its train of palace cars climbs over or pushes its way through the titanic mountain walls in whose hearts are treasure houses of gold and silver, whose caverns glitter with jewels." The writer Eugene Smalley also attributed the "new life that is stirring in Mexico" to the railways that had enabled U.S. influence to reach Mexico. From the Mexican view the railways had offered the "easy means of communication" that would eliminate "errors" in U.S.-Mexican relations and Mexican fair organizers had even crowned their cargo train with a statue representing progress. For Americans, however, the rail lines were not bearing progress up from the South; the railways merely extended the reach of the U.S. to the riches of Mexico.[14]

The disappointing response to the Mexican exhibits should not have been a surprise given the context of the Centennial Fair. The American planners had organized the fair to promote Louisiana commerce, not relations with Mexico. Editor E.A. Burke of the *New Orleans Times Democrat*, the chief promoter behind the Centennial, had approached the fair from the beginning as an opportunity to further New Orleans' position in Latin American trade. Isaac Avery, charged with publicizing the fair in Latin America, simultaneously championed the U.S. construction of a canal through Nicaragua. The *New York Times* journalist at the Exposition evaluated the fair only as a showcase for American trade, since "our goods have never been properly placed before Mexican buyers." And Eugene Smalley of *Century Magazine* walked away feeling that an "honest effort" had been made to instruct him as to what "resources their country [Mexico] possesses inviting foreign development."[15]

While the fair revealed increasing U.S. interest in economic opportunities for Americans in Mexico, it also exposed the overwhelmingly dismissive American attitude toward her history and culture. Days before the Mexican Exhibit arrived the *Times Picayune* recapped a recent proposal of the *Galveston News* to purchase "nine or ten" Mexican states. The Picayune minced few words when it stated that the chief drawback (besides the probability of violent resistance) was that the territory contained two million Mexicans. The fair organizers even displayed the gun of Cortés, appropriated from Mexico during the U.S. invasion of 1846, in the U.S. armament tent at the fair. Edward Bruce of *Lippincotts Magazine* tactfully suggested that it would be a "graceful act" for the U.S. to return the gun to Mexico at the conclusion of the exposition as Cortés "belongs to her; he is a part of her history. We have nothing to do with him." The U.S. has long been interested in acquiring Mexican land without Mexican people; at the fair it became clear that the U.S. also wanted Mexican commerce without Mexican culture.[16]

The experience of the Mexican band clearly revealed the limits to the American welcome as the band members walked a narrow line in accommodating themselves to the racial climate of New Orleans. Lester Smalley gave guarded praise to the "swarthy musicians," who "represent most of the types of Mexico's much mixed races." Although the band was a popular attraction, praised for its spirited music and dashing outfits, its members were criticized by local residents for socializing with white American women. The fair's management, later accused of cheating the band out of eight hundred dollars worth of gate receipts, obviously held no greater regard for the musicians. The band, like other Mexican exhibits, had proven popular, but popularity offered no guarantee of respect.[17]

Although the Mexican government reduced its investment in international displays in the years following the New Orleans Exposition, the Mexican nation continued to enjoy a high profile at American fairs as fair organizers and entrepreneurs recognized the potential profitability of Mexican exhibits. Mexican or more generic "Latin" exhibits were often organized with little input from the featured nations and little regard for accuracy. At the conclusion of the New Orleans Fair, the most popular cultural exhibits were quickly purchased and reassembled by a entrepreneur for a travelling exhibit called the "Aztec Fair," which promised a "minstrel fandango" among other attractions, and otherwise exploited the carnivalesque appeal of the curiosities. The "Aztec village," hurriedly erected on the Chicago Midway in 1893, was populated with Sioux Indians, not natives of Mexico, and decorated with no attempt at imitating Mexican style. Similarly generic "Mexican" villages were featured at Atlanta in 1895, Buffalo in 1901 and St. Louis in 1904.[18]

Educational displays on Mexico and Latin America also continued to appear at subsequent fairs, but these were increasingly organized not by Mexican but American officials, and elaborated different themes from those promoted by the Mexican government in 1876 and 1885. American Archaeologist E.H. Thompson created replicas of Mayan temples for Chicago visitors in 1893, while William E. Curtis coordinated the material presented in the Latin American Bureau. Curtis provided his own captions for the photo collection, including the mistaken observations that the first recorded ascent of the Orizaba Volcano was by American officers in 1848 and the not-very-scholarly revelation that Mexicans could play the horn and dance perfectly after they leave the cradle. At the Tennessee Centennial in 1897 the Mexican building was organized entirely by Frederick Starr, an anthropologist from the University of Chicago. Nor would Mexico have had a chance to showcase her architecture in Chicago as she had done in New Orleans; in Chicago the Latin American republics were allotted pavilions designed by American architects, while the European nations were permitted to fashion their own buildings.[19]

By the late Porfiriato the portrayal of Mexico abroad had taken on a life of its own. Fair organizers in Buffalo in 1901 were unusual in asking the Mexican government for permission to erect their own version of a Mexican village with peons, burros, bazaars and dancing girls. Díaz consented with the stipulation that the "concession should not in any way bring ridicule upon Mexico, her inhabitants or buildings" and ordered that the fair organizers guarantee the return of all employees to Mexico at the conclusion of the fair.[20] Díaz's permission and stipulations were virtually meaningless, however. His concerns revealed his recognition that the image of Mexico had passed beyond the bounds of Mexican control.

Díaz, for example, had no control over the way in which Mexican exhibits were physically framed in the setting of the fair, or in controlling the way in which Americans incorporated the Mexican material into their own perspective on America's place in the world. The spatial and thematic organization of fairgrounds strongly influenced the way exhibits were evaluated by visitors. Music and dance exhibitions from non-European nations, for example, were often relegated to the portion of the fairgrounds reserved for sideshows, animals or anthropological villages. Sometimes the nations and culture of the world were deliberately presented to illustrate stages of evolution. Even the art and architecture of the fairs played a role in shaping the visitor's perspective. C.Y. Turner, the artist charged with the overall color scheme of fair installations at Buffalo, used the opportunity to evoke the journey of man from the primitive ("using the strongest primary colors") to the civilized (portrayed in "the lightest and most delicate in color"). 'Colorful' Mexican exhibits paid a stiff price for their popularity in this framework; the villages, bullfights,

cavalry shows, feast day celebrations and bands were guaranteed to attract
an audience, but they were presented in the spirit and zones of entertainment,
not education.[21]

The organizers bear only part of the responsibility for the failure in cross-
cultural communication. Fair visitors were certainly influenced by the organization and presentation of exhibits, but they also pursued their own goals and
created their own patterns of interaction at the fair. As Mr. Dooley, the fictitious Chicago columnist, noted at Buffalo, "f'r wan man that goes to a wur-
ruld's fair to see how boots is made, they'se twenty goes to see th'hootchy-
kootchy an' that's where th' wan lands fin'lly." Dooley's prediction that the
arts and sciences building would soon be squeezed into a corner where "no
man'd find it unless they thripped over it on their way to the merry go round"
did not come true completely, but over the years the entertainment section
of fairs expanded in a nod to the power of consumer preference. Moreover,
the inability to dictate visitors' responses to exhibits gradually erased the line
between education and entertainment throughout the fair. One visitor to the
Pan Am exposition of 1901 found the "the Mexican, in his preposterously
wide-brimmed sombrero...rich in mirth-provoking possibilities." He was convinced that the "Rainbow City was conceived in a spirit of humor."[22]

The exhibit that best illustrated the complex relationship between organizers, exhibitors and fairgoers was that which showcased the maneuvers of the
Mexican rural mounted police, the Rurales. The Díaz administration willingly
contributed elite dress units of Rurales to American fairs, where their dashing
outfits and skilled cavalry demonstrations easily attracted cheering crowds.
Mexico exhibited the Rurales abroad as personifications of the Díaz pursuit
of order and progress. Their international role was an outgrowth of their domestic symbolism; within Mexico Rurales also served as visible reminders
of the power of the Díaz administration, ostensibly employed to reduce crime
yet more often forestalling regional political challenges through action and
intimidation.[23]

Within the U.S. the Rurales appeared in a different context. Staged recre-
ations of frontier "savagery" had become a staple segment of fair entertainment after 1885. Like the Buffalo Bill shows and Indian Congresses, the
Rurales captured the visitors' imagination because they offered fairgoers
a sanitized brush with the primitive. The Rurales, with their exaggerated
reputations as reclaimed outlaws holding the thin line between savagery and
civilization in Mexico, probably did little to convince Americans of Mexico's
domestic stability. Of course Díaz was not naïve and must have realized that
the sight of gun-toting, galloping horsemen hardly complemented commercial overtures. By the latter half of his regime, however, Díaz had found an
alternative public relations use for the Rurales. By flaunting the specter of

banditry before U.S. audiences Díaz helped cultivate the political identity he had chosen as keeper of the peace in Mexico. The wilder Mexico appeared, the more essential (and forgivable) seemed the strongman rule of the Díaz regime.

Mexico originally participated in American expositions as a means of educating Americans on historical and contemporary Mexico. In the long run, however, the participation did not prove the simple pedagogical exercise Mexico anticipated. The international fairs did not provide a neutral meeting ground between the two nations. Instead, they offered Americans a rehearsal for their encounter with the outside world as fairgoers struggled to impose a familiar order on the bewildering array of merchandise and cultures strewn before them. Not surprisingly, expositions financially dependent upon the patronage of American audiences increasingly favored American values and expectations, and, consequently, American interpretations of foreign material. The patterns of interpretation that emerged (western vs. nonwestern, civilized vs. savage, industrial vs. primitive, educational vs. entertaining) provided a preview of how Americans would incorporate Mexico into their vision of the outside world in the coming years. The fluid and consumer driven environment of the fair worked against Mexico's educational objectives as fair organizers responded to the patronage and interests of fairgoers, yielding an inexact but marketable portrait of Mexico that was exotic, yet politically and culturally non-threatening. At the fair, the "Aztec village" triumphed over the reality of the Mexican nation.

NOTES

1. *Boletín de la Comisión Mexicana, La Exposición Universal de Nueva Orleans*, 15 March 1884 (México: Secretaría de Fomento, 1884), 2–3. Mexico also organized international fairs in Mexico City in 1896 and 1910, and participated in other nation's exhibits. Two works that focus specifically on Mexico at international fairs are Gene Yeager, "Porfirian Commercial Propaganda: Mexico in the World Industrial Expositions," *Americas* 34 (1977): 230–43; and Mauricio Tenorio Trillo, *Mexico at the World's Fairs: Crafting a Modern Nation* (Berkeley: University of California Press, 1996), with some slightly different material included in his dissertation on the same topic, "Crafting the Modern Mexico: Mexico's Presence at World's Fairs, 1880s-1920s" (Ph.D. diss., Stanford University, 1994).

2. See Robert Rydell, *All the World's a Fair: Visions of Empire at American International Expositions, 1876–1916* (Chicago: University of Chicago Press, 1984); and Rydell, "The Culture of Imperial Abundance: World's Fairs in the Making of American Culture," in *Consuming Visions: Accumulation and Display of Goods in America, 1880–1920* ed. Simon Bronner (New York: Norton, 1989), 191–216.

3. Tenorio Trillo, *Mexico*, 24–40; Richard C. McCormick, *The International Exhibition of 1876; Speech in the House of Representatives, 6 May 1874* (Washington, D.C.: n.p., 1874), 7; U.S. Centennial Commission, *International Exhibition of 1876, Official Catalogue*, Part II, (Philadelphia: U.S. Centennial Catalogue Co., 1876), 123.

4. Rydell, *All the World's a Fair*, 10; Frank H. Norton, *Illustrated Historical Register of the Centennial Exposition, Philadelphia, 1876; and of the Exposition Universelle, 1878* (New York: American News Co., 1879), 242; J.S. Ingram, *The Centennial Exposition* (Philadelphia: Hubbard Bros., 1876), 489; *Mexican Section: Special Catalogue and Explanatory Notes* (Philadelphia: Dan Gillin Printer, 1876); Norton, 242.

5. Ingram, 490; *Mexican Section*; also Norton, 242.

6. Antonio Garcia Cubas, *The Republic of Mexico in 1876. A political and ethnographical division of the population, character, habits, costumes and vocations of its inhabitants* (México: La Enseñanza Printing Office, 1876); Ben C. Truman, ed., *The History of the World's Fair*, (Chicago: Monarch, 1893), 21, 51–4; cited in Reid Badger, *The Great American Fair: The World's Columbian Exposition and American Culture* (Chicago: Nelson Hall, 1979), 44.

7. Porfirio Díaz to Jaime Torres, 20 August 1884, "Exposiciones," Box 71, f.1., R.G. 165, Archive of the Secretaría de Fomento; The Díaz correspondence attests to the high priority he gave to the exhibit as one of the commissioners, but the coordination of Mexico's displays was undertaken by Eulogio Gillow y Zavalza. See Eulogio G. Gillow, *Reminiscencias del Ilmo. Y Rmo. Sr. Dr. D. Eulogio y Zavalza, Arzobispo de Antequera* (Los Angeles: Imprenta y Linotipia de "El Heraldo de México," 1920). Also see Tenorio Trillo, *Crafting*, 29–31; and Yeager, 235–6.

8. Tenorio Trillo, *Crafting*, 32; on the Cotton Centennial in general, see John Findling and Kimberly D. Pelle, eds., *Historical Dictionary of World's Fairs and Expositions, 1851–1988* (New York: Greenwood Press, 1990), 86–90; Samuel C. Shepherd, "A Glimmer of Hope: The World's Industrial and Cotton Centennial Exposition, New Orleans, 1884–85," *Louisiana History* 26 (1985); 271–90.

9. *Boletín de la Comisión Mexicana, La Exposición Universal de Nueva Orleans*, 15 March 1884 (México: Secretaría de Fomento, 1884), 2–3; Antonio Garcia Cubas, *Cuadro Geográfico,,* iii; Santiago Ramirez, *Noticia Histórica de la Riqueza Minera de México y de su Estado de Explotación* (México: Secretaría de Fomento, 1884), ix; José Carmen Segura, *Reseña Sobre el Cultivo de Algunas Plantas Industriales que se Explotan en la República de México* (México, Secretaría de Fomento, 1884); *Boletín de la Comisión Mexicana, La Exposición Universal de Nueva Orleans, 7 June 1884* (México: Secretaría de Fomento, 1884), 3; "Mexican Exhibits," *Two Republics*, 15 March 1884.

10. "The World's Industrial and Cotton Centennial Exposition," *Two Republics*, 18 November 1884; "The Exposition," *Two Republics*, 22 November 1884; "Some Reflections about the Expo," *New Orleans Times Picayune*, 25 November 1884; "World's Expo," *New Orleans Times Picayune*, 7 December 1884; *Times Picayune*, 7 January 1885.

11. Lafcadio Hearn, "Mexico at New Orleans," *Harpers Weekly*, 14 March 1885, reprinted in Albert Mordell, ed., *Lafcadio Hearn: Occidental Gleanings* (New York:

Dodd, 1925), 221–3; *Boletín de la Comisión Mexicana, la Exposición Universal de New Orleans*, 15 March 1884 (México: Secretaría de Fomento, 1884), 2–3.

12. Herbert S. Fairall, *The World's Industrial and Cotton Centennial Exposition, New Orleans, 1884–85* (Iowa City: n.p., 1885); Eugene V. Smalley, "The New Orleans Exposition," *Century Magazine*, (May 1885): 11, 3; Findling, 87; John B. Sillard, *Visitors Guide to the World's Industrial and Cotton Centennial Exposition, and New Orleans* (Louisville, Kentucky: Courier Journal, 1884), 17; Lafcadio Hearn, "Notes of a Curiosity Hunter," *Harpers Weekly*, 4 April 1885; reprinted in Mordell, *Lafcadio Hearn*, 225–230; Hearn, "Mexico at New Orleans," *Harpers Weekly*, 14 March 1885; reprinted in Mordell, *Lafcadio Hearn*, 220–225; *The Visit of the Merchants and Manufacturers of Philadelphia to the World's Expo at New Orleans, February 11–25, 1885* (Philadelphia: McCalla and Stavely, 1885), 50–54; "The Worlds Industrial and Cotton Centennial Exhibition," *Two Republics*, 16 December 1884; Agustín Díaz, *A Brief Report on the Organization, Objects and Development of the Geographical Exploring Commission in the Republic of Mexico* (New Orleans: L. Graham and Sons, 1885). The report also describes the loss of other exhibits following a fire on the steamer from Mexico. Also see R.G. 165, "Exposiciones," Secretaría de Fomento, Boxes 71–79; especially, Box 76, "Un Informe rendido por el C. Ing. Mariano Barcena, Representante de Comisión General de México en la Exposición de New Orleans," (a review of the spaces and displays at New Orleans); and Box 79, "La Memoria de la Exposición de New Orleans por Sr. Lic. E. Zarate," (a review of products exhibited).

13. Sillard, 50; Yeager, 237–8; and Smalley, "The New Orleans Exposition" *New Orleans Times Democrat,* 27 January 1885; *Monroe Bulletin*, 14 January 1885; cited in Shepherd, 284.

14. *Times Picayune*, 21 December 1884; Smalley, "The New Orleans Exposition," 12; Garcia Cubas, *Cuadro Geografico*, v.

15. Shepherd, "A Glimmer of Hope," 273–5; Findling, *Historical Dictionary*, 86–90; Tenorio Trillo, "Crafting," 29–31; "Our Trade with Mexico," *New York Times*, 26 December 1884; Smalley, "New Orleans Exposition," 11.

16. "The Purchase of Mexico," *New Orleans Times Picayune*, 13 December 1884; Edward Bruce, "The New Orleans Exposition," *Lippincotts Magazine*, March 1885, 278.

17. Eugene V. Smalley, "In and Out of the New Orleans Exposition," The Century Magazine (June 1885) 189; "The Exposition and the Mexican Band," *Mascot* 13 June 1885, "Miss Bridget Magee's Society Notes," *Mascot* 16 June 1885; cited in *All the World's a Fair*, 91–93.

18. Orrin Brothers and Benito Nichols, *Orrin Brothers and Nichols Guide to the Aztec Fair: Mexico Past and Present* n.p., 1886 (Smithsonian National Museum of American History Archives, Washington, D.C.). Sheet music for the "Aztec Fair," "Melodias Mexicanas: Aztec Fair, Ancient and Modern Mexico para piano solo executed by the Fandango Minstrels at Orrin Brothers and Nichols," cited in Roberts, 31; *The Dream City: A Portfolio of Photographic Views of the World's Columbian Exposition* (St. Louis, MO: N.D. Thompson, 1893); Dean, T., *White City Chips* (Chicago: Warren Publishers, 1895); cited in Gertrude M. Scott, "Village Performance: Villages at the Chicago World's Columbian Exposition, 1893" (Ph.D. diss., New

York University, 1991), 334–36; Findling, *Historical Dictionary*, 140, 165–71, 178; also see *Guía General de St. Louis y de la Exposición Universal* (St. Louis: Mexican American Commercial Co., 1904); and Comisión Nacional de México, *Exposición Internacional de St. Louis, 1904*, (St. Louis: J. MacCallum Printing Co., 1904).

19. William E. Curtis, *World's Columbian Exposition: Illustrated and Descriptive Catalogue of the Exhibit of the Bureau of American Republics* (Chicago: W.B. Conkey Co., 1893), 6–27; *The Best Things to be Seen at the World's Fair* (Chicago: Columbia Guide Co., 1893); *The Book of the Fair: An Historical and Descriptive Presentation of the World's Science, Art and Industry, as viewed through the Columbian Exposition at Chicago* (Chicago: Bancroft Co., 1895); Rydell, *All the World's a Fair*, 92–93; Eric Sandweiss, "Around the World in a Day: International Participation in the World's Columbian Exposition," *Illinois Historical Journal* 84 (Spring 1991): 2–14.

20. Comisión Nacional de los E.U.M. para la Expo Pan Americana, *A Few Facts about Mexico* (Buffalo: White-Evans, Penford, 1901), 109–131; *Around the Pan with Uncle Hank: His Trip through the Pan Am Exposition* (New York: Nutshell Publisher, 1901), 15–16; Rydell, *All the World's a Fair*, 147–8.

21. Rydell, 93–94, 147–8. For more detailed description of Mexican exhibits within the Pan American Exposition, see Comisión Nacional para la Exposición Pan Americana, Buffalo, 1902, *Official Catalogue of the Mexican Exhibits at the Pan American Exposition at Buffalo, N.Y.* (Buffalo: White-Evans-Penfold, 1901); Richard Hayes Barry, *Snap Shots on the Midway of the Pan-American Exposition, Including Characteristic Scenes and Pastimes of Every Country There Represented* (Buffalo: R.A. Reid, 1901); and *The Rand-McNally Hand-Book to the Pan-American Exposition, Buffalo and Niagara Falls* (Chicago: Rand, McNally and Co., 1899). Also see Curtis Hinsley, "The World as Marketplace: Commodification of the Exotic at the World's Columbian Exposition, Chicago, 1893," in *Exhibiting Cultures: The Poetics and Politics of Museum Display*, ed. Ivan Karp and Steven Lavine (Washington, D.C.: Smithsonian Institution Press, 1991), 344–365; and Timothy Mitchell, "The World as Exhibition," *Comparative Studies in Society and History* 31 (1989): 217–236. Mitchell's essay focuses on the depiction of the Middle East at American expositions, but his conclusion, that the commercial nature of the fair distorted even "educational" exhibits, is equally applicable to the Latin exhibits. C.Y. Turner, "Organization as Applied to Art," *Cosmopolitan* 31 (September 1901): 495. Turner's article appeared in an issue of *Cosmopolitan* devoted to the Pan American Fair, alongside William I. Buchanan, "The Organization of an Exhibition," 517–21, which detailed the view of the director general. Also see Hamilton Wright Mabie, "The Spirit of the New World as Interpreted by the Pan-American Exposition," *Outlook*, (10 July 1901): 529–47.

22. F.P. Dunne, "Mr. Dooley on the Midway," *Cosmopolitan* 31 (1901): 476; "Around the Pan," 15.

23. Although the Porfirian administration cultivated the image of the Rurales at home and abroad, in reality they were seldom deployed outside of central areas and more effective as symbolic rather than practical tools of the regime's power. See Paul J. Vanderwood, "Mexico's Rurales: Reputation vs. Reality," *The Americas* 34 (July 1977): 102–112.

Chapter Eight

Writing the Revolution

By 1910 the Porfirian system was more than thirty years old and the man himself in his eighties. Still, with youthful vigor Díaz was quick to imprison challenger Francisco I. Madero, a northern Liberal who had declared his own candidacy for the presidency, and rig yet another election. Despite Díaz's predictable victory, the Mexican state began to unravel in the face of mounting challenges. Madero spearheaded the movement for change and in 1911 assumed power as Porfirio Díaz vanished into a European exile.

Unfortunately, the change of regime proved to be the beginning of an era of disorder and not the final act. The transition from the Díaz to the Madero administration spiraled rapidly out of control as the accumulated resentments and injustices of thirty years overwhelmed the nation's new leaders. Madero was deposed, then assassinated, and in the following years battles disfigured the cities and countryside of Mexico. American military intervention in Veracruz in 1914 and in northern Mexico in 1916 failed to tame the revolution, but by 1917 the completion of a new constitution signaled the birth of a new political order. Eventually the government that emerged in the aftermath of what became known as the 1910 Mexican Revolution took its identity from the rejection of the Porfirian model and the cultural and economic hierarchies it had come to symbolize. While political struggles would persist into the 1920s, by the beginning of that decade it was clear that a reinvented Mexico confronted the United States across the border.

Despite the reorientation of the Mexican state, it was impossible to change longstanding economic and political patterns overnight and both historians of Mexican history and historians of U.S.-Mexican relations have traced these continuities across the revolutionary divide. Cultural studies of U.S.-Mexican relations, however, have tended to interpret cultural relations as undergoing a reinvention in the post revolutionary decade of the 1920s.[1] Certainly the Revolution, with its refreshing rediscovery and glorification of America's ancient cultures and Indian present, provided a welcome alternative to the disillusionment many Americans felt with Western tradition in the wake of the first World War. The cultural renaissance spearheaded by José Vasconcelos, Diego Rivera, Antonio Caso and others attracted new kinds of attention as well. During the 1920s American social scientists, artists and writers flocked to Mexico to revel in this Mexican rebirth and made Mexico City a bohemian alternative to the Paris of the Lost Generation.

Yet the primitivist vision of Mexico that would captivate so many Americans in the early twentieth century was less revolutionary than it hoped. Certainly there were new categories of interaction and writing about Mexico, but the themes and tones voiced by authors unconsciously echoed the concerns and fantasies of earlier eras. From the earliest reports on the challenge to the Porfirian state through the delirious enthusiasms for the muralist movement, American writing on revolutionary and post-revolutionary Mexico was imbued with tropes familiar to Victorian era accounts. Magazines and newspapers that had run steady streams of local-color stories on Mexican customs and scenery replaced them after 1910 with colorful accounts of the martial strife raging beyond the border, but in neither case did writers attempt to examine the political and economic intricacies of Mexican events. American writing on the revolution would ultimately continue a pattern of interpretation that excluded Mexican developments, even revolutions, from serious consideration and preserved Mexico instead as a wonderland refuge from American preoccupations.

American writing on the Mexican Revolution began to appear in 1911 as the political turmoil in Mexico provoked new patterns of American attention. The American travel writers contemplating Mexican flower vendors were quickly eclipsed by would-be-war correspondents, who coalesced along the U.S.-Mexican border waiting for news of the political contests to the South. They described the distant skirmishes, the pathos of the Mexican refugees, and the routine of the U.S. troops called out to contain the Mexican disorder and crowded report after report with accounts of the heat, dust and guns around them, but they included little discussion of the underlying reasons for the upheaval. Edith O'Shaugnessy, who accompanied her husband to his diplomatic post in Mexico City in 1911, was frustrated by her failure to find any substantive U.S. news coverage of the conflict. The Boston *Transcript*, she reported to her family, claimed that the "difficulty of finding out what is happening in Mexico is that of telling which are the names of the Generals and which those of the towns." Only a few periodicals such as the *Review of Reviews* made a cursory effort to explain the politics of events in Mexico, most coverage left readers with the sense that the confusion and disorder were reflections of the national character. Edwin Emerson, writing for *Outlook* in May 1913, credited Constitutionalist victories to the presence of American mercenaries and insisted that all truly Mexican warfare was only on "a primitive Indian basis." William Carson, author of the 1909 travel account, *Mexico the Wonderland of the South*, no longer found Mexico quite so wonderful. "The 'Generals' and 'Colonels' are simply barefoot, ignorant Indians wearing the straw sombrero and red serape," he sneered, "who ride at the head of their forces, machete in hands." These were hardly neutral comments given the racial hierarchies of the age.[2]

American coverage of the Revolution would not only be influenced by older racial categorizations, but by the more recent experience of the Spanish-American War of 1898. Most Americans recalled the intervention in the Cuban war for independence from Spain as an untarnished example of speedy and effective American military action. Americans attributed their victory in Cuba to American technological and moral superiority and saw the subsequent U.S. occupation of the island as a monument to the American talent for organizing and sanitizing societies. By the summer of 1913 Wilson was coming under increasing pressure to do something about the deteriorating situation in Mexico, and the allusions to the American experience in Cuba were never far afield.

Journalists along the U.S.-Mexican border (who also recalled how the 1898 war had boosted the careers of many correspondents) penned emotional portraits of poverty-stricken families fleeing the fighting, and, just as in 1898, presented intervention as the humanitarian obligation. "The question before the American people today is this:" asserted the editors of *Outlook*, "what duty, if any, does a rich, strong nation owe to a weaker nation at its door which is being plundered by bandits?" Press coverage assured Americans that U.S. intervention would not only be welcome, but militarily uncomplicated. Another editorial in *Outlook* reported that "the military opinion in this country seems to be confident that the superiority of our military knowledge, training and organization is such that if we find it necessary to enter Mexico it would be a comparatively easy task." It could be an inexpensive task as well, added an anonymous American resident, who claimed that "the financial expense to the United States will in the end be nothing. Mexico is a rich country and, well administered, she will have no trouble in paying the interest and principal of the hundred million or so she will finally owe this country." "Conviction is growing," summed up the *Review of Reviews*, "that armed intervention is inevitable, and that the United States must eventually, and very soon, abate the international nuisance at its door."[3]

President Wilson had been keeping a watch on Mexican events since taking office in the spring of 1913, and had been quietly moving to isolate the dictatorship of General Victoriano Huerta, whose murderous coup against Madero shook the U.S. president. In April 1914 Huerta provided Wilson with an excuse for intervention when several American sailors were arrested in the port of Tampico. Although they were quickly released, Wilson accused the Huerta government of offering insufficient apologies. In particular, complained Washington, Mexico refused to conduct a ceremony to honor the American flag as an official act of apology. As the editors of *Outlook* noted, "Americans as a rule have detested the idea of intervention in Mexico. No American, however, is indifferent where the honor of country is at stake." In the wake of the Tampico incident Wilson went before a sympathetic Congress to request permission to "maintain the dignity and authority of the United States" and in April the U.S. navy attacked and occupied the port of Veracruz.[4]

The choice of Veracruz signaled Wilson's intention to do away with Huerta's "government of butchers" by taking control of the principal railroad to the capital and the most lucrative customs house in the nation, and thus starving the Huerta government of revenue and supplies. The script was a familiar one for American policymakers in the Caribbean. As soon as the Americans had established control over the port city they repeated the Cuban and Philippine pattern of enacting sanitation and administrative reforms as both a practical measure and a symbol of the blessings of civilization. Enthusiastic cartoons of Uncle Sam striding into Mexico armed with soap and water seemed to imply that all the nation of Mexico needed to set it right was a good scrubbing. Political parallels to the protectorate the U.S. had established over Cuba in the wake of the Spanish-American War motivated some readers to demand similar concessions from Mexico. The *Review of Reviews* argued that Americans "should not leave without exacting guarantees, very much in the same plan as that which gives us the right to see that the people of Cuba are protected." Other editorials expressed the hope that Wilson would consider a long, American-led administration to teach good governance, hygiene, industry, and other lessons of the Philippine and Cuban experiences to the Mexican nation. Wilson encouraged the parallel (and public support for his policy) by publicly praising America's noble and disinterested motives for bringing order to Mexico. His private communications were phrased in more pragmatic terms, but Wilson recognized that the themes of carrying civilization to Mexico and defending American honor were compatible with the American view of U.S. foreign relations.[5]

There was one final parallel to the Spanish-American War of 1898, and that was the prominent place of the press in both engagements. While there is a popular myth that the press, and particularly the publications of William Randolph Hearst, drove Wilson into war by harping upon his impotent responses to Mexican depredations, the power of the Hearst empire was less decisive than Hearst claimed. Hearst was one of the largest foreign landholders in Mexico as well as one of the largest publishers in the U.S., but the rumors of his influence on U.S. foreign policy was part of a deliberately crafted Hearst public relations strategy. Hearst enjoyed his reputation as the author of U.S. policy, but he habitually overstated his influence.[6]

Hearst, for example, can hardly be accused of inventing the denigrating tone used by American papers toward Mexico during the crisis; the same tone could be found in U.S. writing on Mexico half a century earlier. More importantly, that same tone permeated descriptions of domestic U.S. troubles at the time. These were years filled with turmoil on both sides of the border and readers turning past coverage on Mexico could go on to read about violent disorder in their own nation. The Lawrence, Massachusetts Bread and Roses strike of 1912, the West Virginia Mine War of 1912–1913, the 1913 Ludlow Massacre in Colorado, and the Paterson, New Jersey Silk Strike of 1913 were all raising public fears of the prospect of social breakdown in the U.S., while along the southern border perennially tense race relations worsened with the fears of a Mexican-inspired "race war." When Edwin Emerson argued that observations had proven beyond a doubt the "necessity of firmness in dealings with an ignorant and unruly people," he could as easily have been referring to Mexico as Massachusetts. Hearst was only one of many Americans who assumed that the U.S. had an obligation to impose order, whether it was in the mining towns of Colorado or the rural roads of Mexico.[7]

Nor was Hearst the only actor seeking to shape American understanding of the Mexican Revolution. Just as Díaz had thirty years before, the principal contenders for power in Mexico initiated public relations campaigns aimed at the American people. Both before and after the fall of Díaz Mexican political activists struggled to place their interpretation of events in Mexico before the American public.

Venustiano Carranza, the governor of Coahuila who opposed Victoriano Huerta's seizure of power in the winter of 1913, quickly recognized the need for a persuasive information campaign directed at the U.S. and from 1913 until his assassination in 1920 Carranza cooperated with American newspaperman George F. Weeks to "get out the truth about Mexico" to the American audience. Weeks, who had settled in Coahuila after running newspapers in California, was acquainted with the Carranza family long before the revolution began. In the aftermath of Huerta's coup both Weeks and Carranza realized it was not enough to release reports and statements from

Carranza's headquarters to achieve their goals. The principal wire services and newspaper chains were interested primarily in the work of their own correspondents and preferred description to analysis. Weeks encouraged Carranza to establish his own wire service (the Pan American News Service) and a Washington based journal, *The Mexican Review*. Carranza supporters who had seized Mexican consulates in the U.S. worked with Weeks to place sympathetic articles in local newspapers. Their goal, a clear echo from the days of Zamacona, was to win U.S. recognition for the Carrancistas as the rightful government of Mexico.[8]

Over the years Weeks countered the American fascination with solving Mexico's problems through U.S. intervention by emphasizing the vast scale of the Mexican nation and the certainty of the anti-American uprising that would follow U.S. military action. Weeks also publicized the goals and accomplishments of the Carrancistas in restoring order as their campaigns progressed. The themes would have been familiar to the Liberals of the early Porfiriato: Weeks highlighted Carranza's accomplishments in reopening the lines of rail, telegraph and mail communication, the reestablishment of industry and commerce, the security of the banking and landholding systems, the protection of foreign interests, etc. Thirty years after Zamacona's campaign to win respect for the Mexican nation-state, Mexico was still pleading its case by showcasing the standards Americans, not Mexicans, had deemed essential to international legitimacy. Unfortunately Weeks mission largely failed. He was successful at placing the Carrancista pieces in Spanish-language papers in the U.S., but the mainstream English-language journals continued to prefer the vivid battle descriptions sent in by their own correspondents.

Francisco, or Pancho Villa (the alias chosen by Doroteo Arango during his early confrontations with the Mexican authorities), was also quick to recognize the crucial role of public relations in winning both American and Mexican support. Villa may have appeared as a simple man-of-the-people in the pages of John Reed's *Insurgent Mexico* (discussed later in the chapter), but he was a shrewd politician and vigilant in courting and threatening the correspondents who followed his army. While Villa was successful in attracting international attention, the reputation he acquired was ultimately at least as harmful as helpful to meeting his goals.

Despite his lack of formal education, Villa was a skilled agricultural and financial administrator in the territories he controlled, but Villa's management policies were seldom the focus of American articles. Instead, U.S. press coverage reiterated the probably apocryphal stories of family humiliation at the hands of the Mexican elite, his Robin Hood-like dispersal of funds and justice, and his disdain for the lifestyle of the wealthy. The journalists complicit in the creation of the Villa legend, recalled writer Gregory Mason, seldom heard these stories of Villa's early life directly from the man himself, but rather from an entrepreneurial former Hearst correspondent, John W. Roberts. "Johnny" Roberts had created an instant career for himself as press agent by convincing American papers of his connections to Villa, and convincing Villa of his connections to the American press. For a while the strategy worked for both Villa and Roberts as the two benefitted from marketing the image of Villa as an untamed force of nature—a theme that resonated with the tradition of romantic American stereotypes of Mexico.[9]

Yet in retrospect it is clear that Villa's carefully crafted but one-dimensional image as the "people's warrior" both made and undermined his career. It was Villa's string of military successes in 1913 and 1914 against Huerta, and not his administrative innovations and political proposals, that drew the press's attention to this apparent personification of a Mexican revolutionary, and disaster struck as a series of battlefield losses in 1915 destroyed Villa's narrow legitimacy before American audiences and encouraged Wilson to recognize Carranza as the official head of government of Mexico. Villa denounced Carranza's new relationship as traitorous, but it gave Carranza access to loans, arms and even U.S. transit rights for his troops.

During the fall and winter of 1915–1916 Carranza used U.S. railways to transport his troops around territory controlled by Villa. In a final effort to regain his Mexican base by proving his credentials as the true nationalist, Villa lashed out at foreigners in mining towns, railways and along the border. When Villa literally crossed the line by launching a raid across the border on the town of Columbus, New Mexico, his fate was sealed in American eyes. The attack mauled the town's small business district and resulted in the deaths of about sixty Villistas and twenty Americans. Villa had hoped to provoke a U.S. response that would embarrass the Carrancistas by making them appear as tools of the Americans, but the resulting U.S. invasion, the Punitive Expedition, attracted surprisingly little attention in Mexico. While the U.S. soldiers wandered for more than a year across northern Mexico in a fruitless pursuit of Villa, the center of political struggle and press attention had moved south to the capital. Although Villa ultimately survived as a regional leader and even outlasted Carranza, his reputation before American circles never recovered from the raid. He remained, even decades after his murder in 1923, the embodiment of the ruthless and reckless *bandido* in American eyes.

The struggle by Mexican revolutionaries for control of their public image has been overshadowed in the U.S. by the fascination with self-styled villains like Hearst and adventure reporters like John Reed and Richard Harding Davis, who rushed to recapture the spirit and sales of America's first "splendid little war" in 1898. Americans may prefer to remember journalists like Reed as heroic and autonomous icons of the active life, but their work was undertaken and promoted within the cultural and economic confines of an industry that looked to the Spanish-American War as a model for successful coverage. Success was measured in sales, not in analysis, and, not surprisingly, in retrospect press coverage of the Mexican revolution appears as an uneasy cross between Victorian travel writing and chronicles of the "Great White Hunter."[10] The topics in American writing on Mexico may have changed after 1910, but the tone had hardly evolved from the 1870s.

Most of these journalists caught their first glimpse of Mexico along the U.S.-Mexican frontier in 1911, where border towns quickly filled with writers hoping to glimpse and record the distant fighting and thus win a place in American letters. They clambered upon hotel roofs in efforts to capture marketable photos that could then be reprinted and sold as post card souvenirs. The cards were popular among the American soldiers posted to the border in an effort to bring order to the crowds of smugglers, refugees and soldiers spilling north. After the first few months, however, the border situation seemed more tedious than thrilling for both soldiers and correspondents. The Mexican armies moved away into the vast expanse of the Mexican north while the American journalists remained behind in the saloons of El Paso, filing stories based on hearsay and padded with quotes from the Americans and Mexicans fleeing north. For the most part the long stalemate along the border was covered by inexperienced stringers who left no bylines and little memorable reporting. A few exceptions were *Outlook*'s young correspondent, Gregory Mason, veteran muckraker Lincoln Steffens, and a young friend of Steffens, journalist John Reed. While most journalists clustered behind the safety of the border, these three set out into the Revolution itself.

Mason was at the beginning of a career that would take unexpected twists through academic and commercial circles. In the decades after the revolution Mason joined archaeological expeditions that ranged throughout the Americas. His ability to convert the discomforts of fieldwork into enthralling accounts of exploration, blending the genres of history, travel writing and scientific reports, won him a wide and loyal audience.[11] In 1914, however, Mason was still merely one of the dozens of correspondents huddled along Mexico's northern frontier, embroidering the rumors that reached them into some kind of story that could be filed with offices in Chicago or New York.

Unlike most of his fellow correspondents, Mason slipped across the river into Mexico itself as the center of the struggle moved south. He joined the forces of Carranza and, like other correspondents he initially employed classic clichés of disparagement. In one of his early dispatches Mason asserted that the shock of seeing the real Mexico would be "painful in the same ratio as the height of your preconceptions of the intelligence and trustworthiness of the native Mexican." Mason claimed that most rebel soldiers were "not patriots, or martyrs to the cause, they are out for a good time and like nothing better than on a dark night to jam the muzzle of a Mauser into the stomach of a Gringo." Andre Tridon, another border journalist who later became a New York psychoanalyst, adopted a similar tone in stating, "I must preface these impressionistic notes with the remark that before visiting Mexico I too felt an ardent sympathy for the Indian and his heroic efforts to free himself." These formulaic disclaimers provided an easy means of highlighting the daring and expertise of the writer at the expense of his subject. They also conveniently buttressed the writer's credibility by emphasizing how much further than the reader the author had travelled in his study of the Mexican situation.[12]

Unlike most other correspondents, however, Mason grew to question the American press's tendency to belittle the revolution. His contacts with expatriate circles left him convinced that the Americans in Mexico were not laudable missionaries of modern know-how, but rather the "kind of Americans we don't want at home—plutocrats, privilege seekers, and mining riffraff," to be specific. After seeing the poverty, distances and discontent of northern Mexico he was more impressed with the task that confronted the constitutionalists and even complemented Carranza by likening him to Abraham Lincoln.[13]

Mason slipped away for a look at a second, equally famous leader of the Constitutionalist forces, Villa, and continued his uneasy accommodation to the bread and butter stereotypes of the Mexican news account. Villa, he dutifully reported, was a "big chunky man of butternut color shuffling his feet and rolling his shoulders like a Negro longshoreman." He was a "superb animal," with cruel mouth, and bloodshot and protruding eyes. Yet Mason again stepped away from stock images and paired his portrait of Villa with unflattering descriptions of the seedy Americans who followed Villa's army, hoping for easy looting in return for their military expertise. Over time Mason grew more impressed with the uneducated Villa. Despite his ignorance, his virtual illiteracy, and his "strain of Negro blood," Mason admitted Villa's talent for inciting loyalty, stoicism and courage from his followers. If only Villa had had access to education, concluded Mason in a complement unlikely to be appreciated by either party, he could have been "another Díaz."[14]

Mason finished his series with another strange set of ambivalent observations on life in Mexico. Once again Mason underlined his credentials first by distancing himself from those who see Mexico only from "the rear platform of a Pullman and go home to write hysterically of the poverty and misery of the country." In Mason's view there was more happiness in

Mexico than in the slums of a large American city or a hard driven Northern factory town. Mason, despite his impatience with earlier travel writers, departed little from the "wonderland" tradition of the Porfirian age; he merely updated the escapist ideal to the age of Revolution. "Nowhere has warfare ever been so picturesque," Mason reported in describing the start for the front, "when, as the long trains gather momentum, the men stand up on the swaying cars, shooting as wildly as they yell, but with more danger to bystanders, while their sweethearts, yelling also, wave serapes or the men's sombreros, or wrest a rifle from a lover's hands and join the fusillading." In Mason's view, there was little need to cover politics as the Mexican soldier was not driven by political programs. He concentrated instead on the sights and sounds of the camp—drowsy waits, the hum of the cicada, the shrill chatter of children, and the low guitar. "Picturesque, the wars of Mexico certainly are," he concluded.[15]

It is easy to trace the ghosts of Victorian travel writing conventions in Mason's work, but they are equally present in the work of John Reed, who is more often associated with a twentieth century model of politically committed journalism. Seen in the larger context of American writing on Mexico, however, Reed's reports, compiled and published as *Insurgent Mexico* in 1914 and still popular today, appear less than revolutionary. Reed's vivid descriptive essays on life with the rebels of Mexico caught America's attention, but in retrospect the rebels in Reed's work differ little from the comical mule drivers of the Victorian travelogues. It was the swashbuckling correspondent at the center of the work that was reinvented in Reed's *Insurgent Mexico*, not the nation.

1913 had been a tremendous year for John Reed, who began an affair with Mabel Dodge, the doyenne of Greenwich Village radical society, joined the staff of Max Eastman's *The Masses*, and organized a pageant at Madison Square Garden to raise awareness and relief funds for the Patterson, New Jersey Silk Strike. By late fall, however, he was feeling a need to move out of the New York fishpond and find new material and new excitement. Lincoln Steffens recommended him to Carl Hovey of the *Metropolitan*, who was then looking for a writer to cover the meteoric rise of Villa's army in Mexico's north. In December 1913, Reed left for El Paso.

Reed (trailed by a persistent Mabel Dodge, who, according to Reed, expected to find in Villa a sort of male Gertrude Stein), quickly sized up El Paso and decided it was not the place to pursue the story of the Mexican Revolution. The mix of arms dealers, police informants, displaced expatriate investors, and ubiquitous spies was fascinating, but unlikely to offer a useful window into the conflict. Reed ridiculed the journalists he found at the border, who daily "concocted two-hundred-word stories full of sound and fury" while rarely leaving their favorite cantinas. Reed had no interest in a tame, ringside seat to the conflict. He wanted to regain the passion he felt working with the Patterson strikers and to see the Revolution from within. Despite explicit warnings from the commanding Federal Officer across the border, Reed waded across the river into Mexico.[16]

From late December 1913 until March 1914, Reed crisscrossed the Mexican north reporting on the life of the rebel soldiers, of their families and of their commanders. He traveled by foot, on horse and atop boxcars. His stories, which appeared in both the New York *World* and the *Metropolitan* between February and April, were crowded with the poor and the rebellious that had been absent in previous American writing on the Mexican conflict. The scenes, smells, and sounds of the revolution spilled out of Reed's reports and brought the Mexican Revolution to generations of American readers.

Before Reed, reporters had treated the revolution as if it were merely an extended coup and dismissed the mass uprising as symptomatic of the chaotic and irresponsible soul of the Mexican native. William Carson, for example, claimed that the Revolution had merely exposed the dormant savagery of the Mexicans. Deprived of the tempering influence of the Western oriented elite, argued Carson, the Indian quickly "becomes transformed into the embodiment of lust and ferocity." Their revolt was no glorious struggle for liberation, but a "crime against law and order."[17] In contrast, Reed centered his accounts on the half-starved, destitute of Mexico, whose tattered clothing and rude living conditions were not dismissed as proof of their semi-civilized status, but lovingly described in an effort to elicit sympathy for their misery. This was more than a squabble over the reins of power, Reed argued, it was a nationwide campaign for retribution.

For Reed the struggle for justice by the Mexican poor was yet another theater of the same struggle that consumed the factory workers of Patterson and the miners of Ludlow, and a precursor to the great radical revolution that would eventually lure him to Moscow. Over the course of his three month visit Reed felt himself increasingly torn between the duty to preserve the detachment of a correspondent and the desire to support the aims of the revolutionaries through sympathetic coverage. By the time Reed returned to the U.S. in April 1914 to work at converting his articles into a book he was reconciled to his support for the revolutionaries struggling in Mexico. Reed had little compunction about rearranging scenes, dates, and even personnel in the quest to convey his sympathetic image of Mexico to the reader. As his biographers and reviewers conceded, in *Insurgent Mexico* the poet won out over the journalist. His friend Walter Lippman congratulated him on "undoubtedly the finest reporting that's ever been done.... The stories are literature."[18]

Insurgent Mexico, debuted in the fall of 1914 to enthusiastic reviews and remains a perennial favorite among Americans interested in Mexico, revolutions, and politically committed journalism even today. Certainly Reed's later life and death in revolutionary Russia have added to the books almost mystical reputation, but it is still his vivid details of "what people eat, and where they sleep, and who with, as well as their political ideas, and how they respond to pain and death," that give the reader a "powerful sense of place and time." It is these details, argued reviewer Richard Elman more than half a century after the original publication of the book, that make it "difficult to persist in seeing Mexicans as subhuman rapists and desperadoes." In the opinion of another reviewer in the 1980s, Reed's was a vivid and graphic style that prefigured the 'new journalism' of the 1960s by half a century, and, in the same spirit of that 'new' journalism, it sought to break through the emotional defenses of the reader through evocative imagery of the great struggle to the South. Even today students encountering Reed's work enthuse over the vibrant depictions of the social tempest that was the Revolution of 1910. In the end, the work became a vivid tribute to the Mexican poor he encountered, who had become literally "symbols of Mexico—courteous, loving, patient, poor, so long slaves, so full of dreams, so soon to be free."[19]

There is something else in Reed's work for the contemporary reader, however. With one hundred years of hindsight it is evident that however much Reed loved and occasionally envied the Mexican campesino, he borrowed more than a dashing aura from the colonialist genre of Richard Harding Davis. Like the travel writers and yellow journalists of the Porfirian era, Reed could not quite bring himself to see the Mexicans as fully human. Like his predecessors, Reed converted the Mexican poor into symbols of a lost childhood of man in familiar vignettes made strange only by the revolutionary setting. Once again the countryside was alive with humble Indian women sheltered modestly behind colorful serapes, while their manly compañeros imparted ancient wisdom to the young "meester" from the North, before setting off on wild and wheeling horseback races.

Reed's exciting and captivating dispatches from the Mexican Revolution were truly artistic masterpieces, but Reed was clearly not inventing a new model of writing on Mexico. Nor did his publishers wish for a new model. In March 1914, the *Metropolitan* ran illustrated ads promoting John Reed's series on the revolution, complete with an illustration of Reed with sombrero, revolver, and cartridge belts above testimonials to "America's Kipling." Mexico, the ostensible subject of the series, was merely an exotic backdrop to American adventure and Reed was praised not as the herald of a new age, but for his resemblance to the bard of English colonialism. Reed's writing thus entered the American popular market in a form long familiar to American readers. Through Reed, the *Metropolitan* advertised, one would "see the beautiful, blood drenched country," including "glorious nights of revelry where mirth is turned to tragedy by jealousy filled with too generous gulps of sotol."[20] This was merely travel literature of a new variety, exploring the revolution as if it were a new nightclub, not a political and economic transformation to be studied.

Reed's reports were filled with every scenic and social embellishment employed in the previous decades. "It is impossible to imagine how close to nature the people live," wrote Reed before projecting his own Greenwich Village-style utopias on the Mexican landscape: "when a man and women fall in love they fly to each other without the formalities of a courtship, and when they are tired of each other they simply part." Victorian travelers had both censured and envied the Mexican's unrestrained 'natural' instincts; Reed was less ambivalent than his predecessors but equally inaccurate. He overlooked the tightly circumscribed courtship traditions of the Mexican communities he visited in favor of a fantasy of the happy, hot-blooded savage. Nor did his portraits of Mexican individuals caught in the maelstrom do much to improve their standing in American eyes. "This day I have lost all that is dear to me," recounted Reed of a conversation with a rebel colonel after a bloody defeat, "They took my woman, who was mine, and my commission and all my papers, and all my money. But I am wrenched with grief when I think of my silver spurs inlaid with gold, which I bought only last year, in Mapimí!' He turned away, overcome."[21]

Consciously or unconsciously, Reed fell fully into the stereotypes of earlier years. For Reed, Mexicans were "delightfully irresponsible;" he left a bar in mid-conversation because "you can never tell what a Mexican will do when he's drunk." American mercenaries he ran into were pitied for being "hard, cold mercenaries in a passionate country." In Reed's eyes Mexico was still filled with bull fights, song and dance, passionate women and generous men, childish generals with infatuations for colorful gifts, and comical desperadoes. Reed was filled with contentment, "I felt my whole being going out to these gentle, simple people—so lovable they were."

Throughout his series, it is only those Mexicans who have remained close to nature who receive praise, and Reed's contrasting treatments of Villa and Carranza showcased his standards. Villa's earthy mannerisms are set against the aristocratic pretensions of Carranza. Villa's immersion among the disorderly but endearing Mexican 'folk' contrasts with Carranza's barren seclusion in ancient palaces. In Reed's work Villa embodied the vibrant and virile energy of true Mexico, while Carranza decayed amid trappings of the past. Reed's intention may have been at odds with those of his

Victorian wonderland predecessors, but the underlying message was little different: authentic Mexico was untutored, untouched and unrestrained by the advances of Western civilization. To move in any direction from nature toward progress was to lose the real Mexico.

Reed saw himself as a champion of Mexico, but his clean demarcation between the essence of Mexico and the march of history froze Mexico in a timeless state of nature as surely as did William Carson in condemning the innate barbarism of the people. In contrast to his later study of revolutionary Russia, *Ten Days that Shook the World*, Reed included little discussion of Mexican political or military strategy. Instead, he filled his work with charming vignettes of camp life that differed little from travel writing of earlier years.

> Up from the river wound a silent line of black-robed girls with water-jars on their heads. Women ground their corn meal with a monotonous stony scraping. Dogs barked. Drumming hooves marked the passage of the *caballada* to the river. Along the ledge in front of Don Pedro's house the warriors smoked and fought the battle over again, stamping around and shouting descriptive matter. 'I took my rifle by the barrel and smashed in his grinning face, just as—' someone was narrating, with gestures. The peons squatted around, breathlessly listening.

In *Insurgent Mexico* the Revolution was no path to the future, but merely a path to Reed's utopian visions of the past.[22]

For Reed, the Mexican Revolution was the perfect escape from the prison of convention, even if that convention was the unconventional salons of bohemian Greenwich Village. In a later memoir Reed examined his irrational decision to head away from safety at the border to immerse himself in the rebel campaigns. "I felt I had to know how I would act under fire, how I would get along with these primitive folks at war," he wrote in a revealing remark that summed up Reed's political analysis of the Revolution. The leisure traditions of the Victorian era had framed Mexico as the antidote to over-civilization and reading about Mexico in the throes of revolt still provided the catharsis Americans needed. In Mexico, Reed found his great adventure, just as in reading about Reed in Mexico (the real subject of *Insurgent Mexico*), Americans found exoticism, romance and heroism. For both, Americans and Reed, the encounter with Mexico was inescapably filtered by the shadows of earlier literary traditions. Even in the violent disorder of a dangerous retreat Reed revealed his debt to Victorian conventions as he insisted that he "wasn't very frightened. Everything was still so unreal, like a page out of a Richard Harding Davis novel."[23]

As Reed was leaving for Mexico in December 1913 another American journalist was escaping permanently into the Revolution. Ambrose Bierce left no writing from his Mexican journey, but his still-unexplained disappearance in revolutionary Mexico created a legend almost equal to that of Reed's, and in which, once again, Mexico provided the primitivist idyll for an American escape story. Ambrose Bierce was seventy-one in the fall of 1913 and feeling as if his long career as a short story writer and journalist was concluding. In September he wrote his daughter that he planned to go to South America, but hoped to "see something going on" in Mexico on the way. A few weeks later he wrote again to tell her he was off. "Goodbye," he wrote, "and if you hear of my being stood up against a Mexican stone wall and shot to rags please know that I think that is a pretty good way to depart this life. It beats old age, disease, or falling down the cellar stairs. To be a Gringo in Mexico, ah, that is euthanasia!" Bierce departed Washington, D.C. in early October, revisited Civil War battlefields from his youth as he traveled south, and crossed into Mexico for his final adventure. He was spotted with Villa's troops, but his fate after 26 December 1913 remains a mystery still.[24]

The most likely scenario is that Bierce died of illness, but the timing of his disappearance and the publication of Reed's exhilarating reports on the revolution generated a legend of the sardonic Bierce escaping from the living death of settled life to an adventurous finale in Mexico. Dozens of fictional treatments of Bierce's death at the hands of bandits, federal troops, rebels, wronged women, and even runaway horses, have been created, but the most famous is easily Carlos Fuentes' novel, *The Old Gringo* (1985). The Mexican revolution, in the Bierce legend, is the ultimate escape from the claustrophobic trappings of modern life; it becomes not so much a political revolution as an alternative to death by boredom.

By the time Gregory Mason and John Reed slipped across the border to pursue their Richard Harding Davis-style adventures in Mexico, the dynamics of capturing the Mexican story were about to change. The long standoff between President Woodrow Wilson and General Victoriano Huerta ended dramatically when Wilson ordered the occupation of Veracruz in April 1914. Publishers rushed to replace the anonymous hacks with familiar and marketable names to cover the expected march on Mexico City and overnight the bland articles on border duty gave way to stirring prose filled with marching soldiers, snapping flags and sun-drenched navy ships heading out to sea. The stage appeared set for a revival of the hyperbole of 1898.

Richard Harding Davis himself, perhaps the most famous war correspondent of his era, enthusiastically supported the American intervention in Mexico just as he had enthusiastically supported real and fictional American interventions for the previous twenty years. He covered the American invasion and occupation of Veracruz in 1914 for *Scribner's* and the *New York Tribune*, and wasted no time before recreating his classic smoke and thunder portraits of manly white men struggling before the steaming background of tropical America. Like Reed, he found no need to waste energy or column space on the particulars of Mexican politics. In Davis's words it was no revolution, but rather "a falling out among cattle-thieves, between Huerta and Villa there was the choice between Lefty Louis and Gyp the Blood."[25]

The generic details of Mexico that did emerge in Davis's writing could have easily been drawn from one of his best-selling novels, *Soldier of Fortune* (1897), set in an imaginary South American republic complete with rebellious militaries, simpleminded peasants, and a corrupt but cowardly president. Davis knew exactly what his selling strengths were and quickly recreated the tenets of his fiction within the new setting of Mexico. Davis turned his pen upon the glories of the American soldiers and sailors around him in Veracruz. Davis contrasted the "Vikings clad in Khaki," as he termed the American occupation force, with the 'unwashed revolutionaries' in articles that made no effort to hide his contempt for the Mexican people. From Davis's point of view, laid out repeatedly in his work over the decades, it was the Americans who had built progress in the Latin Republics in the form of railroads, mines and businesses, and the current invasion of Mexico was little more than an extension of this civilizing tradition.[26]

Jack London was yet another novelist-turned-war correspondent who offered little background on the revolution or the American invasion. London had been approached by Hearst to cover the "Mexican fracas" but the two disagreed on rates and London left from Galveston as a correspondent from *Collier's Magazine* instead. London, according to his wife, was anxious to "redeem himself" as a war correspondent and looked forward to the "march on the City of Mexico."[27] After the initial bombardment and occupation of the port of Veracruz, however, there were few battles to report. President Woodrow Wilson's decision to seek mediation of the dispute drew only scorn from London and other correspondents who saw no honor (or thrilling subject matter) in negotiations.

This was not the first interest London had shown in the Mexican Revolution and while his political stance toward the revolution was more complex than that of Davis, his coverage ultimately differed little in tone. London's interest in the Revolution dated from 1910 when John Kenneth Turner, the journalist who had written the explosive exposé of Mexican labor practices in 1908, had become involved in raising money for the Mexican opposition in the U.S. and encouraged London and others to lend their talents to the cause. In response London wrote and published a short story, "The Mexican," in the *Saturday Evening Post* that explored the fury of the Mexican poor through the eyes of a young revolutionary, Felipe Rivera. Rivera uses his angry memories of family humiliation at the hands of the Porfirian elite to drive him to victory in prize fights. Wordlessly, he turns the money he wins over to the revolutionary leadership for the purchase of the guns that will avenge his family. As in all his writing, London was alert to class injustice and an ardent advocate of the underdog, but London's ingrained racism undermined his efforts to create sympathy for the revolution. In the story, Felipe Rivera's eyes were "venomous and snakelike." In the words of one character Rivera was "the Revolution incarnate," in the words of another, "the primitive, the wild wolf, the striking rattlesnake..." and, in the words of the narrator, London, "they [his co-conspirators] could not like him." On a level of political ideals the socialist London declared his solidarity with the revolutionaries, but in Veracruz it became obvious that he could not quite bring himself to like them.[28]

Despite his professed sympathy for the revolution, London had no difficulties professing his admiration for the American occupation of Veracruz. London's descriptions of the American troops as boyish, well proportioned bodies filled with 'Anglo-Saxon' enthusiasm and commitment cast a clearly idealistic and racialized glow over the U.S. military mission. In contrast, his descriptions of the Mexican poor elicit no class or race compassion. When London saw the city beggars scrambling to salvage goods tossed aside in the aftermath of the occupation, he encouraged the reader to laugh not to sympathize. "It was the women who fought fiercest and most vociferously," recorded London, "and, to the accompaniment of much hair pulling, many a pair of linen trousers and its legs irrevocably separated. They struggled and squabbled and ran hither and thither like ants about a honey-pot." Although many of London's socialist sympathizers wondered at his support for the occupation, London was confident that the U.S. troops had left "Veracruz cleaned and disinfected as it had never been in its history." London confidently concluded that the Mexicans would "yearn for the blissful day when the Americans will conquer them again.[29]

London and Davis were not the only American correspondents accompanying the American forces in Veracruz. Among the press pool were J.B. Connolly, a prolific writer of sea stories, Arthur Brown Ruhl of *Collier's*, Rufus Zogbaum, renowned painter of cowboys, frontier warfare, and the Cuban-American War, Burge McFall of the Associated Press, Frederick Palmer and Medill McCormick of the *Chicago Tribune*, and R. H. Murray and his wife of the New York *World,* who all joined Davis and London for drinks under the arcades of the central plaza. The correspondents were there for an invasion, but passed their time much as earlier tourists had done. They set out on horseback rides and for swims, they shopped for laces, blankets and opals, danced in the patios of their hotels, attended bullfights, and gossiped over lunch and dinner with the equally bored army and navy officers around them.

London and Connolly were amused to find the wounded aboard the Hospital ship reading their adventure stories, just as the patients were amused to find the authors amongst them. The overall tone of reporting was centered within this American perspective, with American achievements in Veracruz at the foreground in a dimly illuminated Mexican setting.[30]

The correspondents and the American troops they reported on were playing two roles on one Veracruz stage. In Mexico, they hoped they were remaking a city and redirecting a revolution; in America, however, the role they played was one of restoring faith in American honor at home and abroad. American cities were crowded with disease and political bosses, labor conflicts exposed savage violence, and anxieties about the 'mongrelization' of America haunted public discussions. But in the coverage from Veracruz Americans found their faith restored in familiar racial hierarchies, and American energy, expertise and efficiency.

Unlike Davis and London, John Reed had never sympathized with the occupation of Veracruz. He condemned it not because it would jeopardize Mexico's independence and distort the outcome of the people's revolution, but simply because it would bring development to his primeval utopia. "We want to debauch the Mexican people and turn them into little brown copies of American businessmen and laborers, as we are doing to the Cubans and the Filipinos," he lamented in the summer of 1914.[31] Yet he had never written anything that suggested Mexico possessed an alternative to the American way. His sentiments jarred with those of Davis, but his conclusion was little different as he agreed that any change in Mexico reflected American initiative. Mexico, by Reed's definition, was and should remain a colorful but static preserve of the childhood of man.

By the fall of 1914 the show was over—at least from the perspective of the American audience. Journalists raced from Mexico to cover the deteriorating situation in Europe and Wilson moved slowly to withdraw his troops from Veracruz. The evacuation would drag on for months as Wilson and Carranza haggled over the terms of U.S. recognition, but by then only the Mexicans were watching. If the Americans thought of the Mexican Revolution at all, it was more likely from the perspective of Wilson, who closed the U.S. occupation with the comment that the U.S. had given the nation "a valuable lesson in municipal order, in sanitation, and in disinterested control of a city to the benefit of its people."[32] The Mexican revolution, depending upon who one read, had been either an annoying riot or a colorful pageant, but few expected it to help them understand the newest phase of human history, the trenches of Europe.

The writers departing Veracruz crossed paths with a late but famous arrival, Lincoln Steffens, the muckraker who had been both a friend and mentor to

Reed in the radical circles of New York. Steffens was in Italy when the world war broke out in the summer of 1914 and he expected a world revolution to follow. Steffens set out quickly to study the situation in Mexico, but felt frustrated by his inability to analyze the ongoing revolution through the political theories of Europe. But, he comforted himself, "it is a rich experience because it shows me that the problem rises differently from what the books lead one to expect." Mexico was a great but unruly laboratory and Steffens didn't seem sure whether he admired or despaired of Mexican life, "All is fun to them, or a bore. They enjoyed the revolution. They must enjoy everything or hate it and neglect it." He was frustrated by his difficulty in interesting American magazines in Mexican material but took heart in his belief that he was "putting ideas in the heads of the Mexican leaders and they like them and me." As the years went by Steffens, like his colleagues, retreated further into the primitivist vision of the nation. Mexico, claimed Steffens in 1921, was like a great runaway train. "She wouldn't stay on the narrow crooked road you damn foreigners laid out for her," Steffens opined, "and so, she jumped the track. She sprang back into space and went crashing back into barbarism."[33] For Steffens, as for Reed, London and Davis, the barbaric essence of Mexico was never far beneath the Western veneer.

The Mexican Revolution was a watershed for the history of Mexico, the Americas, and the world, but had surprisingly little effect on U.S. visions of their southern neighbor or on their confident vision of America's role before the world. Only a minute fraction of Americans had direct interests in Mexico and the rest read of events to the south through the prism of earlier rhetorical traditions. Images of revolutionary Mexico, both childlike and barbaric, rested comfortably within the cultural framework raised during the Porfirian years. For the correspondents who covered the revolution, Mexico was still the timeless wonderland it had been for those Porfirian-era tourists who rejected historical substance in favor of sunny scenes of human color. Just as in the days of Díaz, Americans saw themselves as both emissaries of and refugees from the future. Davis and London, like the investors of an earlier era, judged the Revolution a deviation from the inexorable path of U.S. style modernization and looked for a restoration of U.S. leadership. For them and for other critics, the violence of the revolution was a consequence of Mexican racial characteristics, not of inequitable political or economic situations. Reed, Bierce and Steffens, like the escape travelers of the Porfiriato, praised Mexico for that same racial difference, locating the Mexican superiority in genes and temperament, and not cultural or intellectual legacies. Despite their different judgments on the American way, these two groups of writers shared a vision of Mexico's intrinsic difference from their own world. Americans could vacation in Mexico, they could work their development magic across the surface of the nation, but they could never fundamentally alter the Mexican soul.

Unfortunately, walling Mexico's experience off beyond a racial barrier was as effective a compartmentalization of misgivings as the work/leisure divide of earlier years. Just as Americans had safely indulged their flirtation with the preindustrial during vacation jaunts away from their normal routine, Americans successfully neutralized the Mexican revolutionary challenge to their development models. The Mexican Revolution was a fascinating and/ or violent eruption, but, viewed across the imagined chasm of racial distinction it held no political or social relevance to the American experience. The revolution, like the Orizaba Volcano above Veracruz, was part of the unique scenery of Mexico and as unlikely to be exported.

Even after years of turmoil, American images of the U.S. place in Mexico and the world remained fundamentally unaffected by the challenge the Mexican Revolution posed to U.S. assumptions of cultural and political order. Harry Carr, traveling in Mexico in the late 1920s, concluded that the revolution had done little to rattle the confidence of Americans in Mexico. "The planters live a life that reminds me of Rudyard Kipling's stories of the life of the English in India," Carr wrote, "They have their tennis clubs, polo fields, golf links, dances, bridge parties. It is as though they lived on a gay island in a sad and changeless ocean called Mexico."[34] Americans continued to exempt themselves from any responsibility for Mexican misery, in fact the misery of Mexico made a satisfying backdrop to American events. Back in the U.S. labor strikes, nativist anxieties, political turmoil and the banalities of industrial culture wore away at American confidence. In Mexico, however, Americans could still look to what they considered American achievements highlighted against the stagnation of Mexico for a corroboration of American superiority.

On the other side of the spectrum enthusiasts of the revolution praised the new Mexico as if it were a harmless antidote to their own malaise and a refuge from all that had gone awry in civilization. During the 1920s artists, writers, and academics flocked to Mexico to experience the energy of the Mexican renaissance. Ultimately, the antidote to modern disaffection could be found in a two-week or ten year vacation among the tropical splendor and quaint handicrafts of Mexico's happy poor. Americans enjoyed visiting the Mexico of flowers and muralists and markets, but, apart from pottery, there was little they would bring back to their world from the revolution. Mexico, enthusiasts of the Revolution assured themselves, had shaken off its Western trappings and preserved its authentic soul—but to what authenticity could Americans return? Americans enamored of the Revolution wanted to be primitives; they became consumers of the primitive instead.

In the end, neither the battle portraits of John Reed nor the humorous sketches of Richard Harding Davis led Americans to think that the Mexican Revolution had any relevance for their world. It remained, like the picture postcards Americans purchased of revolutionaries and refugees, a controlled encounter with an alien world. While Americans living in Mexico during the years of the revolution were confronted with the human and financial disasters of warfare, most Americans experienced the revolution by turning the pages of their favorite magazines. Safe in their homes they thrilled at descriptions of bandoliered gunmen and shawl-draped women riding the rails. For those Americans who clung to the vision of an American-led system, the Mexican disorder was proof of American superiority; while for those who critiqued the American model of development, Mexico offered a virtual nature preserve for the preindustrial soul. The Revolution was a disaster because it was Mexican, or it was glorious because it was Mexican, but in neither vision was there potential for the Mexican Revolution to offer universal lessons for humankind. It remained safely quarantined beyond a wall of imagined difference. Viewed within the long perspective of the American discovery of Mexico begun in the Porfiriato, the revolution became merely another illustration of curious Mexican ways, alternately maddening or charming, but in the end inconsequential to American visions of the world.

NOTES

1. For discussion and examples see Mauricio Tenorio Trillo, "The Cosmopolitan Mexican Summer, 1920–1949," in the *Latin American Research Review*, 32 (1997): 224–242; James Oles, *South of the Border: Mexico in the American Imagination, 1917–1947* (Washington, D.C.: Smithsonian, 1993) and Helen Delpar, *The Enormous Vogue of Things Mexican: Cultural Relations between the United States and Mexico, 1920–1935* (Tuscaloosa, AL: University of Alabama, 1992).

2. Edith O'Shaugnessy to her family, 20 May 1911, in *Diplomatic Days*, (New York: Harper, 1917) 31; Edwin Emerson, "How Mexicans Fight," *Outlook*: 104 (May 1913): 199–207; Carson, 201.

3. "Mexico," *Outlook* 107 (May 1914): 12–4; "The War in Mexico," Outlook 106 (April 1914): 822–823; "The Situation in Mexico: By an American Resident," *Outlook*, 104 (Aug. 1913): 1003–1006; "Is Intervention Near?" *American Review of Reviews*: 49 (Feb. 1914):150.

4. "Mexico and American National Honor," *Outlook*: 106 (April 1914): 880–881; Robert E. Quirk, *An Affair of Honor: Woodrow Wilson and the Occupation of Veracruz* (Lexington: University of Kentucky, 1962); John S. D. Eisenhower, *Intervention: The United States and the Mexican Revolution, 1913–1917* (New York: Norton, 1993).

5. See, for example, "Not going to be any war, but there's going to be a fine housecleaning." reprint from *New York Herald*, in *Current Opinion*, 56 (June 1914): 411; and "The Unexplainable Gringo," reprint from the *Dispatch*, Columbus Ohio, in *Review of Reviews*, 49 (1914): 644; "There Must Be Permanent Results," *Review of Reviews* 49 (June 1914): 644–645; "Can Mexico Redeem Itself?" *Outlook* 107 (1914): 276–277; and Dean C. Worcester, "The Mexican Question in the Light of the Philippine Experience," *Outlook* 107 (1914): 602–608; on Wilson's rhetoric, see Mark T. Gilderhus, Diplomacy and Revolution: United States-Mexican Relations under Wilson and Carranza, (Tucson: University of Arizona, 1977).

6. W.A. Swanberg, *Citizen Hearst* (New York: Scribner, 1961) 296–298; and David Nasaw, *The Chief: The Life of William Randolph Hearst,* New York: Houghton Mifflin, 2000) 58–60, 228–230.

7. On border tension, see Linda B. Hall and Don M.Coerver, *Revolutionaries along the Border: The United States and Mexico, 1910–1920* (Albuquerque: University of New Mexico Press, 1988) ; Edwin Emerson, "The Iron Hand in Mexico," *Outlook* 104 (May 1913): 288–292. Mark Cronlund Anderson discusses how Americans viewed U.S. policy in Mexico as part of the struggle of civilization vs. savagery in "The Mythical Frontier, the Mexican Revolution and the Press: An Imperial Subplot," *Canadian Review of American Studies/Revue canadienne d'études américaines* 37 (2007):1–22.

8. Michael M. Smith, "Gringo Propogandist: George F. Weeks and the Mexican Revolution," *Journalism History* 29:2–11. Weeks' published memoirs include *California Copy* (1928), *Mexico from Muleback* (1925) and *Seen in a Mexican Plaza* (1918).

9. Mark Cronlund Anderson, *Pancho Villa's Revolution by Headlines* (Norman: University of Oklahoma, 2000); Friedrich Katz, *The Life and Times of Pancho Villa* (Stanford: Stanford University Press, 1998) and William K. Meyers, "Pancho Villa and the Multinationalists: U.S. Mining Interests in Villista Mexico, 1913–1915," *Journal of Latin American Studies* 23 (1991):339–363; Gregory Mason, "Reed, Villa and the Village," *Outlook* 140 (May 1925): 1–2. On Villa's administration, see William K. Meyers, "Seasons of Rebellion: Nature, Organization of Cotton Production, and the Dynamics of Revolution in La Laguna, Mexico, 1910–1916," *Journal of Latin American Studies*, 30 (1998): 63–94.

10. For a discussion of the links between the esthetics of fiction and journalism, see Michael Robertson, *Stephen Crane: Journalism and the Making of Modern American Literature* (New York: Columbia University Press, 1997).

11. Mason's works include *Green Gold of Yucatan*, (New York: Duffield, 1926), *Silver Cities of the Yucatan* (New York: Putnam, 1927), *Mexican Gallop* (New York: Green Circle Books, 1937) and *South of Yesterday* (New York: H. Holt, 1940).

12. Mason, "Going South with Carranza," *Outlook* 107 (May 1914): 19–25; Andre Tridon, "Mexican Revolutionists," *Outlook* 107 (July 1914): 612–613.

13. Mason, "Going South," 19–25.

14. Gregory Mason, "With Villa in Chihuahua," *Outlook* 107 (May 1914): 74–78; Gregory Mason, "The Mexican Man of the Hour," *Outlook:* 107 (June 1914): 292–306.

15. Gregory Mason, "Campaigning in Coahuila," *Outlook* 107 (June 1914): 391–7.

16. John Reed to Eddy Hunt, December 16, 1913, reprinted in Rosenstone, 151.

17. Carson, 430–3.

18. Walter Lippman to John Reed, March 25, 1914, Rosenstone, 167.

19. Richard Elman, "Partisan Journalist," *Nation* (17 April 1982): 469–470; Jerry W. Knudson, "John Reed: A Reporter in Revolutionary Mexico," *Journalism History*, 29 (Summer 2003): 59–68; Reed, 130, 138.

20. *Metropolitan*, March 23, 1914, in Rosenstone, 166. On Reed, see David C. Duke, *John Reed*, (Boston: G.K. Hall, 1987); Granville Hicks, *John Reed: The Making of a Revolutionary* (New York: Benjamin Blom, 1936); and Robert A. Rosenstone, *Romantic Revolutionary: A Biography of John Reed* (New York: Knopf, 1975); Advertisement insert, March 23, 1914, *Metropolitan*, cited in Richard O'Connor and Dale L. Walker, *The Lost Revolutionary: A Biography of John Reed*, (NY: Harcourt Brace, 1967) 117–8.

21. Reed, *Insurgent Mexico*, 34, 86.

22. *Ibid.*, 82, 131, 87.

23. John Reed, "Almost Thirty," unpublished manuscript, John Reed Papers, Houghton Library, Harvard University, cited in Rosenstone, 152; Reed, *Insurgent Mexico*, 76.

24. Ambrose Bierce to Lora, 10 September 1913, 1 October 1913, from Bertha Clarke Pope, ed. *The Letters of Ambrose Bierce* (New York: Gordian Press, 1967) 195–7; Carey McWilliams, *Ambrose Bierce, a Biography* (New York: Archon Books, 1929) and Adolphe de Castro Danzinger, *Portrait of Ambrose Bierce*, (New York: Beekim, 1929).

25. Richard Harding Davis, "When a War is not a War," *Scribners* 56 (30 April 1914): 43.

26. Richard Harding Davis, "Army at Veracruz marks time under the Portales," *New York Tribune*, 14 June 1914; "Vera Cruz marvels at Khaki Clad Men," *New York Tribune*, 3 May 1914; *Soldier of Fortune*, (New York: Scribners, 1897); also see John Seelye, *War Games: Richard Harding Davis and the New Imperialism* (Amherst: University of Massachusetts, 2003).

27. Jack London, "Mexico's Army and Ours," *Colliers* 53 (30 May 1914): 5–7; Jack London, "Our Adventures in Tampico," *Colliers* 53 27 June 1914): 5–7; Charmian London, *The Book of Jack London*, Vol 2, (New York: Century, 1921): 289–300; also see Drewey Wayne Gunn, *American and British Writers in Mexico, 1556–1973* (Austin: University of Texas Press, 1974); 56–7, 64–6.

28. W. Dirk Raat. *Revoltosos: Mexico's Rebels in the United States, 1903–1923* (College Station: Texas, A & M. 1981); Jack London, "The Mexican," *Saturday Evening Post*, 184 (19 August 1911) 6–8, 27–30.

29. Jack London, "Mexico's Army and Ours," *Colliers* 53 (30 May 1914): 6.

30. "Vera Cruz: A Crusade for Decency, from a special correspondent with the U.S. expeditionary force," *Outlook* 107 (1914): 527–528.

31. John Reed, "What about Mexico?" *Masses* (June 1914): 11, 14.

32. "The Withdrawal from Vera Cruz," *Outlook* 108 (1914): 149.

33. Lincoln Steffens to Mrs. J. James Hollister, 2 March 1916, Granville Hicks, ed., *Letters of Lincoln Steffens, Vol. II* (Westport, CT: Greenwood Press, 1966), 369; Lincoln Steffens, *The Autobiography of Lincoln Steffens*, (New York: Harcourt Brace, 1931), 741–2; Lincoln Steffens to Lou and Allen Suggett, 10 December 1915, *Letters*, 366; Lincoln Steffens, "The White Streak," *Colliers*, (15 January 1921): 21.

34. Harry Carr, *Old Mother Mexico* (Boston: Houghton Mifflin. 1931), 52.

Conclusion:
Trading Progress for Paradise

The construction of the international railroad linking Mexico and the U.S. marked the end of an era as it literally threw the two nations into an abrupt and iron-bound embrace. The effect not only increased communication, it completely changed the context of U.S. Mexican relations. Whereas Mexico had once appeared accessible only to diplomats and daring commercial agents on professional missions, the new Mexico was accessible to a wide variety of Americans who consumed Mexico through their pleasure reading and their visits to the nation and its expositions. In the railroad era of the 1880s Americans finally entered into a leisure relationship with the Mexican republic and the wonderland image of Mexico sketched out in that era continues to shape interaction today.

On the surface the emergence of the wonderland image of Mexico appears unremarkable. After all, Mexico was beautiful, her customs and people curious, and her weather delightful. But the romantic image was neither inevitable nor innocent; it revealed a choice made by Americans in the face of alternative interpretations encouraged by Mexican nationalists. The wonderland image viewed Mexico as timeless rather than progressive, exotic rather than civilized, and happy rather than hardworking. It substituted a package of inaccurate stereotypes of the Mexican people for the complex and varied reality.

Changes in leisure and literary styles, evident in the ascendance of escape tourism over educational travel and the rise of the carnival-like midway in competition with the informative exhibition halls, did not so much facilitate the rise of the wonderland stereotype as reflect it. In isolation they cannot explain why Americans developed different travel practices in Europe and in Mexico, or why fairgoers assumed one form of comportment in the educational exhibits and European galleries, and another in the "Aztec villages." Nor can they explain why news reporting on the war in Mexico and the war in Europe should differ so in style and content. Yet together the divisions between these styles of interaction suggest that Americans had begun to mentally compartmentalize the world, just as they physically compartmentalized the fairgrounds, into zones of education and zones of escape.

The illusion of a Mexican wonderland could only be maintained through a similar mental compartmentalization within the varieties of American experience with Mexico. Psychologically distancing themselves from their diplomatic and business relations with the outside world, the American traveler and travelogue reader enjoyed the fantasy of participating in a purely personal encounter with the 'primitive' soul of Mexico. It was easy for tourists, writers and fairgoers to forget that even a simple, apparently personal act, like the purchase of a souvenir, was enmeshed in a larger economic and political relationship. The purchasing power or the American dollar, the location of the railroads, and even the esthetics guiding both the production and consumption of souvenir items, reflected the influence of increasingly inequitable national positions. The most telling and unexamined reflection of this asymmetry was the American traveler's ability to set off for Mexico with the most minimal preparation in the expectation that local facilities would accommodate American needs. Even those self-styled tramp tourists, who sought to break out of the beaten path of package tours and press circles, were protected by the implied power of their culture and their citizenship.

In the end, romanticized visions of primitive Mexico helped Americans alleviate the tension caused by their own ambivalence toward progress. As members of an industrializing society Americans benefitted from the fruits of modernity; yet as individual travelers, readers and fairgoers escaping into the primitive, they deceived themselves with the illusion that they were uncorrupted by wealth and could return to the childhood of mankind at any moment. In their leisure relationship with the fragments of Mexico they considered authentic, Americans created a non-threatening, but personally satisfying, form of dissent against progress.

Americans had found in their illusions of Mexico an antidote to their industrial malaise, but in fulfilling their emotional needs they had to ignore the historic heritage and contemporary life of the Mexican nation arrayed before their eyes. John Reed, like his Porfirian predecessors, introduced his reporting from revolutionary Mexico with a stylized Victorian travel reflection on life in a "timeless" village. Reed lamented that "already around the narrow shores of the Mexican Middle Ages beat the great seas of modern life—machinery, scientific thought, and political theory."[1] In the American mind modernity and progress still came only from the West, and Mexico, for good or ill, could only remain Mexico by remaining the same. This reductionist vision, developed in the pages of Porfirian-era travel writers and surviving intact in the writing on the revolution, eliminated Mexico as a possible alternative to the American vision of progress by equating it with the absence of development. It undermined Mexican legitimacy in the international arena as surely as the bandit-filled accounts of Mexican savagery had in the past. Linking Mexico to the pre-modern soul left Americans with the impression that the nation possessed but two unappealing options—struggling for survival against a world of industrializing nations, or adopting the path of change and losing what American considered the essence of Mexican identity. In neither imagined future was allowance made for a viable, distinctively Mexican nation, which left open (and perhaps still leaves open) the question of whether there was space in the American vision of the world for a viable, distinctively Mexican state. Through their leisure practices Americans created a wonderland image of Mexico that froze the Mexican people in an imaginary past that served American emotional needs, at the expense of Mexican national interest.

NOTE

1. Reed, *Insurgent Mexico*, 3.

Epilogue:
The Illusion of Ignorance

In the 1870s the United States and Mexico entered into a new stage of bi-national relations as each nation sought to replace the hostility of the past with a framework of cooperation for the future. Hopes were high that the new forms of contact prompted by changes in trade, tourism and communications would erase the ugly stereotypes of earlier years and result in the birth of an era of cross-cultural respect and international harmony. Even as late as 1898 former Ambassador to the U.S. and Minister of the Interior Matías Romero, who had already spent a lifetime attempting to explain Mexico to Americans, remained hopeful that "trustworthy information" would eventually prove the key to "avoiding misunderstandings."[1]

Yet by the end of the thirty year regime of Porfirio Díaz it was clear that the proliferation of connections that transformed U.S.-Mexican relations during the Porfiriato had made few inroads on American ignorance of Mexico. In 1911 Marie Wright pessimistically observed that the American public still had only "meager" knowledge "of the beauties and resources of this marvelous country."[2] Even at the height of the Mexican revolution Henry Fyfe found Americans throughout the U.S. who knew next to nothing about events in Mexico—some even thought Mexico lay in South America.[3] Despite early Porfirian hopes, neither the establishment of a vigorous economic compact between the two republics nor the explosion of personal contact made possible by new transportation links initiated the hoped-for age of bi-national harmony. Contact and interaction did little to promote respect or understanding between the neighboring nations.

More than a century later, the paradox is even more apparent. Americans are investing in, buying from, and traveling through Mexico more than ever before, but they continue to think of Mexico as an unintelligible and even irrelevant nation to their lives. Americans eat Mexican food, vacation on

Mexican beaches, and hire Mexican workers, but they cannot be bothered to keep track of the political, historical or social conditions of their neighbor beyond parroting the most sensational headlines of the day. Americans are not merely dismissive of Mexico as a nation, but they have willfully chosen forms of limited interaction and interpretation that preserve American illusions of global leadership.

This pattern of intimacy and ignorance emerged during the Porfiriato and persists today because both the profession of ignorance and the stereotyped U.S.-Mexican interchanges that provide the foundation for the American cultural relationship with Mexico remain relevant to modern American life and to the larger American encounter with the world. During the Porfiriato Americans created a mental framework for understanding their changing relationship with Mexico that answered not only the physical and financial needs of an expanding American economic empire, but the political and psychological needs of a nation in the throes of a dramatic reorientation toward the outside world. The self-portrait that Americans preferred during this age of increasing global integration was of themselves in control and in the vanguard of the new foreign activism; it was a portrait that had little in common with their complicated experiences in an unsettled world. It was also a self portrait that Americans could only preserve then and now through a highly selective memory of their experiences in that world.

American tributes to John W. Foster's diplomatic triumphs in Mexico, for example, reassured Americans with testimonials to the orderly expansion of American interests and influence abroad, but only by ignoring the messy reality of Minister Foster's mission to Mexico. In the American memories of the era Foster appears as the architect of the Porfirian-U.S. partnership; in reality he was a talented but limited individual caught in a disorienting moment of diplomatic flux. In a similar way, Americans claimed sole credit for having awakened the commercial spirit of Mexico, sustaining their belief in the singularity of American entrepreneurial talent while overlooking Mexican initiatives. Americans also reveled in their self-image as political mentor to Mexico; American discussion of Mexico highlighted the political failings of the southern republic in ways that enabled Americans to play down their own political shortcomings. Finally, evolving leisure relationships with Mexico provided Americans with a means to indulge in, but never succumb to, their carefully circumscribed longing for an alternative to the modernizing civilization surrounding them. Americans reading about or travelling in Mexico treated themselves to temporary escapes from the stress of the industrialized world, but only by fabricating a "true" Mexico relegated to an imagined zone of perpetual underdevelopment. Together these two modes of contact, that which exaggerated America's role as prophet of progress in Mexico, and that which idealized the eternally primitive attractions of authentic Mexico, offered Americans a way of understanding their place in a shifting world and provided an intellectual model for future American encounters with the world beyond U.S. borders.

The contradictions and compartmentalization revealed in the business-diplomatic/tourist-fairground genres of contact also echoed the emerging division between work and leisure within U.S. domestic life, and served similar functions. In channeling misgivings with U.S. life into marginalized patterns of interaction such as tourism, recreation and consumption, Americans created a refuge from progress and a space for personal experimentation and rebellion that never threatened the underpinnings of the emerging economic order. Dichotomization in domestic and international life has helped Americans quarantine the radical threat of dissent from the cult of progress. Even today the polarization of attitudes continues as Americans chide other nations for not duplicating American political and economic styles, while simultaneously romanticizing those failings in their leisure pursuits. Americans feel free to dip into an alternative cultural format for a week's holiday or to indulge their fascination with the savage in the realm of domestic decoration, while still marching ahead with the persistent upgrades inherent to high tech society. Confining escape and protest to vacation time trivializes the existence of alternatives to American-style progress.

Only the carefully cultivated illusion of ignorance has helped Americans paper over the awkward inconsistencies in their relationship with Mexico and the outside world. The disclaimer of ignorance provides Americans with a convenient scapegoat for the chronic tension between the two neighbors; it offers a guilt-free explanation of discord that stresses the unfortunate absence of intercultural knowledge rather than the existence of actual conflicts of interest. The perennial American assertion that contact and communication will improve relations and dissolve ignorance even lends a convenient tinge of inevitability to American foreign relations, relieving Americans of the obligation of improving their knowledge of the world. In essence, ignorance appears in American discussions of the world as if it were a lamentable but fading legacy of the past, not a constantly reinvented tool for managing the contradictions of contemporary cultural relations.

The mantra of ignorance plays one additional role in the American relationship with Mexico and the world by preserving the possibility of personal exemption from the inequities of the larger relationship. By highlighting the national sins of intolerance and misunderstanding in contrast to their personal communion with Mexico, individuals then and now have sought to absolve themselves from responsibility for more substantive imbalances in the relationship. Yet the convenient cosmopolitanism that equates familiarity with the food, music, or vacation havens of foreign nations with the chimera of virtuous world citizenship seldom translates into deeper intercultural understanding; nor does it threaten the benefits that individuals gain from the uneven relationships between nations. For too many Americans, an unexamined affection for the romantic Mexico of the American imagination substitutes for a closer analysis of the personal advantages they derive from their inequitable national relationship with the other nations with whom they share the planet.

In sipping Mexican beer and decorating with Mexican folk art, Americans today incorporate Mexican products into their own cultural consumption patterns, just as in their selective memory of U.S.-Mexican history Americans selectively constructed an image of the U.S.-Mexican relationship that harmonized with their view of the American nation before the world. In both their condemnations and romanticizations of Mexico, Americans defined authentic Mexico as a static society in a world consumed by American progress. The American ability to create this flattering vision of U.S.-Mexican relations out of the muddled reality of the Porfirian encounter foreshadowed the ability of Americans to fashion global fantasies of world leadership in subsequent years. Despite profound levels of economic, cultural and political engagement with the world, Americans have maintained their myopic vision of a world driven by American initiative. The ignorance and stereotypes that mark American cultural communication with the world beyond will not gradually fade as the world becomes more closely connected because they are not so much barriers to communication as the form of communication Americans have chosen in their approach to globalization. In a complex and increasingly integrated world only the illusion of ignorance can preserve the American illusion of leadership.

NOTES

1. Matías Romero, *Mexico and the United States* (New York: G.P. Putnam, 1898), vii.

2. Wright, *Mexico: A History*, 13.

3. Fyfe, 22–3.

Selected Bibliography

Allen, Henry Ware. "President Díaz and the Mexico of Today." *Review of Reviews* 6 (January 1893): 676–696.

Anderson, Arthur D. *Mexico from the Material Standpoint*. New York: Brentano Brothers, 1884.

Anderson, Mark Cronlund. "The Mythical Frontier, the Mexican Revolution and the Press: An Imperial Subplot*," Canadian Review of American Studies/Revue canadienne d'études américaines* 37 (2007):1–22.

———. *Pancho Villa's Revolution by Headlines*. Norman: University of Oklahoma, 2000.

Arreola, Daniel David. "Landscape Images of Eastern Mexico: A Historical Geography of Time Travel." Ph.D. diss., UCLA, 1980.

Badger, Reid. *The Great American Fair: The World's Columbian Exposition and American Culture*. Chicago: Nelson Hall, 1979.

Baldwin, Deborah. *Protestants and the Mexican Revolution: Missionaries, Ministers and Social Change*. Urbana: University of Illinois Press, 1990.

Ballou, Maturin. *Aztec Land*. Boston: Houghton Mifflin, 1890.

Bandelier, Adolph Francis. *A Scientist on the Trail: Travel Letters of A.F. Bandelier, 1880–81*, eds. George Hammond and Edgar F. Goad. Berkeley: The Quivira Society, 1949; reprint, New York: Arno Press, 1967.

Barrett, Robert. *Modern Mexico's Standard Guide to the City of Mexico and Vicinity*. 3rd. ed. New York: Modern Mexico, 1903.

Barry, Richard Hayes. *Snap Shots on the Midway of the Pan American Exposition*. Buffalo: R.A. Reid, 1901.

Barton, N.H. "Mexico: Treasure House of the World." *National Geographic Magazine* 18 (1907): 493–519.

Bates, James Hale. *Notes of a Tour in Mexico and California*. New York: Burr, 1887.

Baxter, Sylvester. *The Cruise of a Land Yacht*. Boston: Author's Mutual, 1891.

———. "A Mexican Vacation Week." *Atlantic Monthly*, July 1885, 45–52.

————. Baxter, Sylvester. "A Plunge into Summer," *The Atlantic Monthly*, March 1885, 308–318.

Baz, Gustavo Adolfo. *Historia del Ferrocarril Mexicano*. 1874; reprint, México: Cosmos, 1977.

Becher, Henry, C.R. *A Trip to Mexico*. Toronto: Willing and Williamson, 1880.

Beezley, William H. *Judas at the Jockey Club and Other Episodes of Porfirian Mexico*. Lincoln: University of Nebraska Press, 1987.

Beisner, Robert L. *From the Old Diplomacy to the New, 1865–1900*. Arlington Heights: Harlan Davidson, 1975.

Benjamin, Thomas and Ocasio Melendez. "Organizing the Memory of Modern Mexico: Porfirian Historiography in Perspective." *Hispanic American Historical Review* 64 (May 1984): 323–64.

Bigelow, John. "Railway Invasion of Mexico." *Harpers* 65 (1881): 745–7.

Bilateral Commission on the Future of United States-Mexican Relations. "Education for New Understanding." *The Challenge of Interdependence: Mexico and the United States*. New York: University Press of America, 1989. 173–205.

Bishop, William Henry. *Old Mexico and Her Lost Provinces*. New York: Harper, 1883.

Blake, Mary Elizabeth and Margaret Francis Buchanan Sullivan. *Mexico: Picturesque, Political and Progressive*. Boston: Lee and Shepard, 1886.

Boletín de la Comisión Mexicana, La Exposición Universal de Nueva Orleans. 15 March, 7 June 1884. México: Secretaría de Fomento, 1884.

The Book of the Fair: An Historical and Descriptive Presentation of the World's Science, Art and Industry, as viewed through the Columbian Exposition at Chicago. Chicago: Bancroft Co., 1895.

Bowler, Peter. *The Invention of Progress: The Victorians and the Past*. Oxford: Basil Blackwell, 1989.

Brooks, Henry. "Our Relations with Mexico." *Californian* 1 (1880): 210–223.

Brown, Jonathan C. "Foreign and Native Born Workers in Porfirian Mexico." *American Historical Review* 98 (June 1993): 786–818.

Bruce, Edward. "The New Orleans Exposition." *Lippincotts Magazine* 35 (March 1885): 275–85.

Butler, William. *Mexico in Transition: From the Power of Political Romanism to Civil and Religious Liberty*. New York: Hunt and Easton, 1892.

Caballero, Manuel. *México en Chicago*. Chicago: Knight, Leonard & Co., 1893.

Callahan, James Morton. *American Foreign Policy in Mexican Relations*. New York: MacMillan, 1932.

Callcott, Wilfred Hardy. *The Caribbean Policy of the United States, 1890–1920*. New York: Octagon, 1966.

Campbell, Joseph and Jill Rosen. "You Furnish the Legend, I'll Furnish the Quote." *American Journalism Review*. 23: (Dec. 2001): 16–17.

Campbell, Reau. *Mexico and the Mexicans: The Material Matter and Mysterious Myths of that Country and Its People*. Mexico: Sonora News Company, 1892.

————. *Reau's Campbell's Complete Guide and Descriptive Book of Mexico*. Chicago: Rogers and Smith, 1907.

Carr, Harry. *Old Mother Mexico*. Boston: Houghton Mifflin. 1931.

Carson, William English. *Mexico: The Wonderland of the South*. New York: Macmillan, 1909.

Case, Alden Buell. *Thirty Years with the Mexicans in Peace and Revolution*. New York: F.H. Revell, 1917.

Casillas, Mike. "The Cananea Strike of 1906." *SouthWest Economics and Society* 3 (Winter 1977/78): 18–32.

Castillion, Katherine and Ruth B. Wright. *Centennial: A History of the American School in Mexico City, 1888–1988*. Mexico City: American School Foundation, 1988.

Cerutti, Mario and Miguel A. Gonzalez Quiroga, eds. *Frontera e Historia Económica: Texas y el Norte de México*. México: Instituto Mora, Universidad Autónoma Metropolitana, 1993.

Cerutti, Mario. "El Gran Norte Oriental y la formación del mercado nacional en México a fin de siglo XIX." *Siglo XIX* 2 (1987): 53–80.

———. "Estudios Regionales e Historia Empresarial en México, 1840–1920, Quince Años de Historiografía." *Inter-American Review of Bibliography* 43 (1993): 375–94.

Channing, Arnold. *The American Egypt: A Record of Travel in Yucatán*. New York: Doubleday, Page Co., 1909.

Chapman, John. "Steam, Enterprise and Politics: The Building of the Veracruz-Mexico City Railway, 1837–80." Ph.D. diss., University of Texas, 1972.

Church, John H.C. *Diary of a Trip Through Mexico and California*. Pittsfield, Mass.: M.H. Rogers, 1887.

Coatsworth, John. "Características Generales de la Economía Mexicana en el siglo XIX." *Ensayos sobre el desarollo Económico de México y América Latina, 1500–1975*. Ed. Enrique Florescano. México: Fondo de Cultura Económica, 1979. 171–186.

Cochrane, Elizabeth. *Six Months in Mexico, by Nellie Bly*. New York: Munro, 1888.

Coffin, Alfred Oscar. *Land Without Chimneys*. Cincinnati: Editor Publishing Co., 1898.

Cole, G.B. "An Old Imperial Residence, Castle Chapultepec in Mexico," *Overland Monthly and Out West Magazine*, April 1885, 379–386.

———. "Street Scenes in Mexico," *Overland Monthly*, March 1887, 265–273.

Cole, Garold. "The Birth of Modern Mexico, 1867–1911: American Traveler's Perceptions." *North Dakota Quarterly* 45 (1977): 54–72.

Comisión Nacional de los E.U.M. para la Expo Pan Americana. *A Few Facts About Mexico*. Buffalo: White-Evans, Penford, 1901.

Comisión Nacional de México. *Exposición Internacional de St. Louis, 1904*. St. Louis: J. MacCallum Printing Co., 1904.

Comisión Nacional para la Exposición Pan Americana, Buffalo, 1902. *Official Catalogue of the Mexican Exhibits at the Pan American Exposition at Buffalo, N.Y.* Buffalo: White-Evans-Penfold, 1901.

Conkling, Alfred R. *Appleton's Guide to Mexico: Including a Chapter on Guatemala, and a Complete English-Spanish Vocabulary*. New York: D.Appleton and Co., 1883.

Conkling, Howard. *Mexico and the Mexicans: Notes of Travel in the Winter and Spring of 1883*. New York: Taintor Brothers, Merrill and Co., 1883.

Conley, Edward M. "The Americanization of Mexico." *Review of Reviews* 32 (December 1905): 724–5.

Cosío Villegas, Daniel. *El Porfiriato: Vida Política Exterior*. Vols. 5 and 6, *Historia Moderna de México*. México: Hermes, 1963.

———. *The U.S. vs. Porfirio Díaz*. Translated by Nettie Lee Benson. Lincoln: University of Nebraska Press, 1963.

Cott, Kennett. "Porfirian Investment Policies, 1876–1910." Ph.D. diss., University of New Mexico, 1979.

Crawford, Cora Hayward. *The Land of the Montezumas*. New York: J.B. Alden, 1889.

Creelman, James. *Díaz: Master of Mexico*. New York: Appleton, 1911.

———. "President Díaz: Hero of the Americas." *Pearson's Magazine* 19 (March 1908): 231–277.

Curtis, William E. *The Capitals of South America*. [c.1889]; reprint, New York: Praeger, 1969.

———. *World's Columbian Exposition: Illustrated and Descriptive Catalogue of the Exhibit of the Bureau of American Republics*. Chicago: W.B. Conkey Co., 1893.

Danzinger, Adolphe de Castro. *Portrait of Ambrose Bierce*. New York. Beekim, 1929.

Davis, Ethelyn Clara. "The American Colony in Mexico City." Ph.D. diss., University of Missouri, 1942.

Davis, Richard Harding. "When a War is not a War," *Scribners* 56: 30 April 1914, 43.

———. "Army at Veracruz Marks Time Under the Portales," New York Tribune, 14 June 1914.

de la Pena y Reyes, Antonio. *La Labor Diplomatica de D. Manuel Maria de Zamacona, Como Secretaria de Relaciones Exteriores*. México: Publicaciones de la Secretaría de Relaciones Exteriores, 1928.

de Lameiras, Brijitte B. *Indios de México y Viajeros Extranjeros, Siglo XIX*. México: SEP Setentas, 1973.

De Leon, Arnaldo. *They Called them Greasers: Anglo Attitudes toward Mexicans in Texas, 1821–1900*. Austin: University of Texas Press, 1983.

Delpar, Helen. *The Enormous Vogue of Things Mexican: Cultural Relations Between the U.S. and Mexico, 1920–35*. Tuscaloosa: University of Alabama, 1992.

Denman, Kathy. *La Elite Norteamericana en la Ciudad de México*. Cuaderno de la Casa Chata, No. 34. México, Centro de Investigaciones Superiores del Instituto Nacional de Antropologia e Historia, 1980.

Devine, Michael. *John W. Foster: Politics and Diplomacy in the Imperial Era, 1873–1917*. Athens, Ohio: Ohio University Press, 1981.

Díaz y de Ovando, Clementina. *Crónica de una Quimera: Una Invasión Norteamericana en México, 1879*. México: Coordinación de Humanidades, Universidad Nacional Autónoma de México, 1989.

Díaz, Agustín. *A Brief Report on the Organization, Objects and Development of the Geographical Exploring Commission in the Republic of Mexico*. New Orleans: L. Graham and Sons, 1885.

Díaz, Porfirio. *Archivos del General Porfirio Díaz*. Edited by Alberto María Carreño. México: Elede, 1947–1961.

Diccionario Porrúa: Historia, Biografía, y Geografía de México. México: Editorial Porrúa, 1964.

Dictionary of American Biography. New York: Scribner, 1957.

d'Olwer, Luis Nicolau. "Las Inversiones Extranjeras." In *Historia Moderna de México: El Porfiriato, La Vida Económica*, 973–1177. México: Hermes, 1965.

Duke, David C. *John Reed*. Boston: G.K. Hall, 1987.

Dunbar, Edward E. *Mexican Papers*. New York: J.A.H. Hasbrouck, 1860.

Dunne, F.P. "Mr. Dooley on the Midway." *Cosmopolitan* 31 (1901): 476–82.

Dyer, Brainard. *The Public Career of William Evarts*. New York: DaCopa Press, 1969.

Eisenhower, John S.D. *Intervention: The United States and the Mexican Revolution, 1913–1917*. New York: Norton, 1993.

Elman, Richard. "Partisan Journalist." *Nation* 234: (17 April 1982): 469–470.

Estadísticas históricas de México. México: Instituto Nacional de Estadística, Geografía e Informática, Instituto Nacional de Antropologia e Historia, 1985.

Emerson, Edwin. "How Mexicans Fight," *Outlook* 104, May 1913.

Evans, Albert S. *Our Sister Republic: A Gala Trip through Mexico in 1869–70*. Hartford: Columbian, 1870.

Evans, T.B. *From Geneva to Mexico: A Record of a Tour through the Western Part of the U.S. and the Greater Part of Old Mexico*. Geneva, Illinois: Geneva Republican, 1893.

Fairall, Herbert S. *The World's Industrial and Cotton Centennial Exposition, New Orleans, 1884–85*. Iowa City: n.p., 1885.

Ferguson's Anecdotal Guide to Mexico, with a Map of the Railways: Historical, Geological, Archaeological and Critical. Philadelphia: Claxton, Remsen, and Haffelfinger, 1876.

Ferrocarriles Nacional. *Mexico from Border to Capital: A Brief Description of the many interesting places to be seen en route to Mexico City via the Laredo, The Eagle Pass, and the El Paso Gateways*. Mexico City: Ferrocarriles Nacional, n.d. [c.1914].

Ficker, Sandra, Kuntz. *El Ferrocarril Central Mexicano, 1880–1907*. Mexico City: El Colegio de Mexico, 1993.

Findling, John and Kimberly D. Pelle, eds. *Historical Dictionary of World's Fairs and Expositions, 1851–1988*. New York: Greenwood Press, 1990.

Finerty, John F. *John F. Finerty Reports from Porfirian Mexico*. Edited by Wilbert Timmons. El Paso: Western Press, 1974.

Fitzgerrell, James. *Fitzgerrell's Guide to Mexico*. 3rd ed. Mexico: Imp. de la Secretaría de Fomento, 1906.

———. *Fitzgerrell's Guide to Tropical Mexico*. 2d. ed. Mexico City: By the author, 1905.

Flandrau, Charles Macomb. *Viva Mexico!* Edited by C. Harvey Gardiner. New York: D. Appleton, 1908; reprint, Urbana: University of Illinois Press, 1964.

Flippin, John R. *Sketches from the Mountains of Mexico*. Cincinnati: Standard Publishing Co., 1889.

Foote, Mary Hallock. "A Diligence Journey in Mexico," *Century Magazine* (Nov. 1881) 1–15.

———. "From Morelia to Mexico City on Horseback,*"* *Century Magazine* (March 1882) 643–655.

———. "A Provincial Capital of Mexico," *Century Magazine* (Jan. 1882) 321–333.

Ford, Isaac. *Tropical America.* New York: Scribners, 1893.

Foster, John W. *Diplomatic Memoirs.* 2 vols. Boston: Houghton Mifflin, 1909.

Franck, Harry A. *Tramping through Mexico: Being the random notes of an incurable vagabond.* New York: Century, 1916.

Fyfe, Henry Hamilton. *The Real Mexico: A Study on the Spot.* New York: McBride, Nast, 1914.

Garcia Cubas, Antonio. *Cuadro geográfico, estadistico, descriptivo e histórico de los Estados Unidos Mexicanos.* México: Secretaría de Fomento, 1885.

———. *The Republic of Mexico in 1876. A political and ethnographical division of the population, character, habits, costumes and vocations of its inhabitants.* México: La Enseñanza Printing Office, 1876.

Gardiner, Clinton H. "Foreign Travellers Accounts of Mexico, 1810–1910." *Americas* VIII (1952): 321–351.

Garner, Paul. *Porfirio Díaz: Profiles in Power.* London: Longman, 2001.

Gibbs, William E. "Diaz Executive Agents and United States Foreign Policy." *Journal of International Studies and World Affairs* 20 (May 1978): 165–90.

———. "Spadework Diplomacy: U.S. Mexican Relations during the Hayes Administration, 1877–81." Ph.D. diss., Kent State University, 1973.

Gibson, Charles. *The Black Legend: Anti-Spanish Attitudes in the Old World and the New.* New York: Knopf, 1971.

Gilderhus, Mark T. *Diplomacy and Revolution: United States-Mexican Relations under Wilson and Carranza.* Tucson: University of Arizona, 1977.

Gillpatrick, Owen Wallace. *The Man Who Likes Mexico: The Spirited Chronicle of Adventurous Wanderings in Mexican Highways and Byways.* New York: Century, 1911.

Gillow, Eulogio G. *Reminiscencias del Ilmo. Y Rmo. Sr. Dr. Eulogio y Zavalzo, Arzobispo d Antequera.* Los Angeles: Imprenta y Linotipia de "Heraldo de Mexico," 1920.

Godkin, E.L. "What is Mexicanization?" *Nation,* 21 December 1876.

Godoy, José. *Porfirio Díaz: President of Mexico: the Master Builder of a Great Commonwealth.* New York: Putnam, 1910.

Gonzalez Navarro, Moises. *Los Extranjeros en México y los Mexicanos en el Extranjero, 1821–1970.* 2 Vols. México: Colegio de México, Centro de Estudios Históricos, 1993–94.

Gooch, Fanny Chambers. *Face to Face with the Mexicans.* New York: Howard and Hulbert, 1887.

Goodhue, Bertram Grosvenor. *Mexican Memories: The Record of a Slight Sojourn Below the Yellow Rio Grande.* New York: Geo. M. Allen, 1892.

Gordon, Leonard. "Lincoln and Juárez—A Brief Reassessment of Their Relationship" *Hispanic American Historical Review* 48 (Feb. 1968) 75–80.

Gordon, Sarah Herbert. "A Society of Passengers: Rail Travel, 1865–1910." Ph.D. diss., University of Chicago, 1950.

Gorsuch, Robert B. *The Republic of Mexico and Railroads.* New York: Hosford and Sons, 1881.

Grant, Ulysses S. *Memoirs and Selected Letters of Ulysses S. Grant.* New York: Library of America, 1990.

———. *The Papers of Ulysses S. Grant.* Edited by John Y. Simon. Carbondale, Ill.: Southern Illinois University Press, 1967.

Gray, Albert Zabriskie. *Mexico as it is.* New York: E.P. Dutton, 1878.

Gregg, Robert Danforth. *The Influence of Border Troubles on Relations Between the United States and Mexico, 1876–1910.* Baltimore: Johns Hopkins University Press, 1937.

Griffin, Solomon B. *Mexico of Today.* New York: Harpers, 1886.

Gunn, Drewey Wayne. *American and British Writers in Mexico: 1556–1973.* Austin: University of Texas Press, 1973.

———. *Mexico in American and British Letters: A Bibliography of Fiction and Travel Books Citing Original Editions.* Metuchen, New Jersey: Scarecrow Press, 1974.

Hackett, Charles W. "Recognition of the Díaz Government by the United States," *Southwestern Historical Quarterly Online,* 28, no. 1 (2006). http://www.tsha.utexas.edu/publications/journals/shq/online/v028/n1/contrib_DIVL424.html.

Hale, Charles. *The Transformation of Liberalism in late 19th Century Mexico.* Princeton: Princeton University Press, 1989.

Hall, Linda B. and Don M. Coerver. *Revolutionaries on the Border: The United States and Mexico, 1910–20.* Albuquerque: University of New Mexico, 1988.

Hamilton, Leonidas Le Cenci. *Hamilton's Mexican Handbook: A Complete Description of the Republic of Mexico.* Boston: Lothrop & Co., 1883.

Harding, George Canady. *The Miscellaneous Writings of George C. Harding.* Indianapolis: Carlon and Hollenbeck, 1882.

Hart, John Mason. *Empire and Revolution: The Americans in Mexico Since the Civil War.* Berkeley: University of California Press, 2002.

Hatfield, Shelley Ann Bowen. *Chasing Shadows: Indians along the U.S.-Mexico Border.* Albuquerque: University of New Mexico, 1998.

Haven, Gilbert. *Our Next Door Neighbor: A Winter in Mexico.* New York: Harper, 1875.

Hayes, Rutherford Birchard. *Hayes: The Diary of a President, 1875–1881.* Edited by T. Harry Williams. New York: McKay, 1964.

Hearn, Lafcadio. *Lafcadio Hearn: Occidental Gleanings.* Edited by Albert Mordell. New York: Dodd, 1925.

Heaven, Louise Palmer. "Flood and Quarantine," *Overland Monthly,* November 1884, 512–518.

———. "Nine Days Travel in Mexico," *Overland Monthly,* September 1884, 224–235.

Henderson, Peter. "Modernization and Change in Mexico: La Zacualpa Rubber Plantation, 1890–1920." *Hispanic American Historical Review* 73 (1993): 235–60.

Hesseltine, William B. *Ulysses S. Grant, Politician.* New York: Dodd, Mead and Co., 1935.

Hicks, Granville, ed. *Letters of Lincoln Steffens.* Westport, CT: Greenwood Press, 1966.

Hicks, Granville. *John Reed: The Making of a Revolutionary.* New York, Benjamin Blom, 1936.

Hietala, Thomas R. *Manifest Design: Anxious Aggrandizement in late Jacksonian America.* Ithaca: Cornell University Press, 1985.

Hinsley, Curtis. "The World as Marketplace: Commodification of the Exotic at the World's Columbian Exposition, Chicago, 1893." In *Exhibiting Cultures: The Poetics and Politics of Museum Display*, eds. Ivan Karp and Steven Lavine, 344–65. Washington, D.C.: Smithsonian Institution Press, 1991.

Hinton, A.R. "Shall We Annex Northern Mexico?" *Independent* 79 (27 July 1914): 124–5.

Hoogenboom, Ari A. *The Presidency of Rutherford B. Hayes.* Lawrence, Kansas: University Press of Kansas, 1988.

Horsman, Reginald. *Race and Manifest Destiny: The Origins of American Racial Anglo-Saxonism.* Cambridge: Harvard University Press, 1981.

Howe, Daniel Walker. "American Victorianism as a Culture." *American Quarterly* 27 (December 1975): 507–32.

Hunt, Michael. *Ideology and U.S. Foreign Policy.* New Haven: Yale University Press, 1987.

Icazuriaga, Carmen. *El Enclave Sociocultural Norteamericano y el Papel de los Empresarios Norteamericanos en México.* Cuaderno de la Casa Chata, No. 35. México: Centro de Investigaciones Superiores del Instituto Nacional de Antropologia e Historia, 1980.

Ilchman, Warren F. *Professional Diplomacy in the United States, 1779–1939: A Study in Administrative History.* Chicago: University of Chicago Press, 1961.

Ingram, J.S. *The Centennial Exposition.* Philadelphia: Hubbard Bros., 1876.

Jackson, H.H. "By Horsecars into Mexico." *Atlantic Monthly*, March 1883, 351–366.

Jacobson, Matthew Frye, *Barbarian Virtues: The United States Encounters Foreign Peoples at Home and Abroad, 1876–1917.* New York: Hill and Wang, 2000.

Jakle, John. *The Tourist: Travel in Twentieth Century America.* Lincoln: University of Nebraska Press, 1985.

Janvier, Thomas A. *The Mexican Guide.* New York: Charles Scribners and Sons, 1886.

Johannsen, Robert. *To the Halls of the Montezumas: The Mexican War in the American Imagination.* New York: Oxford, 1985.

Johnson, John L. *A Hemisphere Apart: The Foundations of U.S. Policy toward Latin America.* Baltimore: Johns Hopkins University Press, 1990.

Jules, David. "American Political and Economic Penetration of Mexico, 1877–1920." Ph.D. diss., Georgetown University, 1947.

Kagan, Richard L. "Prescott's Paradigm: American Historical Scholarship and the Decline of Spain." *American Historical Review* 101.2 (1996): 423–46.

Kaiser, Chester. "John Watson Foster: The United States Minister to Mexico, 1873–80." Ph.D. diss., The American University, 1954.

Kaplan, Amy. *The Anarchy of Empire in the Making of U.S. Culture*. Cambridge, Harvard, 2002.

Katz, Friedrich. *The Life and Times of Pancho Villa*. Stanford: Stanford University, 1998.

Kautz, A.V. "Notes of Travel in Mexico, II," *California and Overland Monthly*, May 1883, 478–488.

———. "Notes of Travel in Mexico" *California and Overland Monthly*, April 1883, 397–407.

Keen, Benjamin. *The Aztec Image in Western Thought*. New Brunswick: Rutgers University Press, 1971.

Kirkham, Stanton Davis. *Mexican Trails: A Record of Travel in Mexico, 1904–07*. New York: Putnam, 1909.

Kitchens, John W. "Some Considerations of the Rurales in Porfirian Mexico." *Journal of Inter-American Studies* 9 (July 1967): 441–455.

Knudson, Jerry W. "John Reed: A Reporter in Revolutionary Mexico," *Journalism History* 29: (Summer 2003): 59–69.

Krauze, Enrique. *Porfirio*. México: Clio, 1993.

Kroeger, Brooke, *Nellie Bly: Daredevil, Reporter, Feminist*. New York: Times Books, 1994.

Kuntz Ficker, Sandra. *El Ferrocarril Central Mexicano, 1880–1907*. México: El Colegio de México, Centro de Estudios Históricos, 1993.

Lamborn, Robert. "Life on a Mexican Street," *Century Magazine* (October 1882) 803–815.

Lee, S.M. *Glimpses of Mexico and California*. Boston: G.H. Ellis, 1887.

Leonidas, Hamilton. *Mexico's Mexican Handbook*. Boston: D. Lothrop, 1883.

Lester, Charles Edwards. *The Mexican Republic: An Historic Study*. New York: American News Company, 1878.

Lewis, Alfred Henry. "The Maligners of Mexico." *Cosmopolitan* 48 (March 1910): 432a-e.

London, Charmian. *The Book of Jack London*. New York: Century, 1921.

London, Jack. "Mexico's Army and Ours." *Colliers* 53, 30 May 1914.

Love, Eric T.L. *Race Over Empire: Racism and U.S. Imperialism, 1865–1900*. Chapel Hill: University of North Carolina Press, 2004.

Luconi Moroni, Francesca. "Análisis de dos estudios de caso de la estructura religiosa de la colonia norteamericana residente en el Distrito Federal: Union Evangelical Church y la Lutheran Church of the Good Shepherd." Tesis, Lic. Antropología Social, Universidad IberoAmericana, 1979.

Lueck, Beth L. *American Writers and the Picturesque Tour: The Search for National Identity, 1790–1860*. New York, Garland, 1997.

Lummis, Charles F. *The Awakening of a Nation: Mexico* (London: Harper and Brothers, 1898).

Mabie, Hamilton Wright. "The Spirit of the New World as Interpreted by the Pan-American Exposition." *Outlook*, 10 July 1901, 529–47.

MacCannell, Dean. *A New Theory of the Leisure Class*. New York: Schocken Books, 1975.

Manero, Vicente G. *Guide for Mexico*. Mexico City: Tip. Gonzalo Estévez, 1878.

Martin, Percy F. "Porfirio Díaz, Soldier and Statesman." *Living Age*, 1 January 1910; 3–18.

———. *Mexico's Treasure House: An Illustrated and Descriptive Account of the Mines and Their Operation in 1906*. New York: Cheltenham, 1906.

Mason, Gregory. "Reed, Villa and the Village." *Outlook,* 140, May 1925.

Matthews, John Francis. "Little Favors from My Government: U.S. Consuls in Mexico, 1821–65." Ph.D. diss., Texas Christian University, 1993.

Mayer, Brantz. "The City of Mexico," *Frank Leslie's Popular Monthly* (February 1878)144–158.

McCarty, J. Hendrickson. *Two Thousand Miles through the Heart of Mexico*. New York: Phillips & Hunt, 1886.

McClure, Alexander Kelly. *To the Pacific and Mexico*. Philadelphia: Lippincott, 1901.

McCollester, Sullivan Holman. *Mexico Old and New: A Wonderland*. Boston: Gardiner, 1899.

McCormick, Richard C. *The International Exhibition of 1876; Speech in the House of Representatives, 6 May 1874*. Washington, D.C.: Government Printing Office, 1874.

McGehee, Richard V. "Sports and Recreational Activities in Guatemala and Mexico, Late 1800s to 1926." *Studies in Latin American Popular Culture* 13 (1994): 7–32.

McWilliams, Carey. *Ambrose Bierce, a Biography*. New York: Archon Books, 1929.

Metwalli, Ahmed. "Americans Abroad: The Popular Art of Travel Writing in the Nineteenth Century." In *America: Exploration and Travel*, ed. Steven Kagle, 68–82. Bowling Green: Popular Press, 1979.

Mexican Section: Special Catalogue and Explanatory Notes. Philadelphia: Dan Gillin, Printer, 1876.

México y las Colonias Extranjeras en el Centenario de la Independencia. México: Bouligny and Schmidt, 1910.

Meyer, Lorenzo and Josefina Zoraida Vázquez. *The United States and Mexico*. Chicago: University of Chicago Press, 1985.

Meyer, Lorenzo. "The U.S. and Mexico: The Historical Status of their Conflict." *Journal of International Affairs* 43 (Winter 1990): 251–70.

Meyers, William K. "Pancho Villa and the Multinationalists: U.S. Mining Interests in Villista Mexico, 1913–1915." *Journal of Latin American Studies* 23 (1991): 339–363.

———. "Seasons of Rebellion: Nature, Organization of Cotton Production and the Dynamics of Revolution in La Laguna, Mexico, 1910–1916." *Journal of Latin American Studies* 30 (February 1998): 63–94.

Miller, Daniel R. "The Frustrations of a Mexican Mine Under U.S. Ownership." *Historian* 55 (1993): 483–500.

Miller, Robert Ryal. "Matías Romero: Mexican Minister to the United States During the Juárez-Maximilian Era." *Hispanic American Historical Review* 45 (May 1965) 228–245.

Milliken, James. A Voyager's Letters from Mexico. Philadelphia: Lippincott, 1876.

Mitchell, Timothy. "The World as Exhibition." *Comparative Studies in Society and History* 31 (1989): 217–236.

Monsivais, Carlos. "La Nacion de unas Cuantos y las Esperanzas Románticas: Notas Sobre la Historia del Término 'Cultural Nacional' en México." *In En Turno a la Cultura Nacional.* México, Fondo de Cultura Economica, 1982.

———. "Travellers in Mexico: A Brief Anthology of Selected Myths." *Diogenes* 125 (1984): 48–74.

Morales, Vicente and Manuel Caballero. *El Señor Root en México: Crónica de la visita hecha en Octubre de 1907 al pueblo y al gobierno de la República Mexicana, por su excelencia el Honorable Señor Root.* México: Imprenta de Arte y Letras, 1908.

Morgan, John T. "Mexico." *North America Review* 168, May 1883.

Morris, Ida Dorman. *A Tour in Mexico.* New York: Abbey, 1902.

Moses, Bernard. *The Railway Revolution in Mexico.* San Francisco: Berkeley Press, 1895.

Nasaw, David. *The Chief: The Life of William Randolph Hearst.* New York: Houghton Mifflin, 2000.

Niblo, Steve. "The Political Economy of the Early Porfiriato." Ph.D. diss., Northern Illinois University, 1972.

Nichols, Benito. *Nichol's Guide to Mexico: Commercial and Official Guide of the Republic of Mexico.* Mexico: By the author, 1884.

Niess, Frank. *A Hemisphere to Itself: A History of U.S.-Latin-American Relations.* London: Zed, 1990.

Norton, Frank H. *Illustrated Historical Register of the Centennial Exposition, Philadelphia, 1876; and of the Exposition Universelle, 1878.* New York: American News Co., 1879.

Nueva Galicia: A Subtropical Switzerland: Describing the Regions of the Western Sierra of Mexico Now Being Opened by the Mexican Central Railway. Crawford, Colorado: Wynkoop and Mallerbach, n.d.

O'Connor, Richard and Dale L. Walker. *The Lost Revolutionary: A Biography of John Reed.* New York: Harcourt Brace, 1967.

O'Shaugnessy, Edith. *Diplomatic Days.* New York: Hapter, 1917.

Ober, Frederick. *Mexican Resources: A Guide to and through Mexico.* Boston: Estes and Lauriat, 1884.

———. *Travels in Mexico and Life Among the Mexicans,* Boston: Ester and Lauriat, 1884.

Oñate, Abdiel. "El Surgimiento de la supremacia estadounidense en los mercados latinoamericanos: el caso de México, 1870–1914." In *El Dilema de dos Naciones: Relaciones Económicas entre México y Estados Unidos.* Edited by Thomas Noel Osborn and Miguel S. Wionczek. México: Trillas, 1981.

Orrin Brothers and Nichols Guide to the Aztec Fair: Mexico Past and Present. n.p., 1886. Collection Relating to Worlds Fairs, National Museum of American History Library, Smithsonian Institution, Washington, D.C.

Ortega Noriega, Sergio. *El Eden Subvertido: La Colonización de Topolobambo, 1886–1896.* México: Instituto Nacional de Antropología e Historia, 1978.

Oswald, Felix Leopold. *Summerland Sketches, or Rambles in the Backwoods of Mexico and Central America.* Philadelphia: J.B.Lippincott, 1880.

Palmer, Frederick. "Richard Harding Davis." *Scribners* 80(Nov. 1926): 472–477.

Paredes, Raymund. "The Origins of Anti-Mexican Sentiment in the United States." *New Scholar* VI (1977): 139–165.

Parkinson, Edward S. *Wonderland: or, Twelve Weeks in and out of the United States.* Trenton, N.J.: MacCrellish and Quigley, 1894.

Parlee, Lorena M. "Porfirio Díaz, Railroads and Development in Northern Mexico: A Study of Government Policy Toward the Central and National Railroads, 1876–1910." Ph.D. diss., University of California, San Diego, 1981.

Paz, Ireneo and Manuel Tornel. *Nueva Guia de México: en Ingles, Frances, y Castellano.* Mexico: Imp. de. I. Paz, 1882.

Pennsylvania Railroad Company. *Pennsylvania Tour to Mexico: Affording Four Weeks in the Land of the Aztecs.* Philadelphia: Allen, Land & Scott, 1891.

Pike, Frederick B. *U.S. and Latin America: Myths and Stereotypes of Civilization and Nature.* Austin: University of Texas Press, 1992.

Pletcher, David. "México, Campo de Inversiones Norteamericanas, 1867–80." *Historia Mexicana* 2 (1953): 564–574.

———. "Mexico Opens the Door to American Capital." *Americas* 16 (July 1959): 1–14.

———. "Warner P. Sutton and American Mexican Border Trade." *Southwest Historical Quarterly* 79 (1976): 373–99.

———. *Rails, Mines and Progress: Seven American Promoters in Mexico, 1876–1911.* Ithaca: American Historical Association, 1959.

Pope, Bertha Clarke, ed. *The Letters of Ambrose Bierce.* New York: Gordian Press, 1967.

Powell, Phillip Wayne. *Tree of Hate: Propoganda and Prejudices Affecting U.S. Relations with the Hispanic World.* New York: Basic Books, 1971.

Prantl, Adolfo and José Groso. *La Ciudad de México.* México: Juan Buxo y Cia., 1901.

Pratt, Mary Louise. *Imperial Eyes, Travel Writing and Transculturation.* London: Routledge, 1992.

Prendergast, F.E. "Railroads in Mexico." *Harper's Monthly* 63 (1881): 276–281.

Price, Thomas W. *Notes of a Plain Businessman: Originally published as letters in the Hartford Churchman.* Hartford, Conn.: n.p., 1878.

Prieto, Guillermo. *Romancero Nacional.* With a Preface by Ignacio Altamirano. México: Secretaría de Fomento, 1885.

Pritchard, G.S. "The Mexico of the Mexicans." *International Review* 5 (1878): 170–84.

Quirk, Robert E. *An Affair of Honor: Woodrow Wilson and the Occupation of Veracruz.* Lexington: University of Kentucky, 1962.

Raat, Dirk W. *Revoltosos: Mexico's Rebels in the United States, 1903–1923.* College Station: Texas A&M., 1981.

Ramirez, Santiago. *Noticias Historicas de la Riqueza Minera de México y de su Estado de Explotación.* México: Secretaría de Fomento, 1884.

The Rand-McNally Hand-book to the Pan-American Exposition, Buffalo and Niagara Falls. Chicago: Rand McNally and Co., 1899.

Randall, Robert. "Mexico's Pre-revolutionary reckoning with the railroads." *The Americas: Academy of American Franciscan History* 42 (1985): 1–28.

Rangel Frias, Raúl. *Gerónimo Treviño: Héroes y Epígonos.* Monterey, México: n.p., 1967.

Reed, John. *Insurgent Mexico.* New York: D. Appleton and Co, 1914.

Rénique, Gerardo. "Frontier Capitalism and Revolution in Northwest Mexico, Sonora, 1830–1910." Ph.D. diss., Columbia University, 1990.

Rice, John H. *Mexico: Our Neighbor.* New York: J.W. Lovell, 1888.

Richardson, D.S. "Two Nights in a Crater," *Overland Monthly and Out West Magazine,* March 1888, 307–316.

Rippy, J. Fred. *The U.S. and Mexico.* New York: Crofts, 1926.

Rittenhouse, Mignon. *The Amazing Nellie Bly.* New York: E.P. Dutton, 1971.

Robertson, Michael. *Stephen Crane, Journalism and the Making of Modern American Literature.* New York: Columbia University Press, 1997.

Robinson, Cecil. *Mexico and the Hispanic Southwest in American Literature.* Tucson: University of Arizona Press, 1977.

———. *The View from Chapultepec: Mexican Writers on the Mexican-American War.* Tucson: University of Arizona, 1989.

Roeder, Ralph. *Hacia el México Moderno: Porfirio Díaz.* México: Fondo de Cultura Económica, 1973.

Rolle, Andrew F. *The Lost Cause: The Confederate Exodus to Mexico.* Norman: University of Oklahoma Press, 1965.

Romero, Matías. *Mexican Lobby: Matías Romero in Washington, 1861–67.* Edited by Thomas Schoonover. Lexington: University Press of Kentucky, 1986.

———. *Mexico and the United States,* New York: Putnam, 1898.

———. *Romero Railways in Mexico: An Article in Answer to the Article of the Honorable John Bigelow entitled 'the Railway Invasion of Mexico' published in Harpers, October 1882.* Washington, D.C.: H.W. Moore, 1882.

———. *Report of the Secretary of Finance of the U.S. of Mexico on the 15th of January, 1879 on the actual condition of Mexico, and the increase of commerce with the U.S., Rectifying the Report of the Honorable John Foster Envoy Extraordinary and Minister Plenipotentiary of the U.S. in Mexico.* New York: Ponce de Leon, 1880.

Rosenstone, Robert A. *Romantic Revolutionary: A Biography of John Reed.* New York: Knopf, 1975.

Rosenzweig, Fernando. "El Comercio Exterior." In *Historia Moderna de México: El Porfiriato, La Vida Económica,* 635–670. México: Hermes, 1965.

Ruiz, Ramon. *The People of Sonora and Yankee Capitalists.* Tucson: University of Arizona, 1988.

Ryan, Howard. "Selected Aspects of American Activities in Mexico, 1876–1910." Ph.D. diss., University of Chicago, 1964.

Rydell, Robert. *All the World's a Fair: Visions of Empire at American International Expositions, 1876–1916.* Chicago: University of Chicago Press, 1984.

———. "The Culture of Imperial Abundance: World's Fairs in the Making of American Culture." In *Consuming Visions: Accumulation and Display of Goods in America, 1880–1920*, ed. Simon Bronner, 191–216. New York: Norton, 1989.

Said, Edward. *Orientalism.* New York: Pantheon, 1978.

Salvucci, Richard J. "The Origins and Progress of U.S.-Mexican Trade, 1825–1884: 'hoc opus, hic labor est'." *Hispanic American Historical Review* 71 (November 1991): 697–735.

Sanborn, Helen Josephine. *A Winter in Central America and Mexico.* Boston: Lee and Shepard, 1886.

Sánchez Andrés, Agustín et. al. *Artífices y Operadores de la Diplomacia Mexicana Siglos XIX y XX.* (México: Porrúa, 2004).157–172.

Sanders, Frank. "Mexico Visto por los Diplomaticos del Siglo XIX." *Historia Mexicana* 20 (1971): 368–411.

Sandweiss, Eric. "Around the World in a Day: International Participation in the World's Columbian Exposition." *Illinois Historical Journal* 84 (Spring 1991): 2–14.

Scanlon, Arlene Patricia. *Un Enclave Cultural: Poder y Etnicidad en el Contexto de Una Escuela Norteamericana en México.* With a Preface by Guillermo de la Peña. Editorial de la Casa Chata, No. 18. México: Secretaría de Educación Pública, 1984.

Schell, William. "American Investment in Tropical Mexico: Rubber Plantations, Fraud and Dollar Diplomacy." *Business History Review* 64 (Spring 1990): 217–54.

———. *Integral Outsiders: The American Colony in Mexico City, 1876–1911.* Wilmington: Scholarly Research Books, 2001.

Scott, Gertrude. "Village Performance: Villages at the Chicago World's Columbian Exposition, 1893." Ph.D. diss., New York University, 1991.

Sears, John F. *Sacred Places: American Tourist Attractions in the 19th Century.* New York: Oxford University Press, 1989.

Seelye, John. *War Games: Richard Harding Davis and the New Imperialism.* Amherst: University of Massachusetts, 2003.

Shelden, L.A. *Governor Shelden's Jaunt: A Series of Readable Letters on Old Mexico: Letters of Governor Shelden Written to the Santa Fe New Mexican Review While on a Visit to the City of Mexico.* n.p., 1884.

Shepherd, Grant. *The Silver Magnet.* New York: Dutton, 1938.

Shepherd, Samuel C. "A Glimmer of Hope: the World's Industrial and Cotton Centennial Exposition, New Orleans, 1884–85." *Louisiana History* 26 (1985): 271–90.

Sherratt, Harriet W. *Mexican Vistas Seen from the Highways and Byways of Travel.* Chicago: Rand, McNalley, 1899.

Sillard, John B. *Visitors Guide to the World's Industrial and Cotton Centennial Exposition and New Orleans.* Louisville: Courier Journal, 1884.

Sillitoe, Alan. *Leading the Blind: A Century of Guidebook Travel, 1815–1914.* New York: MacMillan, 1998.

Sinkin, Richard N. *The Mexican Reform, 1855–1876: A Study in Liberal Nationbuilding.* Austin: University of Texas Press, 1979.

Skowronek, Stephen, *Building a New American State: The Expansion of National Administrative Capacities, 1877–1920*. New York: Cambridge University Press, 1982.

Slotkin, Richard. *The Fatal Environment: The Myth of the Frontier in the Age of Industrialization, 1800–1890*. New York: Atheneum, 1985.

Smalley, Eugene. "The New Orleans Exposition." *Century* 30 (May 1885): 3–14.

Smalley, Eugene. "In and Out of the New Orleans Exposition," *Century* 30 (June 1885): 185–99.

Smith, Ann Eliza Brainerd. *Notes of Travel in Mexico and California*. St. Albans, Vermont: Messenger and Advertiser Office, 1886.

Smith, Francis H. *A White Umbrella in Mexico*. Boston: Houghton Mifflin, 1889.

Smith, Henry Erskine. *On and Off the Saddle: Characteristic Sights and Scenes from the Great Northwest to the Antilles*. New York: Putnam, 1894.

Smith, Michael M. "Gringo Propagandist: George F. Weeks and the Mexican Revolution." *Journalism History*. 29 (Spring 2003) 2–11.

Spring, Arthur L. *Beyond the Rio Grande: A Journey in Mexico*. Boston: J.S. Adams, 1886.

Spurr, David. *The Rhetoric of Empire: Colonial Discourse in Journalism, Travel Writing and Imperial Administration*. Durham: Duke University Press, 1993.

Stanton, Davis Kirkham. *Mexican Trails: A Record of Travel in Mexico, 1904–07; and a Glimpse of the life of the Mexican Indian*. New York, G.P. Putnam, 1909.

Stevens, Otheman. "Mexico the Progressive." *Cosmopolitan* 48 (March 1910): 444–46.

Stevenson, Catherine Barnes. *Victorian Women Travel Writers in Africa*. Boston: G.K. Hall, 1982.

Stowe, William. *Going Abroad: European Travel in Nineteenth Century American Culture*. Princeton: Princeton University Press, 1994.

Strother, David Hunter, and John E. Stealey. *Porte Crayon's Mexico: David Hunter Strother's Diaries in the early Porfirian Era, 1879–1885*. Kent, Ohio: Kent State University Press, 2006.

Swanberg, W.A. *Citizen Hearst*. New York: Scribner, 1961.

Takaki, Ronald T. *A Different Mirror: A History of Multicultural America*. Boston: Little, Brown and Co., 1993.

Tenenbaum, Barbara A. "Streetwise History: The Paseo de la Reforma and the Porfirian State, 1876–1910." *Rituals of Rule, Rituals of Resistance*. Eds. William H. Beezley, Cheryl Martin and William French. Wilmington: Scholarly Resources, 1994.

Tenorio Trillo, Mauricio. "Crafting the Modern Mexico: Mexico's Presence at World's Fairs, 1880s-1920s." Ph.D. diss., Stanford University, 1994.

———. *Mexico at the World's Fairs: Crafting a Modern Nation*. Berkeley: University of California Press, 1996.

Thomas, David P. "Porfirio Díaz in the Opinion of his North American Contemporaries." *Revista de Historia Americana* 63 (1967): 79–116.

Thomas, Robert Horatio, ed. *Journalist's Letters Descriptive of Texas and Mexico*. Mechanicsburg, Pa: n.p., 1889.

Timmons, Wilbert, ed. *John F. Finerty Reports from Porfirian Mexico*. El Paso: Western Press, 1974.

Tiffany, Flavel B. *Land of the Aztecs*. Kansas City, MO: Franklin Hudson, 1909.

Tinker Salas, Miguel. *In the Shadow of Eagles: Sonora and the Transformation of the Border during the Porfiriato*. Berkeley, University of California Press, 1997.

Townsend, Mary Ashley. *Here and there in Mexico: The Travel Writing of Mary Ashley Townsend*. Edited by Ralph Lee Woodward, Jr. Tuscaloosa: Alabama, 2001.

Truman, Ben C., ed. *The History of the World's Fair*. Chicago: Monarch, 1893.

Turner, C.Y. "Organization as Applied to Art." *Cosmopolitan* 31 (1901): 493–500.

Turner, John Kenneth. *Barbarous Mexico*. With an introduction by Sinclair Snow. Chicago: C.H. Kern, 1911; reprint, Austin: University of Texas Press, 1969.

U.S. Blue Book, A Register of Offices and Clerkships and other Civil Positions under the United States Government, and their Salaries, 1876–77. Washington, D.C.: Washington Publishing Company, 1877.

U.S. Department of the Interior. *Register of Officers and Agents, Civil, Military, and Naval, in the Service of the United States, on the 30th of September, 1873*. Washington, D.C.: Government Printing Office, 1874.

U.S. Department of State. *Diplomatic Dispatches from Mexico*. Record Group 59, National Archives, Washington, D.C.

U.S. Department of State. *Instructions*. Record Group 59, National Archives, Washington, D.C.

U.S. Department of the Treasury. *Statistical Abstract of the United States, 1880*. Treasury Department Document No. 120. Washington, D.C.: 1881.

Urry, John. *The Tourist Gaze: Leisure and Travel in Contemporary Societies*. London: Sage, 1990.

Valdes-Ugalde, Francisco. "Janus and the Northern Colossus: Perceptions of the United States in the Building of the Mexican Nation," *The Journal of American History* 86 (1999): 568–800.

Van den Berghe, Pierre L. *The Quest for the Other: Ethnic Tourism in San Cristobal, Mexico*. Seattle: University of Washington Press, 1994.

Van Dyke, T.S. "Mexican Politics." *Harpers* 71 (1885): 762.

Vanderwood, Paul. "Mexico's Rurales: Reputation vs. Reality." *Americas* 34 (1977): 102–112.

Visit of the Merchants and Manufacturers of Philadelphia to the World's Expo at New Orleans, February 11–25, 1885. Philadelphia: McCalla and Stavely, 1885.

Visitors Guide to the World's Industrial and Cotton Centennial Exposition and New Orleans. Louisville: Courier Journal, 1884.

Wallace, Dillon. *Beyond the Mexican Sierra*. Chicago: McClurg, 1910.

Warner, Charles Dudley. *On Horseback*. Boston: Houghton Mifflin, 1888.

Warwick, A.W. "Can the Mexican Progress?" *Forum* 51, January 1914.

Wasserman, Mark. *Capitalists, Caciques and Revolution: The Native Elite and Foreign Enterprise in Chihuahua, Mexico, 1854–1911*. Chapel Hill: University of North Carolina Press, 1984.

Weber, David J. *Myth and the History of the Hispanic Southwest*. Albuquerque: University of New Mexico Press, 1988.

Weeks, Charles. *The Juárez Myth in Mexico*. Tuscaloosa: University of Alabama, 1987.

Weeks, George F. *Seen in a Mexican Plaza*. New York: Revell, 1918.

———. *California Copy*. Washington: Washington College Press, 1928.

Wells, David Ames. *A Study of Mexico*. New York: D. Appleton, 1886.

Whitaker, Arthur. *The Western Hemisphere Idea: Its Rise and Decline*. Ithaca: Cornell University Press, 1954.

Whitney, James A. *An Address on the Relations of the US and Mexico*. n.p., 1886.

Wilkins, James Hepburn. *A Glimpse of Old Mexico: Being the observations and reflections of a tenderfoot editor while on a journey in the land of Montezuma*. San Rafael, California: n.p., 1901.

Wilson, C.H. "Through Mexico in a Private Car." *Frank Leslie's Popular Monthly*, April 1899, 637–648.

Wilson, James. *Bits of Old Mexico*. San Francisco: n.p., [c1910].

Winter, Nevin O. *Mexico and her People To-day*. Boston: L.C. Page, 1907.

Wooster, Robert. "The Army and the Politics of Expansion: Texas and the Southwestern Borderlands, 1870–86." *Southwestern Historical Quarterly* 93 (October 1989): 151–67.

Wright, Marie Robinson. *Mexico: A History of its Progress and Development in 100 Years*. Philadelphia: George Barrie and Sons, 1911.

———. *Picturesque Mexico*. Philadelphia: Lippincott, 1897.

Yeager, Gene. "Porfirian Commercial Propoganda: Mexico in the World Industrial Expositions." *Americas* 34 (October 1977): 230–43.

Young, John Russell. *Around the World with General Grant*. New York: The American News Co., 1879.

Zea, Leopoldo. *Positivism in Mexico*. Austin: University of Texas Press, 1974.

Index

CPSIA information can be obtained at www.ICGtesting.com
264814BV00002B/3/P